Danger 79er

NUMBER 160

Williams-Ford Texas A&M University

Military History Series

A Davis Ford Book

Danger 79er

The Life and Times of Lieutenant General James F. Hollingsworth

JAMES H. WILLBANKS

Foreword by Sam Nunn

Texas A&M University Press • College Station

First edition

This paper meets the requirements
of ANSI/NISO Z39.48-1992 (Permanence of Paper).
Binding materials have been chosen for durability.
Manufactured in the United States of America

Library of Congress Cataloging-in-Publication Data
Names: Willbanks, James H., 1947– author.
Title: Danger 79er: the life and times of Lieutenant General James F. Hollingsworth / James H. Willbanks; foreword by Sam Nunn.
Other titles: Danger seventy niner | Danger seven niner
Description: First edition. | College Station: Texas A&M University Press, [2018] | Series: Williams-Ford Texas A&M University military history series; number 160 | Includes bibliographical references and index.
Identifiers: LCCN 2017039908 (print) | LCCN 2017042981 (ebook) | ISBN 9781623496319 (ebook) | ISBN 9781623496296 | ISBN 9781623496296 (cloth: alk. paper) | ISBN 9781623496302(pbk.: alk. paper)
Subjects: LCSH: Hollingsworth, James F., 1918–2010. | United States. Army—Biography. | Generals—United States—Biography. | Agricultural and Mechanical College of Texas—Alumni and alumnae—Biography. | United States—History, Military—20th century.
Classification: LCC E840.5.H66 (ebook) | LCC E840.5.H66 W55 2018 (print) | DDC 355.0092 [B] —dc23
LC record available at https://lccn.loc.gov/2017039908

Dedication

This book is dedicated to Holly's brothers—Gerald, Ross, and Cecil—all of whom, like their brother Holly, served the nation in World War II.

It is also dedicated to our son, Russell T. Willbanks, a veteran of both Iraq and Afghanistan, and to our late daughter, Jennifer Susan Schaad, a loving mother and devoted army wife.

Contents

A gallery of images follows page 106.

Maps

Foreword

During my service on the United States Senate Armed Services Committee, my staff and I were constantly looking for objective experts who could provide wisdom and frank advice on the national security challenges of the day.

Gen. James "Holly" Hollingsworth was one of our most candid and valuable advisors. From South Korea to NATO to conventional weapons capability, he was always willing to face head-on the greatest challenges and speak in plain, blunt language that could not be misunderstood.

General Hollingsworth had a long and storied career in the army, dating back to his days as a young tank battalion commander in WWII. During his distinguished career, he was known for taking care of the troops and his focus on "mission accomplishment." He won the fierce loyalty of all who served under him, particularly in combat. As a corps group commander in Korea, he completely revamped the plan for the defense of South Korea.

He was a legendary leader in the US Army, but he was willing to take on the army and the Department of Defense when he thought they were wrong. After his service in South Korea, he returned to the United States where he served as a special assistant to the Chief of Staff of the Army. In that role, he was asked by me and the Armed Services Committee to go to Europe to evaluate the capabilities of US forces and our NATO allies in Europe in meeting the threat of the Warsaw Pact. To quote author James Willbanks, "He did not like what he found when he got there." *The Hollingsworth Report: Central Europe Assessment* played a major role in influencing and shaping the 1977 report that I wrote with Senator Dewey Bartlett on NATO and the new Soviet threat.

As Willbanks notes in his book, "Although it did not happen overnight, the subsequent buildup of US forces and its NATO partners no doubt contributed greatly to the fall of the Berlin Wall, the demise of the Warsaw Pact, and the shortening of the Cold War."

Holly was an uncommon warrior and patriot who left a lasting legacy. I believe that this book by Jim Willbanks will help inspire future generations of American military leaders.

—Sam Nunn, *US senator from 1972–96*

Acknowledgments

I would like to thank the Hollingsworth family, to include Ross, Betsy, Randy, and the late Gerald Hollingsworth, for their invaluable assistance in getting to know their brother, uncle, and cousin. I would also like to thank the members of the Descendants of Valentine Hollingsworth Sr. Society for the background they provided on the Hollingsworth family line.

A special thanks goes to Phil Bakke for all that he did to make this book a reality; he opened a number of doors that would otherwise have been closed. This book would not have been possible without Phil's support and encouragement.

The assistance of Henry Gole and Scott Wheeler was greatly appreciated; they shared their experience in writing biographies that was very useful and encouraging. I would also like to thank Henry for the oral history he conducted with Lieutenant General (retired) Hollingsworth in the preparation of his book on Gen. William DePuy. Additionally, I must thank both John Votaw of the 1st Infantry Division Museum in Wheaton, Illinois, and Professor Terry Anderson of the History Department at Texas A&M University for their excellent oral histories with the general; both works were invaluable to this study of the general's life.

Special thanks go to Lauren Nelson and Nancy Smith of the Sanger Area Historical Society and Museum in Sanger, Texas, and the staffs of Cushing Library at Texas A&M University; the US Army Center of Military History at Fort McNair, Washington, DC; the Army Heritage and Education Center at Carlisle Barracks, Pennsylvania; the National Archives in College Park, Maryland; the 1st Division Museum in Wheaton, Illinois; the Vietnam Virtual Archive at Texas Tech University in Lubbock, Texas; and the Ike Skelton Combined Arms Research Library at Fort Leavenworth, Kansas.

Lastly, my heartfelt and lasting gratitude goes to my wife, Diana, who for over forty-nine years has provided all the love and support needed to keep me going, in uniform and out.

Introduction

On a bright fall day in September 1999, the 2,000-person Corps of Cadets assembled in the quadrangle on the campus of Texas A&M University. The occasion was the dedication of a bronze statue of Gen. James F. Hollingsworth, Texas A&M class of 1940. Hollingsworth—fiery, outspoken, and often controversial—was the most decorated general officer in the history of his alma mater and, according to the Veterans of Foreign Wars, the third most decorated American soldier in the history of our nation.[1] He was a three-time recipient of the Distinguished Service Cross and also received four Distinguished Service Medals, four Silver Stars, three Legion of Merit medals, three Distinguished Flying Crosses, six Purple Hearts, the Soldier's Medal, four Bronze Stars, and a remarkable thirty-eight Air Medals, among many others. His military service spanned nearly forty years, beginning with seven major World War II campaigns from North Africa in 1942 to the fall and occupation of Berlin in 1945, and continuing with command positions in the continental United States, Vietnam, and South Korea.

In paying tribute to Hollingsworth, Texas A&M University System regent Dionel Aviles said, "He was not just a soldier, he was a warrior." After other tributes by several visiting dignitaries, a statue was unveiled before a crowd of friends, family, and two thousand cheering cadets. The 700-pound, seven-foot-tall statue by Houston sculptor Lawrence Ludtke depicted the general in full battle gear—in fatigues and with a pistol strapped to his side—the way he spent most of his life in war.

The statue stood on a 3,000-pound block of granite. The base of the statue bears the inscription "Danger 79er," which was the general's radio call sign for more than twenty years. The accompanying plaque fittingly reads, "He was revered by his troops and feared by the enemy as a warrior who was always on the scene in times of need or at times of immense peril."

This was a unique honor since only two other soldiers—Gov. Lawrence Sullivan Ross and Gen. James Earl Rudder—have statues on the Texas A&M campus. "A great soldier and a great Aggie, Gen. Hollingsworth's legacy of courage and leadership will inspire countless generations of Aggie cadets," said Maj. Gen. Ted Hopgood, commandant of cadets.

After the unveiling of the statue, an obviously moved Hollingsworth spoke to the assembled crowd, insisting during his opening remarks that others deserved a statue before him. Nevertheless, he jokingly remarked that his statue was taller than George Patton's at West Point by three feet. In a more serious vein, he thanked former Texas governor William Clements for his role in sponsoring the statue and for his support when Clements was an official in the Defense Department. He then spoke directly to the cadets, telling them that they were "role models for the future." He urged the cadets to embrace accountability and responsibility. He related a few "war stories" to emphasize his points; he told of defying orders not to defend US troops from fire coming across the border from Cambodia. He accepted responsibility for his actions and was later vindicated when it became policy to return fire across the border when fired upon. Concluding his farewell to the corps, he charged the cadets to "remember God and country."

Like his statue, Hollingsworth was a larger-than-life figure who had a remarkable career in war and peace. The story that follows traces the life of James F. Hollingsworth from the family farm on the North Texas plain to the battlefields of Europe and Vietnam, to a key role in the defense of Korea, and into a fruitful retirement. It is the story of a brilliant, brash combat leader who was often profane and sometimes impetuous, but always focused on mission accomplishment and taking care of his soldiers. He was a unique individual, who was just as comfortable in the Pentagon and the halls of Congress as he was on the battlefields of Europe and Vietnam. It is the story of an American original who will be remembered as a great American patriot and a superb soldier.

Danger 79er

1

Sanger to 2nd Lieutenant

James Francis Hollingsworth was born on 24 March 1918, the first son of James Newton Hollingsworth and Mamie Ella Hollingsworth. The Hollingsworths owned a 231-acre farm seven miles northwest of Sanger, Texas. The property was located in Denton and Cook Counties, north of Dallas. Sanger was only a few miles south of the Red River and had been founded in 1886 as a watering stop on the Santa Fe Railroad. It boasted a flour mill and a cotton gin. The surrounding area was mostly ranch and farm land, with livestock and wheat, oats, corn, and cotton being the main crops.

The elder Hollingsworth was a direct descendant of Valentine Hollingsworth, who had immigrated to America from what is today Northern Ireland with his family in 1682.[1] Valentine and his family were Quakers and were part of the group led by William Penn that founded the Commonwealth of Pennsylvania. James Newton Hollingsworth was born 28 March 1877 in Fayette County, Alabama, the eldest of seven brothers and a sister. James N. Hollingsworth moved to Texas with his family when he was ten years of age, settling in the Union Hill community northeast of Sanger, where his father paid cash for what became the family farm.

When Francis was born, his father was forty-four years old. His mother, who was twenty years younger than her husband, was from a large Scottish family that Hollingsworth described as "more or less sharecroppers." The younger Hollingsworth adored his mother, whom he described as "a magnificent person." She was a musician, playing piano and singing in the church choir. She tried to teach Francis and his three younger brothers the piano, but they were more interested in outdoor activities.

Hollingsworth's father had completed only the third grade of formal schooling, but his son described his dad as "the hardest working man he had ever met."[2] He also described his father as a "disciplinarian," but not in a pejorative way. Rather, he said that his father emphasized doing things right. He taught Francis, as he was known until he went to high school, and his three younger brothers (Cecil, Ross, and Gerald) to always be honest and to stand up for what they believed in. He also taught the boys how to deal with people, stressing the need to treat others fairly and with dignity, a lesson that stayed with the Hollingsworth brothers for the rest of their lives.

It was a hard life on the farm. Just a month after Francis was born, a tornado struck, destroying part of the house and barn, but the family escaped injury by taking refuge in the storm cellar. On several other occasions, the family's crops were destroyed by sandstorms. Although this was during the Great Depression, the Hollingsworths did fairly well because the elder Hollingsworth abhorred borrowing money. Not owing anything to the bank, they were pretty self-sufficient during the really hard times.

Living on a farm, the boys all had chores when they got home from school. During the summers, they had full-time jobs on the farm, working in the cotton, corn, and wheat fields and tending to the livestock. In this environment, the boys learned the value of hard work and developed a strong sense of personal responsibility.

The Hollingsworths were hardworking farm people, but both parents believed in the value of education; they wanted their sons "to get an education so they wouldn't be farmers." The Hollingsworth boys began that education at Union Hill School, which they attended through the eighth grade. Union Hill was a country school that consisted of three teachers and three rooms. It was about a mile from their house down a dirt road and the Hollingsworth boys walked to school, rain or shine.

After finishing the eighth grade at Union Hill, Hollingsworth went to Sanger High School, which was about seven miles from the family farm. There was another student also named Francis; his last name was Stenchberg. So when the two boys named Francis showed up for the first day of high school, the principal said, "Well, we will call you [Stenchberg] Francis, and Hollingsworth, you will now be called 'Holly,' because we can't very well call the other boy 'Stinky,' can we?" The name stuck for the rest of Holly's life. That was all right with him; he had never liked to be called Francis, which he thought sounded like a girl's name.

When Hollingsworth started high school, the road to Sanger from the farm had not been completed, so during the week he stayed in town with the town constable and his wife, Mr. and Mrs. Baker, and then he would go home on the weekends. Holly was a good student in high school. He excelled at "hands-on" subjects but "had some trouble" with subjects like English. He was popular among his classmates. He played football and basketball at Sanger High and also ran track, lettering in all three sports. After practice, once the road was finished, he would head home to do his farm chores.

During his high school years, Holly was very active in the Future Farmers of America (FFA), an agricultural education and leadership organization. He was elected secretary during his freshman year, vice president during his sophomore year, and then president as a senior. The superintendent of the high school, L. I. Samuels, was also the faculty adviser for the FFA program at Sanger High. He became a mentor to Holly, giving him lots of responsibility. He even let the young man use his car to take five or six friends from the FFA group to a competition at the Agricultural and Mechanical College of Texas (now Texas A&M University) some two hundred miles away, a trip that apparently made an impression on the young man.

Holly routinely came into contact with African Americans who worked on the family farm. He learned a lot from an "old-timer" named Jim Sutton, who lived on their land. From an early age, Holly determined that the color of one's skin had nothing to do with what was in one's heart.

According to his mother, Holly was an avid reader, reading everything he could get his hands on, particularly history. She said, "He read about them a lot [the Civil War]." This was probably because he was "proud of his great-great-grandfather, a Captain in the Civil War. On the Southern side, of course."[3]

The family was religious while Holly was growing up, particularly his mother. She was a Baptist and attended church regularly, where she sang in the choir. Jim's father attended church but not regularly, because the demands of the farm meant that he was often working on Sundays.

The family's first car was a four-door Oldsmobile touring car with side curtains and a cloth top. Holly was fond of telling a story about looking out the kitchen window one day to see that a goat had gotten on top of the car, eaten a hole in the cloth top, and fallen through.

His father was a Democrat, but very conservative. He voted in all the elections but was not active in local politics. Holly said his father was too busy keeping the farm up to get involved in outside activities like politics.

Growing up, Holly developed habits that would stand him in good stead for the rest of his life. He learned early on that in order to deal with people fairly and justly, you could not ask them to do something that you wouldn't do yourself. He was also taught the value of accepting responsibility for one's own actions, and to never make excuses.

Upon Holly's graduation from Sanger High, his father wanted him to become a veterinarian. However, because of the severe impact of the Depression in the Sanger area, the Hollingsworth family did not have the funds to send him to college. The vagaries of farming meant that the family, according to Holly, relied on bumper crops just to pay the bills. These difficulties did not deter Holly, who remained determined to attend college and was prepared to get there through hard work and dedication.

Professor Samuels, his mentor at Sanger High, helped him get into North Texas Agricultural College (which was then part of the Texas A&M System but is now the University of Texas at Arlington). During the academic year 1935–1936, he attended class and worked on campus.

In the fall of 1937, Hollingsworth applied for admission to Texas A&M in College Station. By this time, Professor Samuels had departed Sanger to take a position on the A&M faculty. Samuels helped Hollingsworth get admitted to A&M, and upon arrival on campus, Hollingsworth elected to major in dairy science and vocational agriculture.

Texas A&M opened in October 1876 as the Agricultural and Mechanical College of Texas under the provisions of the Morrill Land-Grant Act. The Morrill Act, passed in 1862, provided for grants of public lands to establish colleges where the "object shall be, without excluding other scientific and classical studies and including military tactics, to teach such branches of learning as are related to agriculture and mechanical arts . . . to promote the liberal and practical education of industrial classes in the several pursuits and professions of life."[4] In 1871, the state of Texas used one of these grants to establish its first public institution of higher education; in turn, Brazos County donated 2,416 acres for the campus, near Bryan. The Agricultural and Mechanical College of Texas, which became known as Texas AMC, opened its doors in College Station on 4 October 1876 with six faculty members and a small group of students.

All of the students were required to participate in the Corps of Cadets and receive military training, establishing a strong military tradition at

A&M. Many Texas A&M graduates served during World War I. By 1918, 49 percent of all graduates of the college were in military service, more than from any other school.[5] In early 1918, the entire senior class enlisted, and many of its members were fighting in France when the war ended later that year. During the Great War, more than 1,200 alumni served as commissioned officers; forty-nine A&M graduates died.

In the years immediately after World War I, the Corps of Cadets at A&M numbered about 2,000. In 1921, an air science flight was added for those cadets who wished to enter the Army Air Corps. By 1926, there were about 2,500 cadets in the corps, organized into twenty-two company-sized units. From that point on, Texas A&M grew rapidly and became nationally recognized for its programs in agriculture, engineering, and military service.

By the time Hollingsworth arrived at College Station, there were around 4,000 cadets in the Corps of Cadets, the largest organization of its type in the United States and one of only three institutions that offered military instruction and commissions in all seven branches of the army—infantry, cavalry, field artillery, coastal artillery, engineers, signal corps, and chemical corps. The school's military tradition and its reputation as an agricultural school were strong. Holly had become interested in the ROTC program while at North Texas, and this influenced him to go to A&M, which had a stronger military tradition and a larger Corps of Cadets, assets that no doubt played a role in his decision.

As the war clouds began to gather in Europe and the Pacific, the military tradition at Texas A&M gained national attention. In the summer of 1937, President Franklin D. Roosevelt visited campus, where he reviewed the cadets and received a 21-gun salute. Roosevelt no doubt realized that if war came, Texas A&M would play a major role in any military mobilization efforts. He spoke on campus and used that rostrum to question the path of pacifism and disarmament; to some twenty thousand assembled in Kyle Field, the football stadium, Roosevelt said that it was time "to think in terms of preservation of the nations. Coming here today is an inspiration to me."[6]

In Roosevelt's annual message to Congress in January 1938, he repeated the main points that he had made in College Station, stressing that America was ill prepared for war and needed to rearm. His remarks seemed extremely prescient later in the year when Hitler and Mussolini signed the Rome-Berlin Axis pact.

Holly's father still wanted him to become a veterinarian, but Holly was not excited about the extra years of school it would take. Therefore, when he arrived at A&M, he focused his efforts on the Corps of Cadets and getting a commission.

By his own account, Holly enjoyed the Corps of Cadets, which by the time of his arrival was organized into five regiments (Infantry, Field Artillery, Engineers, Cavalry, and Coast Artillery). Hollingsworth selected infantry as his required military science course. He was assigned to Headquarters Company, 1st Infantry Battalion, in the Corps of Cadets.

Hazing was a part of the corps experience, and Holly later condemned it as "a foolish prankster sort of thing that didn't contribute a damn thing to anything." Nevertheless, he partook in the hazing. Later, he said he had never beaten anyone with a paddle or harmed anyone in any way. However, he admitted that he had participated in the pranks, like throwing a bucket of water on someone who was sleeping. Although most hazing was pretty mild, Holly did not believe that the practice served any useful purpose.

Despite the hazing, Holly believed that he learned a lot about leadership in the Corps of Cadets. As a second-year cadet, Holly was a squad leader. As a junior, he was a sergeant. During his senior year, he was a cadet captain on the 2nd Infantry Battalion staff.

He later said he learned a lot from leading others in the accomplishment of assigned tasks. He enjoyed standing in front of the other cadets and communicating with them in such a fashion that they all understood what needed to be done and then guiding them to completing the task at hand. He enjoyed the camaraderie and the satisfaction of working on projects with his fellow cadets.

The corps also taught him discipline and leadership. To Hollingsworth, this meant learning to do things well, so well that they become habitual and automatic. He believed this left his mind free to meet ever-changing situations. As for leadership, he learned that he could not ask a subordinate to do anything that he was not prepared to do.

Holly also learned a lot from the enlisted cadre, most of whom had been in the military for fifteen or twenty years. When asked in later years, Holly said he believed that his time in the Corps of Cadets at A&M gave him a firm foundation for the rest of his life. It whetted his appetite for the military and helped prepare him for the demands of a military career.

In addition to being a member of the Corps of Cadets, Holly also worked to put himself through college. Professor Samuels helped him get a job on campus at the creamery, which supplied the campus and surrounding community with milk and cheese products. Holly worked at the creamery for the whole time he was at A&M. Because of his earlier farm and FFA experience, he excelled at the job. Since he also did well in chemistry, he was promoted to laboratory technician at the creamery, receiving a pay raise of twenty-five cents per hour. To keep his job, he had to get up at 4:00 in the morning to get to the creamery early so he could run the chemical analysis of milk as it was brought in by local dairy farmers. He finished with this by 7:45 and headed back to his room for a shower before making his first morning class. After class, he went back to the creamery for a final shift, in which he worked until 8:30 in the evening. The creamery was on the other side of campus from the corps area and he did not have a car, so he spent a lot of time walking between his job and the main campus. It was during this period that Hollingsworth developed a capacity for hard work and long hours, a capacity that would serve him well in his military career.

Because of his work schedule, Hollingsworth was unable to participate in varsity athletics, but he was very active in intramural sports, including football, basketball, cross-country, and track. In 1937, he was light heavyweight boxing champion. Hollingsworth did well academically at A&M but had problems with English. In addition to working and going to class, Hollingsworth was also active in a number of campus activities, including the Denton County Club and the Press Club, and he was associate editor of the *Longhorn* yearbook.[7]

At the end of his senior year, in 1939, Hollingsworth lacked several grade points for graduation, so A&M deferred his diploma for a year. During the following semester, Holly worked for Bewley Mills in Fort Worth, but he still wanted to go into the military. While he was working in Fort Worth, several classmates who had already graduated and been commissioned in the army invited him to visit them at Fort Sam Houston, where they were assigned to the 2nd Infantry Division. These visits only increased Holly's appetite for an army career.

As far as Texas A&M was concerned, the most significant happening later that year was that the Aggies defeated Tulane in football to win the national championship. That was a big deal to Hollingsworth, who would be a lifelong fan of Aggie football.

As war in Europe approached, Holly prepared for the next phase of his life. On 19 March 1940, he married a hometown girl from Sanger, Katherine "Nickie" Nicholson, daughter of John A. Nicholson, the town postmaster. Although they had gone to high school together, they had not dated then. She said in school that she "wouldn't date Hollie Hollingsworth for all the money in the world."[8] She didn't specify why, but she changed her mind after they had a blind date when he was at A&M and she was attending Texas Woman's University in Denton.

In May 1940, Holly completed the required courses and received his diploma. The same day, he was commissioned a 2nd lieutenant in the infantry. He was anxious to get on with his military career, particularly in light of the situation brewing in Europe. Once in uniform, Holly would join the long line of A&M graduates who would make their mark in the coming war. The college would produce more than 20,000 soldiers, sailors, airmen, and marines who would sign up to fight the Germans and Japanese. Of those, 14,123 Aggies served as officers, more than the number from any other school and more than the combined total from the United States Military Academy at West Point and the United States Naval Academy at Annapolis.[9]

2

World War II Begins

The 2nd Armored Division

Lieutenant Hollingsworth was called to active duty in July 1940. He was assigned to Fort Benning, Georgia, to the 2nd Armored Division, commanded by Maj. Gen. Charles L. Scott. The new lieutenant, who was reassigned from the infantry to the armor branch, joined a brand-new division. It had just been formed at Fort Benning on 15 July 1940.

The division was a direct descendant of the World War I American Tank Corps. Upon activation, the division was composed of a skeleton force of about 100 officers and 2,200 enlisted men. At full strength, it would have nearly 10,000 men, including 530 officers. The Table of Organization and Equipment (TOE) called for about 700 armored vehicles. However, it would take the new division some time to achieve these levels in personnel and vehicles.

The 2nd Armored Division was originally organized as a "heavy" division with two armored regiments of four medium tank and two light tank battalions each. Additionally, it had an armored infantry regiment, an armored reconnaissance battalion, three artillery battalions, and an engineer battalion. It also included an ordnance battalion, a supply battalion, a medical battalion, a signal company, an adjutant general company, and a military police platoon.

The early days of the 2nd Armored Division were chaotic as new personnel were assigned to the fledgling organization. Additionally, at the same time, the new division had to acquire equipment and organize its subordinate units. The division's equipment was a mix-and-match affair. Initially, the division had three different types of tanks powered with seven different types of engines, both gasoline and diesel.

By far the most pressing problem for the division was to train the new personnel assigned to the unit. The responsibility for transforming new recruits into an efficient armored fighting force fell to Col. George S. Patton Jr., an officer who would become legendary in the coming war and who would have a tremendous impact on Hollingsworth and the other new young lieutenants.

Upon arrival at Fort Benning, Hollingsworth was assigned to a tank battalion, 3rd Battalion, 68th Armored Regiment. Before reporting to his battalion, Hollingsworth met Colonel Patton at division headquarters. Hollingsworth was very impressed with Patton, who wore a Distinguished Service Cross and Silver Star from World War I on his uniform. Patton told him that the two of them would learn to fight together and that he expected Hollingsworth to meet all the standards of performance that Patton had set for his officers. Hollingsworth saluted and departed for his unit.

Patton left his imprint on everyone who served in the 2nd Armored Division. He seemed to be everywhere, speeding from place to place in his command car or a light tank outfitted with a steamboat siren that he claimed could be "heard eight miles away on a clear day."[1] Patton believed that he could mold the 2nd Armored Division into a force that would be the antidote to the German blitzkrieg that overran France. He was tireless in his efforts to get the division ready for war.

Holly later recalled the impression that Patton left, saying, "I've never seen a more immaculate image of leadership on any man I ever met in my life . . . he was fantastic." Holly remained enamored with Patton for the rest of his life. "I liked the way he operated; I liked the way he could ride a horse; I liked the way he could shoot a shotgun." Once at the 3rd Battalion, 68th Armor, Hollingsworth found that there were only four other officers—the battalion commander, who was a major, and three 1st lieutenant company commanders. Holly was the only 2nd lieutenant. All the other officers were graduates of the United States Military Academy at West Point.

In a battalion with so few officers, Hollingsworth served as the executive officer, the supply officer, the personnel officer, and the operations officer. In addition to these extra duties, he was sent to "I" Company to learn how to be a company commander. During the course of his time in the battalion, he worked with five different noncommissioned officers, all of them seasoned soldiers with many years of experience. Hollingsworth set about learning as much as he could from these NCOs. He later said that these sergeants "had PhDs in the art of soldiering" and that these "five great professors" of his life were responsible for his learning the real art of soldiering, which laid a firm foundation for the rest of his career.

Part of Holly's early development as an officer came on Monday evenings when Colonel Patton ran a "school" from 6:00 to 9:00 p.m. It was in these sessions that the charismatic Patton taught the young officers how to be leaders. Patton made a great impression on Holly, and it appears that he took much of what Patton had to say about leading men in battle to heart.

Patton stressed that leaders had to be firm and set high standards with the troops in training, but at the same time treat them like men. This was in line with the way Holly's father had raised him, and he was able to build on his early experiences and put them to good use as a young officer. He never forgot those lessons and always treated his soldiers, "the little fellers" as he called them, with dignity and respect.

The other thing he learned from Patton reinforced his natural pugnacity. Patton was all about taking the fight to the enemy. Patton taught him that the only way to save soldiers' lives was to kill the enemy before he could kill you; you had to do it as quickly and efficiently as possible. That was the only way to victory on the battlefield. Hollingsworth soon developed the same outlook. The only way to do that was to be up front in the thick of the fighting. Later in life, Holly was fond of saying, "There's only one place to be in war and that's in a fight. It's the only place. Up front. Either in it or looking for it." This would be his personal hallmark for the rest of his career, and he would soon get an opportunity to put those ideas to the test.

Some have claimed that Holly molded himself after Patton, but he disputed this, asserting, "Anybody is foolish if they say you are trying to be another Patton."[2] It appears, however, that the young officer was very much inspired and influenced by Patton and either consciously or unconsciously adopted some of his ideas and approaches to leading men in battle.

In November 1940, Major General Scott was promoted to command of I Armored Corps, and Patton, by then a brigadier general, assumed command of the division. He was fully empowered to stamp his hard-driving, hell-bent-for-leather personality and battle philosophy on the entire division. His biographer Carlo D'Este writes that no detail escaped Patton's personal attention, and he established rules for everything: refueling techniques, road march discipline, maintenance, tank gunnery, camouflage, security, radio discipline, and tactical formations.[3]

Maj. Gen. I. D. White first served under Patton at Fort Riley before joining the 2nd Armored Division as a major, and he later commanded the division in Europe. White recalled after World War II that "General Patton was really the person who instilled the division with great pride in itself and developed a great esprit, as well as a great deal of the aggressiveness which characterized the division throughout its entire service." White remembered a time on the range at Fort Benning when Patton asked a soldier on a rifle range what he was doing. The soldier replied that he was just trying to hit the target. Patton said, "You are like hell! You are trying to kill some German son of a bitch before he can kill you."[4] He was fond of exhorting his troops to "hold 'em by the nose and kick 'em in the ass!"[5] This aggressiveness no doubt influenced the young officers in the division, including Hollingsworth. They were part of Patton's team, and the esprit in the division grew rapidly. Patton was a hard taskmaster, but he made his troops feel like they were part of something special.

Shortly after assuming command, Patton ordered a march from Fort Benning to Panama City, Florida, to test march discipline, supply procedures, air-ground communication and control procedures, and field maintenance. Two columns of more than 100 light tanks and 74 mediums, with 1,000 supply and fuel vehicles and more than 6,400 men, converged on Panama City. The march was day and night (under blacked-out conditions), averaging twenty-five miles per hour.

On arriving at Panama City, Patton gave an interview to a local newspaper, saying, "The march is the first of its kind and the morale and performance of the men could not be excelled. The strain of the operation on the tanks and combat vehicles is terrific and the men have held up wonderfully."[6] Patton, naturally given to hyperbole, did not overstate the case in this instance. The march was a great success; only one tank broke down on the 300-mile round-trip.[7] Additionally, a number of valuable techniques were gained for how to keep fast-moving armored columns supplied and in battle condition over long distances. These techniques would be put to good use when the division went to war, as Patton knew it surely would.

Throughout the spring of 1941, Patton continued to push the division, which trained constantly in the Georgia countryside around Fort Benning. The 2nd Armored Division soon gained an enviable reputation; it was billed in the news media as the best-trained armored force in the world. At about this time (May 1941), reporters for the Columbus, Georgia, *Ledger* dubbed the 2nd Armored Division "Hell on Wheels," and the name stuck.

Despite the growing reputation of the division, Patton, promoted to major general, was not satisfied with the state of his unit. He believed that time was growing short and that the United States would probably soon enter the war that was raging in Europe. Accordingly, he accelerated the pace of division training programs and field maneuvers to get the division ready for war.

In June 1941, the 2nd Armored Division moved to Camp Forest, Tennessee, to take part in what became known as the Tennessee Maneuvers. One objective of these maneuvers was to test a reorganization of the 2nd Armored Division. This new alignment would eliminate the brigade as a command, since training had revealed that a brigade was too large and unwieldy to control effectively in combat. Between 17 June and 26 June, the division participated in six "battles." General Patton noted many mistakes made by the division and took immediate measures to correct the identified shortcomings. The division quickly found out that the armored units did not fare well in massive frontal assaults against a well-armed and dug-in enemy force. Accordingly, Patton and his senior commanders developed a new tactic whereby the attackers pinned down the enemy's frontal forces while probing for weak spots on the enemy's flanks. Once the vulnerable area was found, the tanks and attached infantry charged through the enemy positions to attack deep into the enemy's rear.

Patton placed a premium on initiative. He continually preached that victory went to those who could seize and maintain the initiative. Not to do so was considered a cardinal sin. He drilled this into his troops, and this approach enabled the units of the 2nd Armored Division to move faster than most other units. Patton also emphasized discipline, intending to create a pattern of behavior that would become second nature in times of stress and confusion on the battlefield. Such lessons would serve Hollingsworth and his fellow officers well once the United States entered the war and the 2nd Armored Division was committed in battle against the Germans.

After about a year at Benning, Hollingsworth was sent to automotive school at Fort Knox, Kentucky. There for three months, he learned about tank maintenance and about how to employ large tank formations. Then in February 1942, he was assigned to the 5th Armored Division, which was stationed at Camp Cooke in California, for tests in the desert to determine whether gasoline or diesel engines were best for tanks in a desert environment. These tests lasted about six months.

During this time, Hollingsworth became a father. Nickie gave birth on 9 March 1942 to a son, who was named James Francis Hollingsworth II. He would be known as "Jamie" and became the apple of his father's eye.

According to Hollingsworth, his superiors in the division selected him for a very sensitive mission to South America for an unnamed government agency. He was sent to Belem, Brazil. At this time, there were rumors that the Germans were putting agents ashore in Brazil using submarines. In his oral history, Holly implied that he had been working with the FBI in Brazil to observe submarine activity and monitor the potential for spies entering the area.[8] He stayed in Brazil until December 1942, when he was transferred to North Africa to join the 2nd Armored Division, which had just landed in Casablanca, Morocco.

The Division Prepares for War

US entry into the war was still some months away, but Patton continued to drill the 2nd Armored Division relentlessly. Shortly after Hollingsworth departed for Fort Knox, the division received new vehicles and weapons. In mid-August, the division prepared for another set of maneuvers, which were held in Louisiana and involved larger numbers of units and personnel than any previous training exercise, the equivalent of eight divisions. Patton saw these maneuvers as an excellent opportunity to continue to hone the combat skills of his division. Before the maneuvers began, he told his men, "You will make your shoulder patch something that will cause as much dread to the enemies of your country as it causes pride among your friends."[9]

During the course of the Louisiana Maneuvers, which lasted until September 1941, the division fought six "battles." These were demanding exercises in terrain much more difficult than what the division had experienced in North Carolina. The exercises helped identify lingering deficiencies, particularly regarding the employment of maximum available firepower, but generally, the division under Patton performed very well, conducting a 350-mile end run to outflank the Red force that brought the exercise to a premature halt after just five days.[10] To Leon Kay of the United Press, the ability of the 2nd Armored Division to move and fight "looked like a flashback from a Nazi advance of the European theater."[11]

Following the Louisiana Maneuvers, the division repaired and replaced vehicles, to include the reception of more light and medium tanks and half-tracks for the infantry. More importantly, during this time the division received and installed voice radios in its vehicles. These were much more reliable than the old Morse-code radios, which worked infrequently at best, and greatly improved command and control among the combat elements of the division.

By this time, General Patton was increasingly pleased with the progress of the division and the capability of its tankers. They would have one more opportunity to hone their skills in exercises that were held in South Carolina in November 1941. The tanks were moved from Fort Benning to the maneuver area on railroad flatcars, while the infantry and artillery road-marched from the home station. The 2nd Armored was to act as a defending force with the mission of stopping the advance of an "enemy" force from the south near Columbia, South Carolina. The tactics that were developed in the Tennessee Maneuvers and perfected in the Louisiana Maneuvers worked perfectly. In the first "battle," Patton's tankers found weak spots in the enemy front and penetrated to the depth of the enemy formation.

In the second "battle," the outcome was a replay of the first and was so successful that the exercise was terminated a day early with all objectives achieved. The third "battle" ended in a draw, after certain rule changes were instituted that put the tankers at a distinct disadvantage. Nevertheless, Patton was elated at the performance of his division; he was beginning to believe that the division was ready for war.

Upon returning to Fort Benning, Patton issued a General Order to his command: "You have completed six months of active field training under severe conditions. Through Tennessee, Louisiana, and Carolina maneuvers, you have acquitted yourselves individually and by units as soldiers. You were commended by the highest and most experienced officers in the Army for your appearance, your discipline, your soldierly deportment, and your combat efficiency. By every test short of war, you are veterans."[12] The order was dated 6 December 1941. The following day, the Japanese attacked US forces at Pearl Harbor. By 11 December, the country was at war with Japan, Germany, and Italy.

With the declaration of war on Germany, the 2nd Armored Division prepared for overseas movement and went through several significant changes, not the least of which was a change of commanders. In January 1942, Patton was promoted to command I Armored Corps, and Maj. Gen. Willis D. Crittenberger assumed command of the division.

By the end of January, the 2nd Armored Division had reorganized, forming the organization with which it would go to war. The 68th Armored Regiment was disbanded, sending a company of light tanks to each battalion in the 66th and 67th Armored Regiments. This left those regiments with two medium-tank companies and one light-tank company. Under the new organizations, the two tactical headquarters were Combat Command A (CCA) and Combat Command B (CCB), each of which could be task organized with different mixes of tank and infantry units based on the situation and mission. The 66th Armored Regiment was assigned to CCA and the 67th Armored Regiment to CCB. The two tank regiments included two medium-tank battalions and one light-tank battalion.

The division's 41st Infantry Regiment had three battalions, and the three division artillery battalions each had three firing batteries, for a total of fifty-four howitzers. The division reconnaissance battalion had three reconnaissance companies and a light-tank company. Additionally, there was a tank destroyer battalion and an engineer battalion. For logistical support, the quartermaster and ordnance battalions formed a new maintenance battalion, and together with the supply battalion, they formed the Division Trains. A signal company and a medical company completed the combat service support for the division. Fully reorganized, the division numbered more than 14,600 officers and men.

The situation in North Africa was bad and seemed to be worsening as the British tried to hold off Field Marshall Erwin Rommel's Afrika Korps. British armored units had taken significant losses, and General Crittenberger was ordered to prepare some of his tanks and self-propelled artillery for shipment to the British in North Africa. Maj. Gen. Charles Scott, the division's earlier commander, headed up this contingent, which included trained mechanics to maintain the M4 Sherman tanks and a number of tank crews to reinforce the hard-pressed British.

Upon arrival in North Africa, Scott began to send reports back to the division, which were used to improve training at Fort Benning before the division shipped out. During July and August 1942, the division again conducted major maneuvers in the Carolinas to test and refine the techniques that were developed based on General Scott's reports from the desert.

In July 1942, even before the Carolina maneuvers were completed, General Crittenberger was moved to assume command of III Armored Corps.

Brig. Gen. Ernest N. Harmon, a graduate of Norwich University, assumed command of the division.

With the second set of Carolina maneuvers completed, the division moved to Fort Bragg, North Carolina. There, intensive training continued as the division made final preparations for deployment overseas. By the end of August, it became clear to the senior leaders of the division that they would be headed to North Africa.

Operation TORCH

Operation TORCH, the British-American invasion of French North Africa, began on 8 November 1942. The operation consisted of three task forces: the Western Task Force, under General Patton, would focus on Casablanca in French Morocco; the Center Task Force would be aimed at Oran, and the Eastern Task Force would land at Algiers. When the initial objectives were seized, the follow-on operation would be an attack toward Tunis, some five hundred miles to the east.

The Western Task Force comprised the 2nd Armored Division along with the 3rd and 9th Infantry Divisions. They sailed from several ports in the United States on 23 October 1942. When the convoy joined up in the Atlantic and headed east, it numbered more than 100 ships with some 35,000 men embarked.

OPERATION TORCH
November 1942

The Western Task Force reached its station off the Moroccan coast on 7 November 1942, D minus 1 (one day before the attack was scheduled to begin). The attack force was split into three groups. One group, code named BRUSHWOOD, under the command of Maj. Gen. John P. Lucas, consisting of the 3rd Infantry Division and the 1st Battalion of the 67th Armored Regiment, would land at Fedala, an oil tanker port about twenty miles northeast of Casablanca. Another group, code named GOALPOST, with Brig. Gen. Lucian Truscott commanding the 60th Infantry Regiment from the 9th Infantry Division and the 1st Battalion, 66th Armored Regiment, would go ashore at Port Lyautey, some sixty miles northeast of Casablanca.

The southernmost portion of the attack, code named BLACKSTONE, under the command of General Harmon, along with the remainder of the 2nd Armored Division, was to capture Safi, about 150 miles south of Casablanca and the only deepwater harbor south of the city. Only a part of the 2nd Armored Division would go in the initial landing at Safi, with a number of armored vehicles deemed sufficient to accomplish the mission and about 1,500 selected personnel. In addition, General Harmon would have operational control of the 47th Infantry Regiment of the 9th Infantry Division for the landing and subsequent attack. The plan was to secure the port and then leave Safi in the hands of the infantry while the tanks rolled north along the coast to assist in the capture of Casablanca.

The Western Task Force landed on the French Moroccan coast on 8 November; upon taking their objectives, all forces were to converge on Casablanca for the final attack on the city. The landings were made without covering fire, with the hope that the French defenders could be persuaded to surrender without a major battle. This proved to be a costly mistake, as the French resisted the landings.

Nevertheless, the 2nd Armored Division made the landing at Safi, as planned. Once the infantry and a few light tanks that were landed by lighter had secured the port, the rest of the division's tanks were off-loaded, and after blocking an attempt by French forces to reinforce Safi, the division advanced to the north to attack Casablanca from the flank and rear. The division was in its attack position on the high ground overlooking the city when Casablanca surrendered to Allied forces on 11 November.

The landings at Algiers and Oran, along with those in French Morocco at Port Lyautey, Fedala, and Safi, had accomplished all assigned objectives. The landings had cost more than 500 American lives and resulted in

2,500 French casualties. The 2nd Armored Division lost four killed and five wounded. The division and its subordinate units had acquitted themselves very well in their first test of fire. Still, it was clear that there was a lot to learn in the harder fighting to come.

With French Morocco in Allied hands, the advance elements of the 2nd Armored Division moved into the Mamora Cork Forest, about eighteen miles northeast of Rabat, to await the arrival of the rest of the division. The division was not scheduled to take part in the advance toward Tunis but was ordered to guard the Spanish–French Moroccan border, to prevent attempts by Spain or Germany to attack supply and communication lines and to keep open the single-track railroad between Casablanca and Oran. The division would use this time to conduct training for anticipated follow-on operations.

Meanwhile, the rest of the division embarked on ships and headed for North Africa. Hollingsworth joined the division in early December 1942, returning to the 67th Armored Regiment, where he took command of a medium-tank company, which had three platoons of five tanks each plus two in the company headquarters. By the end of December, the entire division had reunited in North Africa and began to prepare for its next mission.

In February 1943, as Holly was settling in to his new assignment, the Germans mauled elements of the US 34th Infantry and 1st Armored Divisions at Kasserine Pass in Tunisia. After the battle, the II Corps commander, Lt. Gen. Lloyd Fredendall, was relieved and Major General Harmon, the 2nd Armored Division commander, was temporarily put in charge of II Corps. After Harmon stabilized the situation somewhat, General Patton assumed command of II Corps.

After that debacle, there was a desperate need for replacement equipment, but shipping problems prevented resupply from the States. The 2nd Armored was ordered to provide trucks to help reequip the 1st Armored Division. Additionally, the tank companies in the division were tasked to send the equivalent of one tank platoon, one officer, and twenty-four men to the 1st Armored. With the 2nd Armored Division not engaged, General Harmon was ordered to go to the front, where he was named deputy commander of II Corps. He quickly organized an effective defense and then launched a counterattack that drove the Germans out of Kasserine and back to Faid Pass.[13]

Hollingsworth, who had been promoted to captain, was one of those officers who went forward with his tanks to join Harmon and Patton in retaking the lost ground. In his first action, Hollingsworth had fifteen tanks in his area of responsibility. Their position was attacked by ten German tanks dragging antitank guns behind them. As the tanks advanced toward the American lines, they dropped off the antitank guns, whose crews rapidly began to dig them in. Hollingsworth's tanks opened fire and the Germans withdrew; Hollingsworth determined that the Germans were trying to lure his tanks into an antitank ambush. As Hollingsworth cautiously led his tanks forward, they came under fire from the German antitank guns. Hollingsworth massed all his firepower, knocking out all the antitank guns.[14] He held his position until the rest of his unit arrived in the area, and then they continued the attack as the Germans fell back slowly. Hollingsworth and his company were in combat almost every day until they returned to the division.

This was Hollingsworth's baptism of fire, and he passed with flying colors. He was an energetic leader who always led from the front. Naturally aggressive, he was fearless under fire, and taking his lessons from Patton at Fort Benning, he pushed as hard as he could for as long as he could until the enemy was defeated. This early action set the tone for Hollingsworth's performance in combat for the rest of the war in Europe.

When Holly and the others who had gone to the Tunisian front returned to the division, they found that the division had begun training for the invasion of Sicily. Hollingsworth and the other returnees from the front shared the benefit of what they had learned in battle against the Germans, which proved invaluable in preparing for operations to come.

In April 1943, General Harmon departed the division to assume command of the 1st Armored Division. He was replaced by Brig. Gen. Allen F. Kingman. However, Kingman was in command for only a month; he was fluent in French so he was transferred to the French Armor School as its American adviser. In May, Brig. Gen. Hugh J. Gaffey, formerly commander of CCB, became the sixth commander of the division. At the same time, Col. Isaac D. White, an officer who would play a major role in Holly's professional development and postwar assignments, assumed command of CCB.

By the middle of May, all German and Italian resistance in North Africa had ceased; a quarter million of the enemy surrendered and the war in North Africa was over. In late April and early May 1943, the 2nd Armored Division moved to Oran to begin amphibious training for what would be known as Operation HUSKY, the assault on Sicily.

Operation HUSKY was to be the largest amphibious operation in history to that point. Three thousand ships of all kinds carried 160,000 men, 600 tanks, and 14,000 other vehicles. It was to be a joint American, British, and Canadian operation with British general Harold Alexander in overall field command under General Dwight D. Eisenhower as supreme commander. Two armies, the British Eighth under Gen. Bernard Law Montgomery and the American Seventh under General Patton, would assault the southern coast of Sicily. Montgomery's forces, consisting of four infantry divisions, part of an airborne division, two armored brigades, and three commando teams, would land from Cape Murro di Porco around to Pozzallo on the southeastern coast. Patton's troops, including the 1st, 3rd, and 45th Divisions, the 2nd Armored Division, and part of the 82nd Airborne Division, would land on the central southern coast from Licata to Cape Scaramia.

Sicily

Operation HUSKY began on 10 July 1943. The 2nd Armored Division supported the 1st Infantry Division in the battle at Gela and the 3rd Infantry Division at Licata. From D-Day to about 14 July, tanks from the 2nd Armored were assigned to a variety of infantry units for the push inland off the beaches. On 16 July, the division pulled all of its attached units back at the order of General Patton, who had devised a plan to capture the northwestern port of Palermo. He formed a "Provisional Corps" under Maj. Gen. Geoffrey Keys, which was made up of elements of a Ranger battalion and the 82nd Airborne Division in addition to the 2nd Armored and 3rd Infantry Divisions. Patton was unhappy with the role that his Seventh Army was assigned, which was initially to protect the left flank of Montgomery's Eighth Army as it slugged its way up the east coast toward Messina. He requested approval from Alexander to take Palermo; although its seizure had no immediate impact on the success of Operation HUSKY, Patton wanted to take the port for the publicity value it would have.

On 20 July, the division attacked westward, with CCA leading and CCB in support. The division overran one town after another, reaching a point just five miles south of Palermo on 21 July. As the lead elements of the division approached the city, the resistance stiffened, but the enemy was no match for the advancing tanks and infantry of the 2nd Armored. The Italian commander of the port defenses at Palermo surrendered on 22 July.

No military unit in history had moved as far and as fast against enemy resistance as had Patton's "Provisional Corps" spearheaded by the 2nd Armored Division.[15]

During the course of the campaign in Sicily, the division suffered 56 killed, 250 wounded, and 32 missing and presumed dead. The 2nd Armored Division alone captured more than 16,000 enemy soldiers in its twelve days of combat.

During the campaign, Hollingsworth, who had been promoted to major, was the regimental maintenance officer for the 67th Armored Regiment, chosen primarily because of his background and schooling at Fort Knox. As such, he was responsible for the maintenance of the entire regiment, but he also commanded the maintenance company, which had three tank platoons organized for combat. During the course of the operation, Hollingsworth's jeep hit a mine; although the vehicle was destroyed, he suffered only a slight concussion. This proved to be only the first time that he would be injured while under fire.

The British, with US support from the American 1st, 3rd, 9th, and 45th Divisions, pushed the Germans out of Sicily at Messina, taking the port on 16 August. The Allies had won a spectacular victory. In thirty-eight days of fighting, they had essentially destroyed thirteen Axis divisions, killed 37,000 enemy soldiers, and captured most of the rest; only a handful of the 200,000 Axis soldiers who garrisoned Sicily were able to escape to the Italian mainland.

After the fighting in Sicily was over, the division spent four months serving as a military occupation force. This transition from combat operations to occupation proved a testing ground for the occupation and military government that was later installed in postwar Germany after September 1945. Additionally, during this time the division repaired its vehicles and continued to train in tactics and amphibious operations.

In late September 1943, the 2nd Armored Division and the 1st Infantry Division were alerted to prepare for embarkation to another theater of operations. The tankers were told to leave everything but their personal items, clothing, and individual weapons. Most of the division's tanks and equipment would be left behind. On 1 November, the division was relieved of all occupation duties and was ordered to prepare to load ships for an undisclosed location. The division was headed for England, but only a few key senior leaders knew its destination.

3

The Fight for Fortress Europe

Preparations for Invasion

The convoys carrying the division arrived at the ports of Liverpool and Greenock, Scotland, on Thanksgiving Day in November 1943. All elements of the division immediately proceeded by rail to Tidworth, England, a former cavalry post on the Salisbury Plain some seventy miles southwest of London and only thirty-five miles from the channel port of Portsmouth. After spending a week settling into its new garrison, the division began to receive its new equipment.

The next few weeks were spent drawing new vehicles and associated equipment. The vast motor parks that grew on the edge of the camp were scenes of feverish activity. All equipment had to be unpacked, thoroughly checked, sorted, and stowed. The waterproofing on the vehicles had to be removed and the vehicles repainted. Then came a series of break-in marches to test the vehicles and to familiarize the crews with the new equipment.

With all elements newly equipped and the equipment and vehicles tested, the division began an extensive training program in preparation for the cross-channel invasion of France. This program began with crew drill and range practice, integrating the lessons learned in North Africa and Sicily. This was followed with field exercises meant to forge the companies and battalions into more efficient fighting units. The focus was on coordinating tanks, infantry, and close air support.

The area around Tidworth had been evacuated and the surrounding countryside had been set aside for training purposes. The Salisbury Plain provided ideal training ground for armored operations and the division took full advantage of the opportunity, conducting large-scale maneuvers and live-fire exercises.

In February 1944, the 2nd Armored was assigned to XIX Corps, commanded by Maj. Gen. C. H. Corlett. Shortly thereafter, General Gaffey was transferred to Patton's Third Army and Maj. Gen. Edward H. Brooks became the division's seventh commander. All passes were cancelled in April, and by the first of May all units were confined to their areas. For the rest of the month, the division practiced amphibious landings.

By early June the waiting was over; the long-anticipated invasion of the European continent was imminent. The 2nd Armored Division was ordered to move from Tidworth to the marshaling areas near Portsmouth and Southampton.

The Normandy Invasion

On 6 June 1944, Allied forces commenced Operation OVERLORD, the invasion of Normandy and the establishment of a lodgment on the continent of Europe.[1] The operation began with a 1,200-plane airborne assault that preceded an amphibious landing involving more than 5,000 vehicles and nearly 160,000 troops.

The 2nd Armored Division was initially held in reserve by Major General Gerow's V Corps, which was part of Gen. Omar Bradley's First Army. The 2nd Armored would not hit the beach on D-Day, but it would be the first Allied armored division to land on the continent after the assault divisions had secured the beachhead.

The first elements of the division landed on the beach at Normandy on 9 June, but the rest of the combat elements did not land until mid-June. The lead elements came under heavy fire from the Luftwaffe and German artillery.[2] Once ashore, the division was to be ready to help expand the beachhead and exploit the successes of the initial landing.

During this period, the division was also responsible for providing assistance to the forces that had already landed. Accordingly, the division soon found one of its combat commands sent to support the 101st Airborne Division at Carentan. It was there that troops from the 2nd Armored saw their first combat on the continent in the bocage, or hedgerow, country. The countryside was dotted with small fields surrounded by thick hedgerows, sunken roads, and many intersections. The hedgerows, which had grown dense over the years, were a particular problem that greatly impeded tank movement out of the beach area. Sgt. Curtis G. Culin of the 102nd Reconnaissance Squadron came up with an innovative answer to the problem. He designed a hedgerow cutter, which consisted of heavy steel prongs salvaged from dismantled German beach obstacles, sharpened and welded to the front of the tanks. A tank with the prongs welded to its bow was able to charge into the hedges, where the prongs cut through the mass of roots and allowed the tank to plow through the hedgerows without exposing the tank's belly. After a few experiments with Culin's "Rhino," First Army locally manufactured five hundred of them.[3]

Having adapted to the situation, the Allies drove the Germans back with heavy losses, but it was a slow and deliberate process. During this bloody war of attrition, the 2nd Armored Division tankers earned the grudging respect of the German army, who nicknamed the division "Roosevelt's Butchers."[4] At the same time, the 2nd Armored Division's reputation among the Allies was also growing. Donald Houston reports a comment by an American military policeman on seeing CCA pass by his road intersection: "That's Patton's old outfit. Toughest bunch in the army. Hitler never saw nothing like them."[5]

On 27 June, Cherbourg fell to American troops and the Cotentin Peninsula was cleared two days later. The next goal was Saint-Lô, which was to be used for follow-on operations to continue the attack eastward. The city finally fell on 18 July after five weeks of bitter fighting.

With the lodgment in Normandy firmly established, the Allies began to build up supplies and troops for the breakout through German lines and the subsequent advance across France toward Germany. The 2nd Armored was pulled from the line and assumed a position as reserve force until the third week of July. During this period, the division focused on repairing and maintaining its tanks in preparation for follow-on operations.

Breakout

With the capture of Saint-Lô, the Allies made plans for Operation COBRA, the breakout from Normandy. The objective of this operation was to secure Brittany, hoping to trap a large portion of the German Seventh Army in the process, and then continue the attack to the Loire River. Leading the operation would be Gen. Omar Bradley, commander of First US Army. Bradley hoped to stage a breakthrough on a narrow front by a single corps, with a corps on each flank to keep the German forces tied down. Bradley summarized the plan for COBRA in his memoirs: "First, we must pick a soft point in the enemy's line; next, concentrate our forces against it. Then after smashing through with a blow that would crush his front-line defenses, we would spill our mechanized columns through that gap before the enemy could recover his senses."[6]

According to the plan, the initial breakthrough would be made by US VII Corps, commanded by Maj. Gen. J. Lawton Collins. The point of the attack would be between Marigny and Saint-Lô, where the 9th and 30th Infantry Divisions would force a penetration in the German lines so that VII Corps' exploitation force, consisting of the 1st Infantry Division and the 2nd and 3rd Armored Divisions, could pivot on Marigny and drive through the penetration west to the sea between Coutances and Bréhal until enemy resistance collapsed. For this attack, the 2nd Armored Division would have 236 M4 medium and 158 M5A1 light tanks.

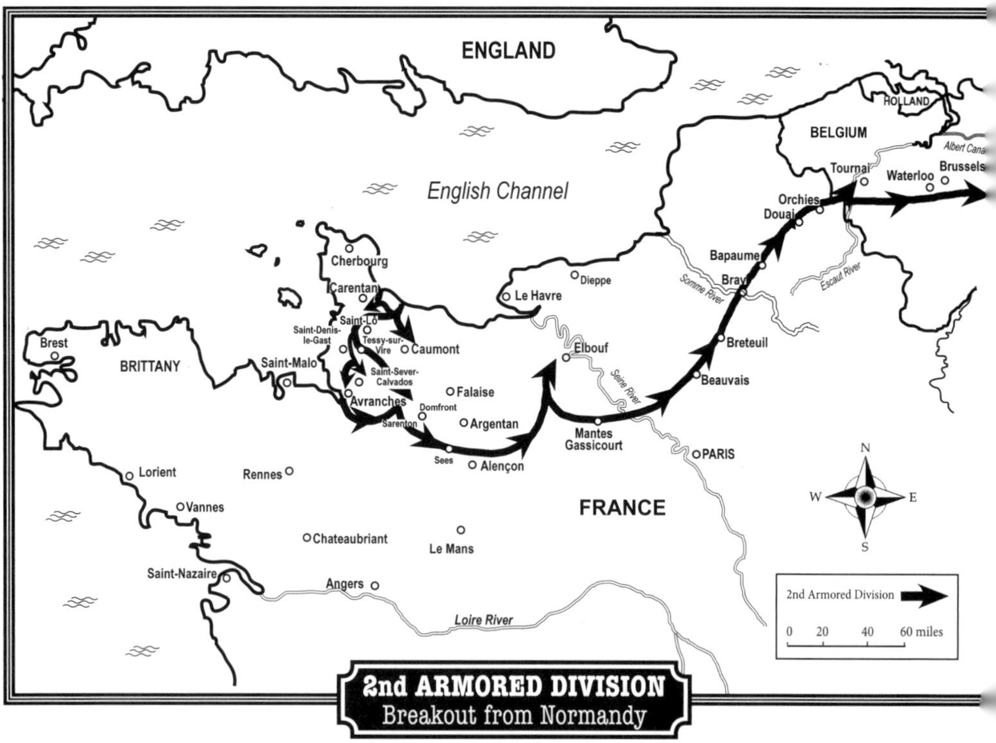

COBRA commenced on 25 July 1944, just fifty days after the initial Normandy beach landings, after an extensive aerial bombardment of the German defensive positions in front of VII Corps' advance. Carpet bombing was originally scheduled to begin at 1:00 p.m. on 24 July, but after the bombers were already in the air it was postponed because of marginal weather. Some of the aircraft did not get the message and carried out the attack along the northern edge of the bomb zone. The 30th Division suffered more than 25 men killed and another 131 wounded from bombs that dropped short during this strike.

When the attack was launched on 25 July, it got off to a good start, but it was seriously disrupted when bombs again accidentally fell on the attackers. Again, the 30th Division took the brunt of the bombing, losing 61 dead and 374 wounded. Gen. Lesley J. McNair, former commander of US Army Ground Forces, who had gone forward to observe the VII Corps attack, was one of those killed by the bombing that day.[7]

Despite this tragic incident, General Collins ordered his lead elements to continue the attack. Meanwhile, he ordered the breakthrough divisions, the 1st Infantry and 2nd and 3rd Armored, to remain concealed in their attack positions until the penetration was made by the lead infantry divisions.

Although the bombing had tragic consequences for the attackers, it proved very effective against the defending Germans. After heavy fighting all across the corps front, the attack resulted in a penetration of the German main line of defense. General Collins decided it was time to order the exploitation forces into action. This was a gutsy call that threw the German command off balance.

On the morning of 26 July, the 2nd Armored Division began its attack on the left flank into the penetration forged by the 30th Infantry Division, attacking with its two combat commands abreast. The lead columns carried two rifle companies on each battalion of tanks and were to drive to the southwest. By midnight, the division had advanced seven miles, losing three tanks in the process. It appeared that the defending Panzer-Lehr Division was collapsing, and General Collins, recognizing that he had the breakthrough he had been hoping for, ordered a continuation of the attack, favoring speed over caution.

By 28 July, the German defenses across the US front were crumbling. As the 2nd Armored Division moved forward, the Germans launched a counterattack, but it was unsuccessful and the Germans fell back in disarray.

On 29 July, Hollingsworth was in command of the service trains (logistical support elements) of Combat Command B (CCB). The forty vehicles loaded with gas and oil were dispersed in the woods near Notre-Dame de Chantilly when they were attacked by Luftwaffe fighter-bombers, which set one of the gasoline trucks on fire. The vehicle exploded, spraying burning fuel all around the area. Hollingsworth jumped into the nearest truck and drove it to a safer area, returning twice to remove other endangered vehicles as the enemy continued to bomb the area.[8] Once again, he demonstrated courage under fire as well as his reluctance to ask his soldiers to do anything that he would not do himself.

During the breakout, Hollingsworth went forward from the trains to locate and evacuate damaged vehicles. As he did, he was repeatedly exposed to intense artillery and small-arms fire. Nevertheless, he persevered and was later decorated for his efforts to keep his command advancing to the east.

On the night of 29 July, elements of the division came under attack from SS troops at Cambray and Saint-Denis-le-Gast, to the east of Coutances. In the bitter fighting that ensued, the American tankers repelled both attacks, inflicting heavy losses in men and tanks on the Germans. One American officer described the carnage from these battles as "the most Godless sight I have ever witnessed on any battlefield."[9] This battle was only a precursor of the carnage that was to come.

CCB continued the attack, cutting the road south out of Coutances near Lengronne and Cambray. Meanwhile, CCA continued covering the eastern flank, reaching Villebaudon. During 26–31 July, the 2nd Armored Division fought elements of more than a dozen German divisions. It is estimated that more than 2,250 Germans were killed and more than 5,000 taken prisoner. Close air support and the attacking "Hell on Wheels" tankers destroyed more than 100 tanks, 150 half-tracks and armored cars, and more than 100 heavy guns. In the process, the division sustained fewer than 100 killed and not quite 300 wounded. According to General Collins, the 2nd Armored Division "had done a magnificent job."[10]

After the breakout accomplished by VII Corps, General Bradley ordered VIII Corps to continue the attack to exploit what had already been gained. Very quickly the German command and control in the area collapsed. On 1 August, First Army became 12th Army Group, and General Patton's Third Army was activated. Commencing immediately, seven divisions from Patton's Third Army, now including the 2nd Armored Division, swept through

Avranches and turned southward to sweep through Brittany and the Loire River.[11]

As the division advanced, Hollingsworth continued to command the service and supply trains of CCB. During this time, he repeatedly exposed himself to enemy small-arms and artillery fire as he moved forward to recover damaged vehicles and remove destroyed tanks from the roadway to clear the path for the advancing columns. Hollingsworth realized that what he was doing was vitally important, but, feeling like he was stuck in the rear and missing the war, he was anxious to get with one of the forward units that were taking the fight directly to the Germans.

During the advance, CCB trains were repeatedly bombed by the Luftwaffe. While the Allies had air superiority, most of the assets were operating at higher altitudes, which gave the Luftwaffe more leeway at lower altitudes, and the German aircraft repeatedly harassed the armored columns as they moved eastward. The tankers fired back but were not very successful against the attacking German fighters. In one unfortunate incident, the Americans shot down a Spitfire that was chasing a German ME-109.

As the trains moved forward, the air attacks continued. At one point, Hollingsworth and his troops were bombed by a German HE-111 with a 4,000-pound bomb. This type of bomb had not been seen before in the war, and Holly later recalled that this "brought out the whole Air Ministry from England to look at the crater," which was forty meters across. This caused a lot of consternation because the troops on the ground had never seen such a large bomb. It damaged five of Holly's half-track armored vehicles and turned over two tanks. Being hit from the air without being able to fight back adequately was very frustrating to Hollingsworth, who redoubled his efforts to move to the front.

The "front" was a fluid concept during the rapid advance through northern France. The speed of the advance put a tremendous strain on the maintenance and service companies, which performed miracles in keeping the division moving eastward. There was no real front, as scattered enemy groups emerged along the axis of advance, sometimes as far as fifty miles behind the leading elements. The enemy was all around and the fighting was bloody and desperate. Hollingsworth had a number of opportunities to employ tanks to overcome the enemy pockets of resistance as the trains moved forward. These small actions only whetted his appetite for the main fight that was going on at the tip of the division's spearhead.

On 7 August, the German XLVII Panzer Corps made a major counterattack on VII Corps in the Mortain area. Although the Germans made initial gains, they were soon halted, and Allied aircraft inflicted severe losses on the attacking troops, eventually destroying nearly half the German tanks involved in the attack. During this battle, the 2nd Armored dispatched its two combat commands to attack the rear of the 1st SS and 116th Panzer Divisions at Saint-Hilaire and Barenton, respectively. Although fighting continued around Mortain for six days, VII Corps eventually turned back the German attack.

By 15 August, the 2nd Armored Division, having fought almost constantly since leaving the beach at Normandy, was pulled out of the line for rest and maintenance. The fighting had been tough on both soldiers and machines. The terrain was too rugged and restrictive for the wide flanking movements that best suited tank operations; the tankers and attached infantry had to fight through every village and hamlet, foot by foot and door by door.

Nevertheless, following the Allied breakout from Normandy, the German forces in northern France had become enveloped in a series of encirclements, starting with the Roncey pocket in late July and followed by the Falaise pocket in mid-August, thereby opening the possibility of a rapid thrust eastward. This was the general situation when, on 18 August, the 2nd Armored Division, now under XIX Corps, was ordered to continue the attack northeast toward Paris. CCA on the southern flank and CCB to its north covered more than a hundred miles in the next forty-eight hours. Resistance increased as the division got closer to the Seine River and Paris. Still, the lead elements of the division rolled on, overrunning German positions and destroying enemy tanks wherever they were encountered.

In the late afternoon of 26 August, CCB captured the crossing on the Seine at Elbeuf. The division had covered more than 125 miles in about a week, destroying elements of the 2nd Panzer, the 116th Panzer, the 17th Luftwaffe, and the 344th Infantry Divisions. For its performance in combat since landing in Normandy, the division was awarded the Presidential Unit Citation.

The Germans in Paris surrendered on 25 August. Operation COBRA had been a resounding success. The German Seventh Army in France had been decimated. More than 200,000 enemy soldiers had been killed or wounded, another 200,000 captured, and 1,300 tanks and 20,000 vehicles destroyed or captured. Additionally, the US Seventh Army had staged a second amphibious landing on the Mediterranean coast of southern France and raced northward to cut off the remainder of the German occupation forces in western and central France. As a result, there was wholesale withdrawal of German forces to the east; the enemy forces were in rout and the Allies wanted to keep the pressure on as they advanced toward Germany.

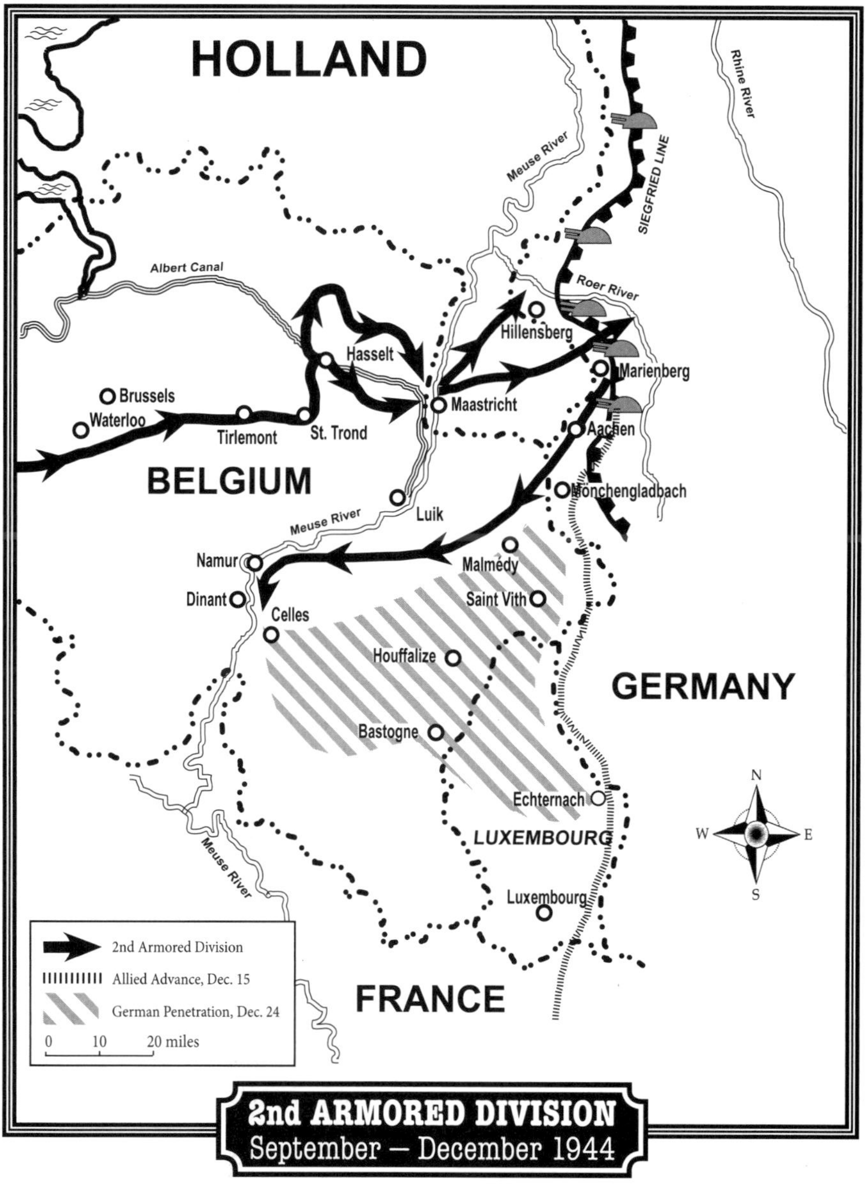

At Supreme Headquarters Allied Expeditionary Force, Gen. Dwight Eisenhower and his staff believed that the German Army was in its death throes. The Allies had advanced much farther and faster than had been anticipated in the original plan for Operation OVERLORD.[12] The order of the day was to press eastward toward Germany. However, the Allies had advanced so rapidly that they had outrun their logistics.

The Siegfried Line

The 2nd Armored Division continued its attack eastward, reaching the Belgian border in the first week of September. However, resupply was becoming critical; the logistics support could not keep up with the rapid advance of the tankers in the lead elements. The fuel situation was the most serious; on several occasions, when the division stopped for the night, the fuel tanks of the half-tracks were drained to get fuel to keep the tanks running so they could man the roadblocks to preclude German counterattacks.[13]

Despite the critical fuel situation, the division resumed its attack east on 5 September, in five separate armored columns. In a number of cases, the Army Air Corps flew in fuel in five-gallon cans, landing wherever it could find a suitable place near the onrushing tank units.

On 6 September, the division's 82nd Reconnaissance Battalion reached the Albert Canal, forty miles east of Brussels. The division hoped to secure crossing sites, but the retreating Germans had blown all the bridges. The rest of the division moved up to an assembly area outside Hasselt to make preparations for forcing a crossing over the canal.

As the division prepared to continue its attack eastward, Maj. Gen. Ernest Harmon, who had previously commanded the division, was back in the States preparing to take command of XXIII Corps, stationed at Camp Bowie, Texas, when he received a call from Gen. George C. Marshall, army chief of staff, directing him to report to Washington immediately. When he arrived, Marshall told him that the current commander of the 2nd Armored Division, Major General Brooks, would be leaving the division to assume command of V Corps. He then asked Harmon whether he wanted his old job back. Harmon was delighted and rushed to Europe to rejoin his old command. Harmon had commanded the division in 1942–1943, including during the TORCH landings in Morocco. Many of the men who had served in North Africa were still in the division, and for Harmon it was like a homecoming. His troops, who called him "Old Gravel Voice," were happy to have him back.

When Harmon assumed command, he was confronted with the daunting task of getting the division across the Albert Canal. The Germans had gained valuable time when the Allied armies were slowed because of the lack of adequate fuel supplies. They had been able to extricate troops from northern France and Belgium that might have been destroyed had the Allies been able to maintain the momentum of their advance. As the Allies got closer to Germany, the enemy resistance increased; it was clear that the Germans hoped to hold the line along the Albert Canal.

Harmon ordered three companies from the 82nd Reconnaissance to cross an intact bridge in the British sector to the north and clear the opposite bank in front of the division's assembly area at Hasselt. After a seesaw battle, the 82nd took Zonhoven, opposite Hasselt. On the morning of 13 September, CCA crossed the canal and cleared the city of German holdouts.

The division continued its attack to the east; both combat commands experienced heavy enemy resistance as they moved eastward. The Germans had established a strong defense in depth, and 2nd Armored tanks and infantry had to fight for every yard of progress. Nevertheless, by 17 September, the lead elements of the 67th Armored Regiment had crossed into Germany and taken the town of Wehr. By 20 September, CCA and CCB had both crossed into Germany. That day, the division was ordered to take up defensive positions and hold; it had outrun the corps' infantry, who needed time to catch up and stabilize the front lines. Additionally, the division needed this operational pause for maintenance, refueling, and ammunition resupply.

The Allied plan at this point centered on capturing the two industrial areas in western Germany, the Ruhr and the Saar Basin. The seizure of the Ruhr was deemed the most important, because the loss of the Ruhr combined with the loss of the Low Countries would eliminate 65 percent of German steel production and 56 percent of its coal production.[14] The Maubeuge-Liège-Aachen corridor provided the most direct route to the Ruhr. With the failure of 21st Army Group's Operation MARKET-GARDEN to seize a key bridge across the Rhine, the task of taking the Ruhr fell to Bradley's 12th Army Group.[15]

However, between the Allies and the Ruhr was the Siegfried Line, a series of fortifications protecting the German border that ran from Kleve on the Dutch border to near Basel on the Swiss border. The Siegfried Line was a complex arrangement of fortifications, tunnels, tank traps, and other barriers designed to provide defense in depth. The first row of defenses included hastily dug antitank ditches backed by five rows of tank obstacles, called "dragon's teeth," that were fashioned out of steel rails and concrete. Then came three rows of concrete pillboxes with walls up to eight feet thick interspersed with infantry fighting trenches. Farther to the rear were prepared artillery positions. Throughout the area, the approaches were seeded with tank and antipersonnel mines. The idea behind the Siegfried Line was not necessarily to stop the Allied attackers, but rather to weaken them and make them vulnerable to German counterattacks.

At this point, Maj. Gen. Charles Corlett's XIX Corps, positioned to the north and west of Aachen, was ordered to attack north of the city and penetrate the Westwall in its zone of operations with forces of the 30th Infantry and 2nd Armored before driving farther eastward toward Duran to link up with VII Corps making the main attack on Aachen. Between the 2nd Armored Division and the Siegfried Line flowed the Wurm River, thirty feet wide in this sector but only about three feet deep. According to the XIX Corps plan, the 2nd Armored Division was to cross the Wurm and then turn north and east to protect the corps' northern flank while the 30th Infantry Division wheeled south to aid VII Corps in capturing Aachen. General Harmon, the division commander, was less than happy about the mission to defend the flank; he thought that the division should be making the main attack on Aachen. Nevertheless, he issued his attack orders to conform to the corps' plan. The division was to advance with CCB following the 30th Division through the Siegfried Line, clearing the area between the Wurm and Roer Rivers and securing a crossing site at Linnich on the Roer. CCA was to also follow the 30th Division to secure a crossing at Jülich. It was hoped that these crossings would then support a follow-on attack to the Rhine River.

On 1 October 1944, as elements of the division prepared to launch the attack, Hollingsworth, now promoted to major, got his wish to join the fight up front when he was made executive officer of the 2nd Battalion, 67th Armored Regiment. The regiment, part of CCB, was commanded by Col. Paul A. Disney. Holly was familiar with the battalion because he had often been attached to it with his maintenance company. The 2nd Battalion, commanded by Lt. Col. John D. Wynne, had fifty-seven tanks, three assault guns, and a company from the 41st Infantry Regiment. Hollingsworth was ecstatic about joining the unit; he could now take the fight to the enemy, something he had been looking forward to since the first day he had set foot in northern France.

It did not take long for Hollingsworth to get into the fray. On 2 October, during poor weather marked by rain, snow, and sleet, the 67th Armored Regiment, along with the 2nd Battalion, began crossing the Wurm at Marienberg-Palenberg under intense mortar and artillery fire. As each vehicle crossed the bridge, it came under fire from an enemy antitank gun located in a pillbox on higher ground to the northeast of the bridge. It was clear that the Germans still had a lot of fight left in them; they were defending their homeland and they resisted stubbornly, fighting from pillboxes and fortified trenches. The "Road March War," as some later characterized the pursuit phase, was over; the division knew that gains would now be made in yards, not miles.

After crossing the Wurm River, the 67th Armored was ordered to push through the German resistance to take Übach, between the Wurm and the Roer Rivers. The regiment attacked on 6 October. At the same time, two German tank regiments launched a counterattack to push the Americans back across the Wurm; what resulted was ten days of desperate yard-by-yard fighting. A unit history described this action as "a slow and savage struggle through mud, rain, and snow" against some of the "most determined resistance faced by the 2nd Armored Division in the European theater of operations."[16]

The two tank forces collided and ended up in something of a bloody standoff near Beggendorf until the German regiments decided to withdraw, leaving the 505th Heavy Panzer Battalion in contact. This unit had twenty-two Tiger Royals, which mounted 88-mm guns and were heavily armored. The 75-mm guns on the American M4 Sherman tanks were incapable of piercing the front slope of the Tiger Royal armor. Holly, in command of a tank and infantry task force, called for a time on target from the supporting 105-mm, 155-mm, and 8-inch howitzers.[17] The massed fire from these guns landed on the German unit at exactly the same moment, destroying three tanks and crippling three more. Holly later recalled, "They [the Germans] all turned tail and left their dead with me on the battlefield."[18] This incident only reinforced the lesson that Hollingsworth had already learned and that stayed with him the rest of his career—kill the enemy with massed firepower to husband your soldiers' lives.

The next day, the 2nd Battalion was ordered to take a town overlooking the Roer River. As it turned out, the retreating Germans had not gone far and they were waiting in ambush for Holly and his tanks on the high ground on the other side of the river. As the Americans approached the town, the Germans opened up with their artillery, hitting five of Holly's tanks in the initial barrage. A round hit near one of the assault guns, setting fire to soldiers' bags stored on top of the vehicle. Seeing this happen, Holly hurriedly dismounted his tank and jumped on board the assault gun, kicking the bags off the vehicle before turning to assist the troops inside. In the process, he was wounded by shrapnel as the German shells continued to fall around them. The medics patched up his wounds and he continued to fight with his unit. This was the first time he was wounded, but it would by no means be the last.

Attacking on a 150-yard front, Hollingsworth's battalion faced a series of fortified, heavily armed concrete pillboxes. His infantry did not have weapons that could penetrate these bunkers, so, after Hollingsworth's lead unit made a hole in the line, he ordered his dozer tanks forward to cover the entrances of the bunkers, isolating the German defenders inside the fortifications.[19] In this fashion, the 2nd Battalion captured its assigned objective.

The other elements of the division had been equally successful. It had been a tough and bloody fight, but the 2nd Armored Division had breached the Siegfried Line and held a firmly established salient in the German defensive line in that area.

For the next week, Hollingsworth's regiment engaged in an aggressive defense of the salient they had forged. German artillery and mortar fire was very heavy, and at the same time, the Luftwaffe pounded the Americans from the air. For the first time since COBRA was launched, the regiment was involved in static warfare; the tanks were generally dug in and outposted by infantry in trenches and foxholes as they guarded against German counterattack. The fight to forge and hold the salient had been costly; the division suffered 126 killed, 737 wounded, and 36 missing. During the battle, the division lost 28 tanks destroyed or so incapacitated they could not be repaired and returned to duty.

On 27 October, the regiment was relieved in place by elements of the 102nd Division. Holly and his battalion moved to the Windhausen-Palenberg area and assumed a reserve mission for the division. The next week was spent in training, with special emphasis on the indoctrination of new replacements.

Although the Siegfried Line had been pierced, it had by no means been smashed. The 2nd Armored Division, now under the command of Lt. Gen. William H. Simpson and the Ninth Army, began preparing for continuing the attack to the east to cross the Roer River. The Germans had erected a hedgehog system of defenses; each village and town on the Roer plain was within direct fire range of two or more similar towns, which had been converted into mutually supporting strongpoints. Each of these strongpoints would have to be taken, and the going would be slow and methodical. In its sector, the 2nd Armored Division would face a Panzer division on the east bank of the Roer, with two more Panzer divisions on the west bank of the river. The division would experience the fight of its life; even the battle to breach the Siegfried Line would pale by comparison.[20]

On 6 November, Hollingsworth's regiment received the order to continue the attack to seize objectives that dominated crossing sites on the Roer River. The attack, Operation QUEEN as it was to be called, was originally scheduled for 11 November. However, it was postponed until 16 November because of bad weather, which prevented the aerial bombardment that was to precede the ground advance. The 1st and 2nd Battalions jumped off the attack from the vicinity of Beggendorf, after air strikes that were only partially successful in softening up the enemy. The Germans reacted strongly to the American attack with artillery and mortars. As the tanks got closer to the German defensive positions, enemy infantry contested the advance with antitank teams using Panzerfaust antitank rockets. Nevertheless, both attacking battalions advanced rapidly, overcoming German resistance. However, the 2nd Battalion soon found itself in a minefield, which blew the tracks off six tanks.

The 2nd Battalion extricated itself from the minefield and joined the 1st Battalion on 18 November for an attack to capture Geronsweiler on the banks of the Roer. They ran into heavy German resistance near Puffendorf, where they were engaged by the lead elements of the 9th Panzer Division, equipped with Panther and King Tiger tanks. Again, the American M4 Sherman tanks were greatly outgunned by the German behemoths. The weather was overcast and the ground was covered with mud and slush from the previous days of cold rain and light snow. The Shermans had a hard time maneuvering in the mud, and their 76-mm guns were largely ineffective against the German tanks (one M4 tanker reported that he fired fourteen rounds at one Panther before finally getting a hit on the thinner side armor).[21] The American tanks withdrew back into Puffendorf to take advantage of the cover provided by the buildings in the town. The Germans tried to advance, but the American tankers, who were joined by tank destroyers from the 702nd Tank Destroyer Battalion, were able to knock out several of the lead tanks while the rest of the enemy tanks and accompanying German infantry were taken under fire by US artillery.

Hollingsworth's battalion moved out but was having a tough time advancing against the heavier Tiger tanks. Resorting to a tactic he had used earlier, Hollingsworth directed his forward observer to adjust three rounds of 105-mm artillery fire on the lead German tanks. Once the target was registered, he called for a time on target by supporting 105-mm and 155-mm howitzers coupled with 155-mm and 8-inch guns. The resulting artillery barrage, falling on the same place at nearly the same moment, disabled eighteen of the Tigers, allowing Hollingsworth's tanks to move forward.[22]

The Germans withdrew, but it had been a costly battle for both sides. The 2nd Battalion lost nineteen tanks to German fire; the Germans suffered an additional eleven tanks destroyed in the subsequent fighting. Like many of the battles along the Roer, this action devolved into a bloody slugfest. It was not until General Harmon committed additional divisional units that the Americans were able to capture Geronsweiler and the surrounding area.

By 28 November, after very heavy fighting that included the repulse of several strong German counterattacks, the 2nd Armored Division had secured its objectives on the approaches to the Roer River. However, in the thirteen days that it had taken the division to advance the ten miles to reach the river, it had lost more than 200 dead, more than 1,000 wounded, and 200 missing. The division had lost 80 tanks, about half unrepairable. The Germans had suffered more, sustaining more than 800 killed in action and an additional 2,400 soldiers captured. During the intense fighting, they lost 86 tanks and had more than 100 other vehicles destroyed.

Despite the high costs in lives and matériel, ultimately the Allied forces had breached the Siegfried Line from Linnich to south of Aachen. This left one more obstacle, crossing the Roer, before the Rhine River and the heart of Germany itself could be reached.

As plans were being made for crossing the Roer, Holly's unit was ordered to move to a small town south of Geronsweiler for refit and resupply. There they would also receive replacements. Holly later noted that most of the new men he received there had been trained as artillerymen; apparently the replacement depot had more artillerymen than tankers.

Holly had to retrain them as tank gunners in preparation for the crossing of the Roer and the advance to the Rhine.

For the next few weeks, the division held in place at the Roer and made preparations to continue the attack to the Rhine, another thirty miles into Germany. However, the next battle for "Hell on Wheels" would not take them to the Rhine. Instead, they would have to backtrack nearly one hundred miles into Belgium.

As the 2nd Armored Division prepared for its next mission, farther to the south, Field Marshal Gerd von Rundstedt and his forces, largely hidden from the probing eyes of Allied reconnaissance by early mists and snow, were making preparations for a stunning new counteroffensive. This offensive would divert the 2nd Armored Division's attention away from the Rhine and involve it in one of the largest and most important battles of the war in Europe.

The Battle of the Bulge

On 16 December, von Rundstedt launched a massive offensive through the Ardennes in Belgium and the tip of northern Luxembourg with fifty-five infantry divisions and fifteen armored divisions, organized in three armies along a 37-mile (60 km) front. The German attack, which would result in what became known as the Battle of the Bulge, caught the Americans off guard and was intended to split the Allied lines in order to capture the vital port of Antwerp and in the process drive a wedge between the British 21st and American 12th Army Groups. The attacking force would strike through the lightly defended Ardennes Forest during a period marked by bad weather and low visibility in order to negate the capabilities of Allied airpower. The Germans planned to secure bridgeheads across the Meuse River and then continue the attack to capture Brussels and Antwerp.

The weather was the worst in northern Europe in recent memory. It was bitterly cold and the ground was covered with deep snow. The roads were either frozen or seas of mud. There was a thick overcast and the constant fog shut down air operations almost completely.

At 5:30 a.m. on 16 December, the Germans launched their attack, breaking through the US VIII Corps sector, commanded by Maj. Gen. Troy Middleton. Before the Allies could react, the Germans had forged a salient, or "bulge," in the Allied lines, some sixty miles deep and forty-five miles wide. The Americans were caught completely off guard, and in rapid order Saint-Vith was under heavy enemy pressure, the town of Bastogne hung by a thread, and German units at the front of the bulge had broken through and were heading for crossings on the Meuse River.[23]

The 2nd Armored Division, temporarily reassigned from the Ninth Army to the First Army, was ordered to move south to the Ardennes to join the 3rd Armored Division in blocking the 5th Panzer Army before it could reach the Meuse. At 11:00 p.m. on 21 December, the 66th and 67th Regiments began to move along parallel columns south to the Ardennes. They traveled all night under radio silence and without lights on icy, muddy roads, hampered by heavy mist and fog. About two in the afternoon, after a march of nearly one hundred miles that took twenty-two hours, they arrived at Huy, fifteen miles west of Liège, Belgium. There they were informed that the VII Corps commander, Lt. Gen. J. Lawton Collins, intended them to serve as the reserve force in accordance with orders he had received from Field Marshal Montgomery, now in command of American troops in the northern half of the Ardennes. Montgomery and Collins wanted the 2nd Armored to avoid contact with the enemy in the hope that they could keep the presence of the division secret until it could be committed to battle later in January; also, Allied commanders did not want the Germans to know that the division had been pulled away from its previous positions along the Roer. Major General Harmon, the 2nd Armored Division commander, was not happy about the division being assigned a reserve role but nevertheless complied with his orders.

Late in the afternoon of 22 December, after Hollingsworth's troops had arrived in their assigned assembly area, a sergeant came up the road from the outpost where the reconnaissance company had occupied forward positions. His dead platoon leader was lying across the hood of the jeep. When asked what had hit the lieutenant, the sergeant replied that a German Panzer force had knocked out an M8 armored car and captured or killed its crew. When Major General Harmon heard of this incident, he realized that the lead elements of the 2nd Panzer Division, the vanguard of the advancing German 5th Panzer Army, were just ten miles away from his position, and it appeared to be out front on its own, having outrun the German units on its right and left flanks. Moreover, the enemy did not appear to know that the 2nd Armored Division was in the area. The always aggressive Harmon, seeing a golden opportunity, contacted General Collins and asked for approval to attack the Germans, who in his mind were clearly on the move and needed to be stopped before they reached the

Meuse. Collins replied, "You are in the Army Reserve and you will remain in Army Reserve until I give you orders to attack!"

Hollingsworth later said that Harmon uttered a four-letter word and, ignoring the corps commander's order, ordered his two combat commanders to attack south toward Haid and Ciney to stop the Germans. He called Collins and told the corps commander that the division was committed to battle.

Within an hour, the lead elements of the 2nd Armored Division ran into a German force of about eight hundred tanks and vehicles from the 2nd Panzer Division coming down the road headed west. The American tanks rapidly deployed on line in the forest and opened up on the column with tank and artillery fire, wreaking havoc on the Germans, who were strung out on the road bumper to bumper. What resulted was a free-for-all as the two forces blazed back and forth at each other with everything they had. The Americans killed the lead tank and the one at the end of the column and then methodically took the rest of the column under fire. The Germans were road bound and could not escape, but the situation remained fluid and uncertain.

At this point, Christmas Eve, the German offensive in the Ardennes had reached its farthest point west when the spearhead of the 2nd Panzer Division came in sight of the Meuse River near Dinant. However, they were just about out of fuel. US units had intercepted German radio messages that made it clear that the Germans were seriously short of fuel. General Harmon, believing he had the enemy trapped, pressed for the authority to continue the attack, but there was considerable confusion between First Army headquarters and VII Corps, where Collins was more concerned with the dangerous situation developing on his east flank. Still Harmon pressed the issue; when no answer was forthcoming from VII Corps, Harmon, refusing to wait any longer, ordered his forces to attack. When he was finally contacted by Collins and given the go-ahead, Harmon told him that he had already launched the attack, proclaiming, "The bastards are in the bag!" Ultimately, Collins, making a judgment call that went against his orders from Montgomery, gave Harmon the green light to press on with the attack.[24]

On 26 December, during the course of the renewed attack, Lt. Col. Lemuel Pope, who had taken command of the 2nd Battalion from Lieutenant Colonel Wynne in November 1944, was wounded by an armor-piercing shell that struck the front slope of his tank; he was evacuated to the rear and Major Hollingsworth assumed command of the battalion. However, Lieutenant Colonel Pope returned on 28 December and reassumed command.

Hollingsworth, now leading a task force composed of two companies, was in the thick of the fighting to stop the German advance to the Meuse. In the battle to take the town of Humain as other elements of the 2nd Armored fought their way toward Celles, a small town just four miles from the Meuse, Hollingsworth was wounded again, this time from shrapnel from enemy artillery fire. Once again, the medics patched up Holly's wounds and he returned to battle.

The fight to take Celles raged for three days. At one point the American tankers were attacked by 45-ton Panther and 57-ton Tiger tanks from the Panzer-Lehr Division, which were trying to break through to rescue their embattled comrades. The American tankers had learned the hard way that their Shermans could not stop the larger, better-armored, and better-armed behemoths. The weather had improved and they were able to call on rocket-firing British Typhoon fighter-bombers that were stationed nearby. The Typhoons were joined by Army Air Corps P-38 fighter-bombers and together, guided by an American spotter plane, they attacked the Panthers and Tigers, evening up the playing field somewhat.

The fighting continued until elements of the division joined at Celles, halting the German advance toward the river. On 28 December, the 2nd Armored Division was relieved by the 83rd Infantry Division, the British 53rd Division, and the 4th Cavalry Group. The division was ordered to the Grandmenil area to prepare for follow-on operations.

The fight between the 2nd Armored Division and the German Panzers had been a bitter battle. According to one observer, the countryside around Celles was "a vast cemetery of vehicles, destroyed or abandoned and of equipment half buried in the snow."[25] The 2nd Armored had suffered 43 killed, 201 wounded, and 26 missing, with 7 light tanks and 2 Shermans destroyed (26 other medium tanks were hit, but soon repaired). The 2nd Panzer Division lost 82 tanks, 83 antitank guns and artillery pieces, and 441 vehicles of various types.[26] The division suffered an estimated 550 killed during the intensive fighting. An additional 1,213 German soldiers were captured.[27] General Harmon triumphantly reported that the battle had resulted in "a great slaughter."[28]

Although the forward movement of the German advance had been stopped and the Germans had been prevented from crossing the Meuse, they retained a salient deep in the Allied lines from which they could potentially launch attacks in any direction, posing a threat to all Allied operations toward Germany. It was important that this salient be reduced so the attack across the Roer to the Rhine could continue. On 2 January 1945, as part of this effort, the 67th Regiment, including Hollingsworth and the 2nd Battalion, was ordered to make a long march to the northeast of Érezée, Belgium, in preparation for an attack southward to Houffalize in an effort to cut the German salient in two and link up with the Third Army, which was attacking north from the area around Bastogne with the intent to trap the Germans in the salient. According to Allied intelligence reports, six German divisions along with a reserve composed of parts of six more divisions were believed to be in the forests of the Ardennes on the way to Houffalize.

On 3 January, the division launched the attack to establish a bridgehead on the Ourthe River at Houffalize, about twenty-five miles into Belgium from the German border. The division was to clear all enemy strongpoints from the line of departure to the town—not the easiest mission for an armored division, which depended on speed for success and survival. This operation promised to be a bitter slugfest that would require the methodical reduction of the German defenses one by one. Compounding the difficulty, the weather had again turned from bad to miserable and the roads were covered with snow and ice. Off road, the infantry would have to contend with heavily wooded terrain that was extremely hilly and frequently veiled in heavy fog or swirling snowstorms.

Once the move began, the American troops encountered stiff enemy resistance. Even as the tankers advanced, the Germans launched repeated counterattacks that took a toll on already understrength units; it would be the worst eighteen miles the division had ever suffered. The going was slow because of the weather and terrain, and the Germans fought back doggedly. By the end of the first day, the division had advanced only about two miles. Both the tankers and the infantrymen were suffering losses not encountered since the Normandy landings. Nevertheless, the division continued its attack.

By 8 January, the forward elements of the division had reached Samrée. The Germans held the high ground that dominated the approaches to the town. Additionally, they had established a strong defense in the town itself, including dug-in infantry, minefields, roadblocks, and booby traps. The fight for Samrée would take four days.

It was during this battle that Hollingsworth was wounded a third time, much more seriously than he had been earlier. On 11 January, as the unit attacked Samrée from the east, Hollingsworth had his head out of the tank turret trying to direct his driver as his column moved through a heavily wooded area. A German artillery shell with a superquick fuse landed in the trees above him. Shrapnel from the shell cut off Holly's thumb and finger and killed his gunner. Another round came in as Holly tried to load the gun, but he had on a thick sheepskin-lined flying jacket that protected him from most of the shell fragments, and this probably saved his life. Then Holly's tank took a direct hit from a German antitank gun and caught fire. Holly's loader got him out and the driver pulled out the dead gunner; they made it about one hundred meters before the tank was hit a second time and exploded.

Incapacitated from his wounds, Holly refused to leave the battlefield until he was ordered to by his commander. He was evacuated to Paris and then on to England. Holly's arm did not heal properly while he was in the hospital and the doctors threatened to evacuate him to the United States, but he was having none of that. Holly, who had been gone from his unit about two weeks by then, was afraid that he would lose his position in the battalion (the rule was that if you were gone more than thirty days, someone replaced you), and he went AWOL (absent without leave) from the hospital. With his arm not completely healed, he made his way to Paris and went to the rear area transportation to ask for a lift back to the front to rejoin his unit. He ended up riding with an African American sergeant who was leading a truck company that was resupplying the 2nd Armored. When they got to Liège, Belgium, he telephoned the division headquarters from a tactical phone in a rear area supply unit. His battalion sent a jeep for him and he rejoined his unit on the high ground overlooking Houffalize. His commander was happy to see him, and nothing ever came of his leaving the hospital without authorization.

His return to the front was just in time to witness the end of the Battle of the Bulge. On 16 January, Holly and the other troops of the 67th Regiment watched the meeting of the 82nd Reconnaissance Battalion from their division with elements of the 11th Armored Division in Houffalize, marking the juncture of the First and Third Armies in the Ardennes and signaling the collapse of the westernmost German salient in the Allied lines.

During the fighting in the Ardennes, the 2nd Armored Division captured 1,742 German soldiers; the number of Germans killed in the bitter fighting is unknown. The defenders, including the 2nd SS Panzer, 116th SS Panzer, and 560th Volksgrenadier Divisions, lost 43 tanks, 8 self-propelled guns, and 25 artillery pieces. The Americans sustained 121 killed, 63 missing, and 484 wounded, while losing 28 medium and 7 light tanks.[29]

The Battle of the Bulge was declared over on 28 January 1945. It had been costly for both sides. The Allied losses totaled 19,000 killed in action among the 600,000 men involved. The Germans, who had expended precious reserves of men and matériel in the Ardennes, sustained casualties approaching 100,000. Nevertheless, the Germans had demonstrated that they were not going to give up without a fight. The overoptimism that had prevailed in November had clearly been misplaced; there was still a lot of hard fighting left to be done before the Germans would be forced to surrender.

Following the linkup with the 11th Armored, the 2nd Armored Division was relieved and moved to new assembly areas near Sprimont, Belgium. From there, the division moved to a new position between Margraten and Gulpen, Holland. There the division conducted a long period of maintenance, rehabilitation, and combat refresher training. Also, the division

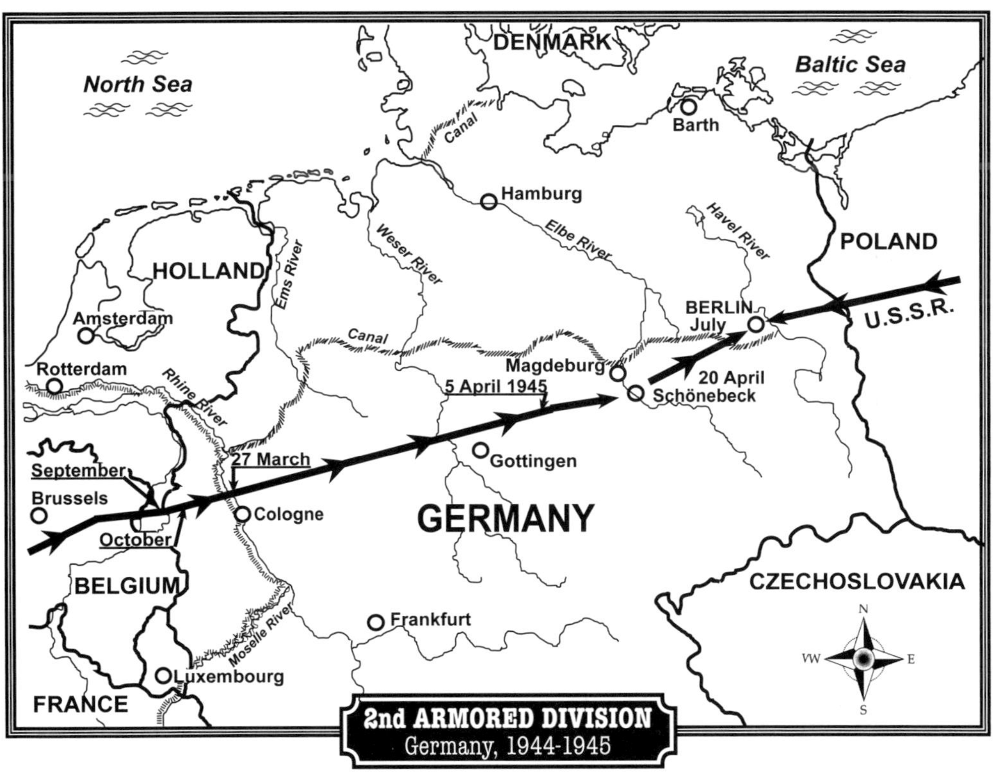

received a number of much-needed replacements who also had to be trained. Meanwhile, planning for the crossing of the Roer, Operation GRENADE, and the advance to the Rhine commenced under the new division commander, Brig. Gen. Isaac D. White, who had replaced Major General Harmon when he had departed to assume command of XXII Corps earlier in January.

Operation GRENADE

In the early morning hours of 23 February, the lead elements of the 29th and 30th Infantry Divisions crossed the river, followed by the 83rd Infantry Division. At 9:30 a.m. on 26 February, the 67th Regiment, including the 2nd Battalion, crossed the Roer River under light enemy artillery fire and occupied an assembly area around Lich, Germany. On the twenty-eighth, the 2nd Battalion and the rest of the regiment launched an attack to the northeast toward the Rhine River.

XIX Corps was attacking with three divisions abreast. The 2nd Armored Division attacked in the center flanked by the 29th and 30th Infantry Divisions. The attack initially went very well against light enemy resistance. The 2nd Armored Division took town after town in its rapid advance. However, resistance stiffened in the area beyond Hemmerden when the lead elements came under heavy antitank fire followed by a strong German counterattack, which was turned back only after bitter fighting and five flights of air corps fighter-bombers that broke up the tank attack. The battle was so intense that at one point, Hollingsworth's tanks engaged German tanks at point-blank range. With the counterattack turned back, Holly's tanks continued moving forward. However, they again encountered very heavy antitank fire in the woods west of Grefath.

After overcoming the Germans there, the column continued attacking toward Büttgen. Once it was taken, they continued toward Holzbüttgen and the Nord Canal. Crossing the canal, Hollingsworth's battalion continued the attack, overrunning every position along its route of march and shooting up everything with a black cross on it.

Meanwhile the rest of the regiment also continued to advance, with the main objective of securing the 1,649-foot-long Adolf Hitler Bridge over the Rhine at Krefeld-Uerdingen. After a mad dash to seize the crossing site and an intense fight outside the town, the regiment reached Krefeld-Uerdingen on 2 March, only to have the retreating Germans once again attempt to blow up the already-damaged bridge before the American troops could capture it. However, the Germans succeeded only in blowing a large crater in one end of the bridge. This precluded passage by tanks but left just enough room that the American infantry could pass over the bridge. About 7:00 p.m., as the infantry prepared to cross over the bridge, the Germans succeeded in exploding another, larger demolition charge that dropped the entire center span in the river.

As preparations were made to cross the river at other sites, division morale was high. The vital area between the Roer and Rhine Rivers had been cleared of enemy forces, and just across the Rhine lay the Ruhr, the heart of Germany's war-making machine; if the Ruhr could be captured, the Germans would not have the wherewithal to continue the war. After a brief pause to reorganize and resupply, elements of the regiment prepared to continue the attack eastward. The grand plan was to surround the Ruhr, attack through the Teutoburger Wald, cross the Elbe, and enter Berlin.

Despite the loss of the Adolph Hitler Bridge, Operation GRENADE had been a resounding success. XXIX Corps counted more than 900 enemy killed in action, some 2,500 captured, and the destruction of 37 German tanks and 225 guns and artillery pieces. In the dash for the Rhine, 150 towns were captured, but the price for the 2nd Armored Division was high, with 90 killed and more than 280 wounded.

The German heartland lay open in the west to attack by eight armies from four nations, some eighty-six armored, infantry, and airborne divisions. In the east, the Russian armies were advancing rapidly through Poland and into eastern Germany. The vise was closing on Hitler and the Nazis.

Crossing the Rhine

Less than three weeks after reaching the Rhine, the US Third, Seventh, and Ninth Armies, along with the British Second, Canadian First, and the French First Armies surged across the river. In the Ninth Army area, the attack into the German heartland began on 24 March when the 17th Armored Engineer Regiment built a 1,152-foot treadway bridge across the Rhine near Wesel, which facilitated the establishment of a bridgehead on the enemy side of the river. Just after 6:00 a.m. on 30 March, lead elements of the 2nd Armored Division began to cross the river and rushed eastward, attacking through the 30th Infantry Division in the vicinity of Haltern, fifteen miles from the Rhine.

This was perfect tank country, characterized by flat plains and good roads. The 2nd Armored units moved rapidly, taking town after town in their path. Initially, the attackers encountered only light resistance, but some German units elected to stand and fight. When that happened, the fighting was bitter and bloody. It was during one of these engagements that Lt. Col. Lemuel Pope, Hollingsworth's battalion commander, was wounded in the shoulder by machine gun fire. Upon Pope's evacuation, Hollingsworth again assumed command of the battalion.

In the drive from the Rhine to the Elbe, Hollingsworth would command a task force that included his own organic unit supported by a battalion of infantry commanded by a lieutenant colonel and a direct support artillery battalion also commanded by a lieutenant colonel. Additionally, he had a tank destroyer company and reconnaissance troops. As the lead maneuver element, Holly was in charge of units that were commanded by men who outranked him. Not letting rank bother him, he believed that he was more than qualified to lead the battalion, and he would prove that in very short order.

Once across the river, Holly headed for Lippstadt and Paderborn, securing the northern flank of the Ruhr Pocket. On 1 April, his unit linked up at Lippstadt with the 3rd Armored Division, which had crossed the river at Köln. Holly promised his troops some rest after they had arrived at Paderborn and serviced their vehicles. About 5:00 p.m., as the troops finished refueling their tanks and were getting ready for a good night's sleep, the division commander, Major General White, arrived in the area. Asking for a map, White directed Holly to move twelve kilometers to the east to conduct a night attack to secure a pass at Haustenbeck in the Teutoburger Wald (forest) by midnight. The division was to follow six hours after the pass was secured.

The area was supposedly a collecting point for SS soldiers and units that had been beaten up in earlier fighting. Holly called the attached reconnaissance company commander and directed him to lead the advance toward the pass. With the recon company leading and Holly following right behind them in a jeep, the tank column moved out under the cover of darkness.

The reconnaissance company ran into a German Army headquarters. The German soldiers guarding the road were asleep. The headquarters was just off the main road, but generators were running and the Americans could see lights. They opened up with the machine guns from the recon jeeps. The Americans took a few prisoners, but most of the Germans were killed or ran away into the woods when the firing started.

Holly continued the attack. They came upon a road that ran perpendicular to their advance. It turned out that this was the outer-perimeter road of a German Panzer training center. The Americans found themselves surrounded by German tanks. The tanks were relics from which the engines had been long removed, but their guns were still in place for use in training recruits, and the Germans inside opened up on Holly and his tanks. Holly's gunner, S.Sgt. Clyde W. Cooley, a veteran of North Africa, knocked out a tank at 1,500 yards and then quickly rotated the turret to blast another at just 75 yards away. Hollingsworth later said of the battle, "All I can remember is that all hell broke loose, as everyone on both sides opened fire."[30] As the tanks engaged the German tanks, Holly moved up his infantry to join them while he called in supporting artillery fire.

During the battle, Holly did not lose any tanks or men. At one point, a German truck full of soldiers came barreling down the road toward Holly's lead element. He directed two of his machine gunners to take the truck under fire that was headed in their direction. They waited until the truck was seventy-five yards away and opened up on it; the truck, riddled by machine gun bullets, ran off the road and turned over, littering the surrounding ground with bodies. When Holly and several of his troopers went forward to inspect the truck and bodies, they discovered that the dead were all uniformed German women, the equivalent of US WACs.[31] The image of those bodies stayed with him for the rest of his life. As one journalist observed, recounting the story, Holly was "a war lover, not a death lover."[32]

Later that day, during the course of the fighting, Holly felt someone punch him in the arm who said, "What's going on here?" Holly turned to the man and said, "Look, you son of a bitch. Don't you know there is a battle going on here? Get the hell out of here." The guy who had punched Holly was Major General White, the division commander. White later called Holly "the greatest battalion commander in the war" and the only man who had called the general "a son of a bitch" and gotten away with it.

The battalion advanced fifty-six miles that day, knocking out more than ten enemy tanks along the way. The German armor was pulling back, leaving their infantry to cover the withdrawal. Although the resistance was light and sporadic, the German infantry launched numerous Panzerfausts at the advancing American tanks, knocking out one. Two of Holly's tanks overturned on the muddy, sloping roads as the going proved difficult.

In one case, Holly in his jeep encountered a German soldier who stepped out from behind a tree. Holly tried to engage him with his carbine, but it malfunctioned. He threw down the carbine and killed the German with his pistol before the German could return fire.

By this time, Hollingsworth had achieved almost legendary status among his troops and had greatly impressed his higher headquarters. His philosophy was to be bold and aggressive, to lead from the front so your soldiers could see you. He came to believe that a rapid, daring attack, rather than a deliberate advance, saved lives in the long run and got them closer to Berlin more quickly. He was all over the battlefield, seemingly fearless and serving as an inspiration to his troops.

Hollingsworth continued to push his unit toward the Elbe as fast as they could go. They bypassed many German positions, firing at them as they rushed eastward. The fight had gone out of many of the Germans, but not all of them. In one case, Holly's battalion came upon a group of dug-in German troops who appeared to be ready to make a stand. Hollingsworth then did something that stunned the Germans. He lined up thirty-four tanks and gave the order "Charge!" His tanks rushed at the German positions with all guns blazing; not surprisingly, the enemy troops broke and ran.[33]

As they continued to move eastward, they came upon a German soldier who threw down his rifle and gave up. Holly's radio operator, Sergeant Hayes, who spoke German, found out that there was an entire German regiment that wanted to surrender, but they could not give up because the SS in the next village was forcing them to fight. The German regiment was deployed between Holly's task force and the village.

Holly told Hayes to get the location of the village where the SS troops were, which turned out to be just a short distance away. The SS troops were in the center of the village, where they had occupied a farmhouse and barn that had a fence around it and farm implements inside. They were apparently up in the loft of the building operating a radio. Holly alerted some of his troops and they set out for the village. On the way, they encountered a German civilian with a horse and a small wagon filled with loaves of bread. They asked the German where the SS troops were and he pointed out the farmhouse and barn, saying that there were about a dozen SS soldiers there.

Holly went into action. Armed with a Thompson submachine gun and wearing his customary twin Colt automatic .45 pistols in low-slung holsters, he grabbed three of his soldiers and headed for the town. They made their way to the back of the building, where they smashed a door in the fence with their shoulders and rushed inside. The surprised SS troops came out firing. Holly dropped the first one with his Thompson. The other SS troops retreated back into the building; the Americans threw grenades in the windows. At the same time, Holly spotted another SS trooper in the door of the adjoining barn's hayloft. The German went for his gun, but Holly beat him to the draw with his pistol. Eight of the SS troops were killed in the gunfight. Holly and his men took the remaining German soldiers prisoner and marched them back to his lines, making them walk in front of his jeep with their hands over their heads. When the other German soldiers saw the captured SS troops, they came out of the woods and surrendered. There were about 1,600 of them, mostly old men from the Volkssturm.[34]

Holly had the Germans stack their weapons and then directed them to march along the road to the west with their hands up. Holly, anxious to continue the attack, determined that the German soldiers had no fight left in them and were not a threat to anyone, so he sent them to the rear on their own.

Holly later told a story about the captured Germans. Supposedly, the regimental adjutant was coming forward in a jeep to deliver mail. According to Holly, the captain had not seen much combat. When he saw all these Germans headed in his direction, he took out his .45 pistol and captured the entire lot. He did not know what to do with them and his jeep radio was not working. The story goes that the captain got in the middle of a circle and made the Germans march around him all night long. Somebody finally came along in the morning and helped him out with the prisoners. This incident was the source of much humor in the division for weeks to come.

One of the problems that Holly and his unit had to deal with was displaced persons, both German civilians and those of other nationalities. Most of them were worn out and hungry; the Americans tried to help and gave them food, but the American rations made many of them sick. Many of the displaced persons, especially those of other nationalities, were very bad about looting and, if not prevented, would go out and ransack every German village and kill every horse and cow. The Americans tried to stop this activity, but the displaced persons were angry that the Americans were treating them like the enemy.

After capturing and clearing a number of small towns and villages, the tankers continued their advance toward Schönebeck, a small town seven miles southeast of Magdeburg overlooking the Elbe River. By this time they had advanced over seventy miles in just twenty-four hours and were just seventy-five miles from Berlin. In the approach to the town, they encountered a regiment of Germans marching along the road searching for someone to accept their surrender. The Germans said they wanted to join in the attack toward Berlin. The German colonel had been on the Eastern Front and knew what would happen when the Soviets took Berlin. Holly gave the Germans food but left a guard detail to secure the prisoners as his tank column rolled on toward Schönebeck. Holly hoped to seize the bridge across the river there before the Germans could destroy it.

Hollingsworth's lead tanks reached the high ground overlooking the town in the early evening of 11 April. Hollingsworth, with twin Colts strapped low on his hips and a Thompson submachine gun slung over his shoulder, made his way forward with his binoculars to a vantage point. He was stunned to see that the highway bridge over the river was still intact; this was because the Germans were using it to flee east across the river. He observed a large column of tanks, truck- and horse-drawn artillery, personnel carriers, and trucks moving south to north on a road running parallel to the Elbe toward Bad Salzemen. There they could swing east at the road junction and head for the bridge. Holly reported the situation to his regimental commander, Col. Paul Disney, who notified 2nd Armored Division headquarters with a simple but "electrifying" message: "We are on the Elbe!"[35]

Holly and his tankers might have been at the Elbe, but there was much more to do. Seeing an opportunity to take the bridge, Holly hastily hatched a bold plan. Using the falling darkness, Holly wanted to sneak his troops in behind the Germans and follow them across the bridge; if they could pull it off, they could gain control of the bridge and keep the Germans from destroying it as they retreated to the east. He ordered one of his company commanders, Capt. Jim Starr, to put a company of infantry on his tanks and move out under the cover of darkness to "chop the column in two." Once Starr tied down the last half of the column and secured the road junction at Bad Salzemen, Holly, along with Capt. Jack Knight's company, would follow the front of the German column across the bridge. Holly hoped that in the darkness the Germans would not realize that the company behind them was American, not their fellow Germans.

The ploy almost worked. Hatches buttoned up, Starr's company roared into Bad Salzemen, blocked the road junction, and engaged the approaching tanks. Meanwhile, Holly and Knight's company slipped in behind the German tanks leading the column that had already made the turn and were heading for the bridge. It looked like the audacious plan might work, but some German gun crews whose pieces were mounted on flatcars in an adjacent rail yard saw what Hollingsworth was trying to do and sounded the alarm, opening fire on the American tanks. An intense firefight broke out, with the American tanks and German guns on the flatcars firing at each other at point-blank range.

Hollingsworth's lead tank turned a corner only to be confronted by a Panther tank, already swiveling its turret to take them under fire. Hollingsworth's gunner knocked out the Panther, which slewed sideways before smashing into a wall and beginning to burn furiously. Hollingsworth's tank could barely get by and had to slow down to make its way through the narrow street, followed by the rest of the column.

By the time they reached the center of the town, according to Hollingsworth, it was "everyone . . . firing at everyone else . . . the damnedest mess. Germans were hanging out of windows, either shooting at us with their *Panzerfäuste* or just dangling in death."[36] Holly remembered that it was so bright from the fires in the burning buildings and tanks that it might as well have been day.

During the course of the raging battle, when Holly found his tanks blocked by stone walls and wrecked vehicles, he dismounted to lead his tanks through the narrow debris-strewn street. Weaving through the burning Panzer tanks and constant enemy fire, his unit made it to the stone wall in front of the bridge. At that point, a Panzerfaust rocket impacted about fifteen yards in front of Hollingsworth, spraying him in the face with hot shrapnel, cutting his lip and forehead. His face covered with blood, he continued advancing toward the bridge, tank telephone handset in one hand and his .45 in another.

His tank collided with a jeep and Hollingsworth called for his infantry to move up. He began to lead them through the maze of roadblocks the Germans had hastily erected. The Germans took them under direct fire, doing their best to stop the American advance. Still, Holly urged his men forward until he took a bullet in the knee. Staggering and half blinded by his own blood, he continued to move forward until the volume of German fire intensified to the point that he and his infantry could go no farther and they were forced to withdraw.

When Colonel Disney, his commanding officer, arrived on the scene, he found the major "unable to walk and bleeding all over the place."[37] A disconsolate Hollingsworth was evacuated to the 4th Station Hospital. He later lamented that he had been so close, and if he could have taken the bridge, the 2nd Armored could have been in Berlin in eleven hours. However, such was not to be. At dawn on 12 April, as infantry and engineers tried once again to capture the bridge, the Germans blew it up in their faces.

Hollingsworth was in pretty bad shape. His lip had been cut all the way through and he also had a serious cut above his eye that was bleeding a lot. The wound to his knee turned out to be a machine pistol bullet that was lodged in the cartilage; the doctors decided to leave it there, where it remained for the rest of his life. Holly stayed at the hospital for eight days until he could talk the doctors into letting him return to his unit. For his actions at the bridge at Schönebeck, Hollingsworth, recently promoted to lieutenant colonel, received his first Distinguished Service Cross for valor.

The destruction of the bridge was a bitter disappointment for the tankers, but there was much joy at Ninth Army headquarters when the 2nd Armored Division reported that its lead units were at the Elbe. The division had covered seventy-three miles in one day to arrive at the river. The next day, the 83rd Infantry Division also reached the Elbe at Barby, a few miles upstream of Schönebeck. At the same time, the Ninth Army's 5th Armored Division also reached the river, at a point only fifty-three miles from Berlin. The US troops thought they were going on to Berlin and were ready to continue the attack. Plans were made to force crossings at Magdeburg to continue the attack toward Berlin, but such was not to be.

By the time Holly arrived back at the unit, it was in the process of withdrawing to Brunswick. On 15 April, with US troops poised to cross the Elbe, Ninth Army commander Lt. Gen. William H. Simpson got a call from Gen. Omar Bradley, who said that he had an urgent message for Simpson, but that he did not want to transmit it on the phone. Simpson, with his plan for the attack across the Elbe to Berlin, flew to Wiesbaden in a light plane. Bradley met him on the ground and told him he had to stop his advance at the Elbe; he was not to advance any farther in the direction of Berlin. Simpson was stunned; Supreme Allied Commander Dwight D. Eisenhower had given the order to halt all US forces at the Elbe so the Soviets could take Berlin.

A deeply disappointed Simpson made his way to the 2nd Armored Division headquarters on the Elbe, where he gave Major General White the word that he was to cease advancing. White could not believe his ears, but it was true; there would be no dash for Berlin, and the war was effectively over for the 2nd Armored Division.

Holly remained bitter about Eisenhower's decision to stop at the Elbe for the rest of his life. He thought that Eisenhower had been deceived by Stalin into letting the Soviets have a free hand in Berlin. He believed that US forces could have taken Berlin and that the postwar situation would have been very different from the way it turned out.

War's End

Victory in Europe Day (V-E Day) was declared on 8 May 1945. In recognition of its contribution to ending the war, the 2nd Armored Division was given the honor of being the first American unit to occupy part of Berlin.[38] On 3 July, the 67th Armored Regiment set out in a driving rain on the long march from its assembly area at Köthen to Berlin. Because of bridge and road difficulties, the trip took over thirty hours. The regiment, upon arriving in the city, took up billets in the Steglitz area and began going about the business of occupation.[39]

By this point in the war, James F. Hollingsworth had been in combat almost constantly since his arrival in North Africa in December 1942; he had fought across two continents and eight countries, concluding with the desperate battles in the hedgerows, the swift pursuit across France and into Germany, the bitter fighting in the miserable cold and over the rugged terrain of the Ardennes, then the Roer, the Rhine, and into the German heartland. He was twenty-five years old and had commanded units from platoon to battalion, culminating with command of a task force of more than three thousand troops in the desperate fighting from the Siegfried Line to the Elbe. In the process, he had received a Distinguished Service Cross, four Silver Stars, and four Bronze Stars. He had also received five Purple Hearts for wounds sustained in battle.

With all this in mind, General White, the division commander, asked Hollingsworth whether he didn't think it was time to go home. White told Holly that he was leaving Germany to become commandant of the Cavalry School at Fort Riley, Kansas, and that he wanted Holly to come along to command a mechanized cavalry regiment there.

With the war coming to an end, it was only natural for Holly to consider his options. As the army was being mobilized, Holly considered several possible avenues. He thought about attending medical school. He was also offered a job as a district manager of a metropolitan life insurance company in one of the larger cities in Texas. He said that he could not see himself "on the street corner begging people to buy insurance," so he quickly discarded that idea. Because of his maintenance experience during the war, General Motors made him several job offers. He later said he gave those ideas some thought, but in the end it came down to the fact that he had found his place in war; he reveled in leading men in battle. "A battle is a real test of a man," he said. "I felt that I had met that test in the face of enemy fire on the battlefield, and that maybe I owed something to my country by serving in the army—a responsibility to my country and to be involved in the training of young men." Holly later explained, "I don't know of any other profession that offers a man who is interested in people [a better] opportunity for leadership . . . training and growth than the Army does."[40] It was an "awesome responsibility," but one he eagerly accepted. Holly's wife was a great encouragement to him and told him that she would be right by his side no matter what he decided. Hollingsworth decided to take up General White on his offer to accompany the general to Fort Riley.

Hollingsworth's World War II experiences molded his character like nothing else. He had found a calling in leading men in combat. He had found that the only way to be victorious in war was to treat his soldiers well, but never to lose focus on the mission. Victory went to the attacker; the only way to win a battle was to push as hard and as quickly as possible, asking and giving no quarter. He had been eminently successful in combat; now it remained to be seen how he would operate in the absence of war.

4

Post–World War II Years

Fort Riley

Hollingsworth was promoted to lieutenant colonel in June 1945 and departed Europe for the States in July.[1] After thirty days of leave and recuperation in Sanger, Lieutenant Colonel and Mrs. Hollingsworth reported to Fort Riley, Kansas, where they would stay for four years. Arriving at the fort, he assumed command of the Cavalry School's cavalry regiment.

The regiment had 2,200 people assigned and was responsible for supporting the school's training mission. It was a difficult unit to command, because it contained all the cadre and students at the school, as well as all the support personnel. General White, having seen Hollingsworth in action, no doubt felt that he was more than up to the task.

After a year in command of the cavalry regiment, Hollingsworth became the chief of combined arms tactics at the Cavalry School in August 1946. An officer efficiency report (OER) from December 1946 gives a very good picture of Hollingsworth as an officer. Col. James H. Polk wrote, "This officer is decisive . . . and possesses a broad background of combat and command experience. His viewpoint is sometimes narrow because of this experience and he is sometimes intolerant and given to snap judgment." A note appended to the OER read, "This officer is a complete extrovert, happy-go-lucky, confident, friendly, raucous, vigorous, and full of fun. He is a definite asset and moral [*sic*] builder in any unit. He obeys direct orders to the letter and has an extremely strong will and forceful personality. He can be serious about his work when the pressure is on but is inclined to be negligent of details and center his interest in self-selected activities. He has great ability and capacity for work if properly directed. He is a top battle-field commander and a poor staff officer."[2] Hollingsworth did not appear to be upset by this last statement; he saw himself above all as a commander of men and not a paper pusher.

During the course of this assignment, Hollingsworth, having decided on a military career, endeavored to continue his military education every chance he got. In the summer of 1947, he completed the G-2/G-3 Air Officer's Course at the Army Air Force Special Staff School at Craig Field in Alabama. In January 1948, he requested the Air Transportability Course at Fort Benning "to further my military education and better prepare me to present and supervise Air Transportability and Air Movements." He completed the course of instruction in May 1948 and was rated a qualified gliderman and authorized to wear the Glider Badge.

It was during his tenure at Fort Riley that Hollingsworth became a Mason, joining Union Lodge No. 7 in Junction City. While at Fort Riley, he completed his Entered Apprentice and Fellowcraft Degrees. He remained active as a Mason for the rest of his life.[3]

In late 1948, General White, who had departed for Germany so he could assume command of the US Constabulary there, recommended Hollingsworth for attendance at the 1949–1950 class of the Command and General Staff College (CGSC) at Fort Leavenworth, Kansas, writing that he "found him [Hollingsworth] to be outstanding in every respect."[4] This was a prestigious assignment that was required for advancement to more senior ranks in the army.

However, the timing was not right for Hollingsworth. In a 23 November 1948 letter from Maj. Gen. F. A. Irving of the War Department Personnel and Administration Division, White was told, "As you know only 50% of all officers can attend this course and competition is very keen. It does not appear at this time that he will be among those officers selected for the 1949–50 course . . . on his return [from overseas] at the age of 33 it is believed that he will be within the preferential age bracket and his chance will be better at that time."[5]

In a 6 December 1948 letter to Hollingsworth, White wrote, "It is apparent . . . that your tender age will limit you from consideration [for the CGSC this next year] at this particular time. However, you should not feel badly about that. A great many of us would like to be told that we were too young instead of the usual remark that we are getting too old!"[6] Hollingsworth was disappointed, but soon General White arranged for Hollingsworth to join him in Germany.

Germany

When World War II in Europe ended, the victorious nations occupied defeated Germany, dividing it into four Zones of Occupation controlled by the Russians, British, French, and United States, respectively. Each of the occupying nations faced difficult and unprecedented challenges. There was no functioning government and the defeated country was flooded with refugees and displaced persons. The question for the victors was how to govern the conquered German territory.

Even before the war ended, the European Theater Headquarters began planning on how to deal with the vanquished. At the end of November 1945, Gen. Dwight Eisenhower, then European commander, announced that the United States Zone of Occupation in Germany would be controlled by a constabulary. This superpolice force would be created to meet the special needs of a successful occupation of Germany; it would eventually be called the United States Constabulary. The US VI Corps Headquarters would furnish the nucleus of the Constabulary Headquarters, but the 1st and 4th Armored Divisions provided most of the personnel that would flesh out the constabulary.

Three regimental headquarters were established in each constabulary brigade. Under the regiments were battalion-sized units called squadrons (modeled after the wartime cavalry squadrons). The squadrons were reorganized as mechanized units for flexibility and mobility.

The constabulary was organized along geographical lines to coincide as nearly as possible with the major divisions of the German civil administration, in order to facilitate liaison and coordination with the German civil authorities and the US military government. Therefore, there would be one Constabulary Headquarters for the entire US Zone of Occupation, and a brigade headquarters at each of the capitals of the three German *Länder* (states). Each brigade headquarters would deploy its assigned squadrons at key points throughout its assigned area.

On 10 January 1946, Maj. Gen. Ernie Harmon, wartime commander of the 1st and 2nd Armored Divisions and the XXII Corps, was appointed commanding general of the United States Constabulary. He established his headquarters at Bad Tölz, a town in southern Bavaria, but it was moved to Bamberg in February.

After extensive training, the constabulary became fully operational on 1 July 1946 with a total of about 55,000 troops. Under General Harmon, the mission of the constabulary was to maintain general military security and civil order, to assist in the accomplishment of the US government in Germany, and to control the borders of the US Zone of Occupation. These proved to be daunting tasks since the area to be controlled was more than 400,000 square miles and included 1,400 miles of international and interzonal boundaries, extending from Austria in the south to the British Zone in the north, and from Czechoslovakia and the Soviet Zone in the east to the Rhine River and the French Zone in the west. More than sixteen million German people lived in the area plus more than a half million refugees, and it included many cities of considerable size. Additionally, there were hundreds of thousands of US soldiers in the area. The constabulary would be responsible for maintaining order in an area about the size of Pennsylvania until a German police force could be trained and become operational.

Harmon was a driving force in fielding the constabulary, devising a motto—"Mobility, Vigilance, Justice"—that was meant to instill pride in the unit and its mission. He wrote in his postwar memoir, "We were to be fast moving to ensure that no part of the American Zone was without the police power it needed; we were to be ever alert for trouble, especially on the borders; and above all, we were to be fair and impartial in our dealings with everyone."[7]

Harmon established a school at Sonthofen in the Bavarian hills to train the new members of the constabulary for their unique mission. Harmon tried to fill the ranks of the constabulary with combat veterans, but this was difficult because the army was demobilizing and sending troops home as soon as possible. Nevertheless, Harmon set about molding the constabulary into the mobile, elite force that he desired.

In addition to building the constabulary from scratch, Harmon was also charged with building the German police force. Harmon wanted to build a force designed along the lines of an American state police organization. With the assistance of a German nobleman, Count von Henneberg, the civilian German police were organized and began training. Eventually, the fielding of this force permitted the constabulary to concentrate its efforts on border control and law enforcement among displaced persons and

American servicemen. Additionally, the constabulary had to concern itself with combating subversion, black marketing, and other criminal activity.

By May 1947, General Harmon had organized the constabulary and trained the German police force, and things were running very smoothly. The general had been overseas continually for more than five years and he asked for a transfer to a new assignment at home in the United States. Accordingly, he relinquished command of the constabulary and returned to the United States to become the deputy commander of Army Ground Forces under Gen. Jacob L. Devers at Fort Monroe, Virginia. Harmon was replaced as commander of the constabulary by Maj. Gen. Withers A. Burress, who would occupy the position until April 1948, when he was in turn replaced by Maj. Gen. Louis A. Craig.

By 1948, the mission of the constabulary had been expanded to include combat readiness of all assigned troops. General White arrived in Germany from Fort Riley in May 1948 to oversee this transition from a police force to the largest armored formation in the US Army. This would be a difficult and complex task, and White reached back to Fort Riley to tap Hollingsworth for his drive and expertise.

In June 1949, Hollingsworth, accompanied by Nickie and nine-year-old Jamie, arrived in Germany. General White placed Holly in charge of the Special Troops Regiment, which did not have a combat table of organization. It was a specially organized headquarters, located in Stuttgart, which was formed to meet the requirements of the higher command. This meant that Holly had command responsibility for all the officers and men assigned to the higher headquarters, to include the generals and colonels on the staff. In addition, he had responsibility for a medical battalion, an engineer battalion, a transportation company, and several other company-sized units.

In his job, Holly had a lot of contact with German nationals, to include local *Bürgermeisters* and a large number of German workers. Hollingsworth was involved in setting up and running care centers for the disabled and providing clothing and food. Relations with the local German populace were very good. Mrs. Hollingsworth could speak and read German, so the Hollingsworths enjoyed the German community. However, there were some uncomfortable moments. On one occasion, when they were trout fishing in a local stream, Mrs. Hollingsworth went to the car to rest while Holly kept fishing. He came to an area that was loaded with trout, but a *Jägermeister* (forest ranger) approached, yelling, "Nein, nein!"

Holly went to get his wife, who told him, without prompting from the *Jägermeister*, "You are fishing in a fish hatchery!" She apologized to the *Jägermeister* and they left. Later, Holly relished telling the story, saying, "I thought they were biting pretty good!"

When the constabulary headquarters was taken over by the reactivated Seventh Army late in November 1949, Hollingsworth was reassigned as chief of operations for the new headquarters. One of his major staff responsibilities was to plan and supervise the buildup of US troops in West Germany. During this period, the 2nd Armored Division and 1st and 3rd Infantry Divisions arrived and became part of the occupation forces.

When the North Koreans poured across the 38th parallel in June 1950, Holly volunteered to join the fighting in Korea. Holly's boss, Lt. Gen. Manton S. Eddy, asked him why he wanted to leave him to run off to Korea. Holly replied that he wanted to get into the war that was raging there. Eddy told him that he was trying to stop a war in Europe and that Holly was needed in that effort and was not going anywhere.

The Seventh Army had an extensive sector that ran from the Austrian border to the Czech border to the East German border. It was a stressful time as the Cold War heated up. With the war raging in Korea, the tensions in Western Europe increased exponentially as the Soviets became very active along the inner German border.

When Holly was at Seventh Army, there was an incident at Hof on the border. Alerted at 2:00 a.m., he rushed to the headquarters to see what was going on. He found out that a Soviet tank company had taken up a position near a border crossing point in the Fulda Gap and appeared to be readying itself for action. The crossing site was defended by a small US cavalry platoon. The situation was very tense, and no one was sure what the Soviets were up to.

During the night, Holly prepared a message for the army commander to send to Joint Chiefs of Staff asking for the authority to begin evacuating civilian dependents from the area. If there was going to be an armed confrontation, the dependents had to be moved out of harm's way. The Soviet tank company stood down and the looming confrontation never occurred, but the incident demonstrated the increasing confrontation between East and West in Western Europe.

With the establishment of the North Atlantic Treaty Organization and the Warsaw Pact, the tension only increased. One of Holly's responsibilities was to conduct joint planning with the French. He was not happy about sharing classified information with the French, because he thought that France was infiltrated with Communists. He was ordered to pass on the information, but he did so on a selective basis. Such is indicative of the growing Cold War tensions, even among allies.

During the course of Holly's tenure at Seventh Army, he helped expand the total number of US forces from 55,000 to more than 225,000 troops. In addition to moving troops to the theater, he also had to find the cheapest way to station them once they were in Germany. A large part of the plan was to use old German army facilities in order to keep costs down. He was tireless in attending to all the myriad details involved; in doing so, he coordinated US military efforts with the German civilian authorities.

Hollingsworth added greatly to his growing reputation while at Seventh Army. Major General White wrote him a letter in March 1951, saying, "Your friendly, pleasing personality and your ability to secure cooperation have gained favorable recognition for you from all whom you have come in contact. . . . The greatest satisfaction a commander may experience is to be served by an officer of your caliber and loyalty."[8]

CGSC

In the summer of 1951, Holly finally received orders for the Command and General Staff College at Fort Leavenworth, Kansas. On 11 July, Hollingsworth and his family departed Bremerhaven for the States on the troop ship *General William O. Darby*. After an auto trip across the country, Hollingsworth reported to the student detachment at Fort Leavenworth in August 1951. The Staff College was for majors and lieutenant colonels. It was a very intense curriculum that included leadership, management, finance, logistics, and tactics. There were about six hundred students in his class, including a number of international officers from some forty nations. Holly studied hard and graduated in the top 10 percent of his class. He also had time for recreation and played golf every afternoon. Additionally, he became a Master Mason and 32nd Degree Scottish Rite.[9]

Hollingsworth attended CGSC as the Cold War intensified. The Soviets had exploded their first atomic bomb in 1949 and the specter of nuclear war was ever present. Good evidence of this was a post-wide briefing held during October "dealing with the effects of the Atomic Bomb upon the individual" that was conducted for the benefit of adult military dependents and civilian employees at Fort Leavenworth. The attendees were told that "the purpose of this lecture is to provide all adult military dependents and civilian employees at this Post with information relative to the dangers inherent in an atomic explosion, how to recognize these dangers, and what emergency measures the individual should take if exposed to an atomic explosion."[10]

As he was completing the Staff College course, he again volunteered for Korea, but once again he was turned down. Hollingsworth then requested that he be reassigned to the 1st Armored Division at Fort Hood or back to the 2nd Armored Division in Germany. Instead, having already commanded a regiment, he was assigned as the chief of combined arms instruction at the United States Military Academy at West Point, New York. Hollingsworth later found out that it was Gen. Maxwell Taylor, chief of operations and plans at the Department of the Army, who personally selected him to go to West Point, largely based on his combat record in World War II.

West Point

Upon Holly's graduation from CGSC in June 1952, the Hollingsworths made their way to New York. They very much enjoyed their time at the Military Academy. There he served as the chief of all tactical instruction and commanded the Combat Arms Detachment. In that capacity, he saw his duty as developing the character of the cadets while providing a broad basic military education to go along with what the cadets received in their academic classes. Additionally, he supervised the administration and discipline of the Corps of Cadets. It was not all work, because he also took the time to teach handball and was responsible for fishing and hunting by the cadets on the West Point reservation.

Hollingsworth was a highly decorated war hero, and his outgoing, larger-than-life personality quickly won him the loyalty, respect, and affection of his cadets, who held him in high esteem for the rest of their lives. He was known for his rousing lectures and ability to motivate the cadets. In one speech, he told them he would like to have a tank battle against a Soviet tank with one of our new tanks. The cadets left the rousing class shouting, "Beat Russia!"[11]

Graduates from the West Point class of 1954 still remember a message he sent to them upon graduation, which read:

> Congratulations to each of you. I sincerely hope and expect you to execute your new assignments with the force, aggressiveness and enthusiastic spirit you have displayed during the past six months. Pursue one great decisive aim with force and determination. Remain faithful throughout to the principles we have laid out for you.
>
> A powerful emotion must stimulate the great ability of a military leader, whether it be ambition as in Caesar, hatred of the enemy as in Hannibal, or pride of glorious defeat of the enemy as in Gen. George S. Patton.
>
> Open your hearts to such emotion. Be audacious and cunning in your plans. Be firm, bold, and persevering in their execution, determined to find a glorious end and fate will crown your brow with glory, and engrave your image in the hearts of your last descendants and countrymen.[12]

Hollingsworth greatly impressed both the cadets and his colleagues on the West Point faculty. One of those on the faculty was Alexander M. Haig Jr., who would later serve under Hollingsworth in Vietnam and then go on to a long and illustrious military and diplomatic career, serving six presidents in one capacity or another. Haig recalled that Holly was "a man's man and a born soldier who lived his life on an all-out, try-anything basis and then, over a drink of the best available bourbon whiskey, recounted its funniest moments in a repertoire of war stories that had few if any equals in the Army."[13]

Haig recalled one time during summer cadet training at Camp Buckner, outside West Point, when Holly explained to the cadets why he kept a round in the chamber of his .45-caliber pistol as well as a full clip of seven rounds. According to Haig, Holly said, "Sometimes you need the eighth round. One day in Germany, I popped the hatch of my tank, stuck my head out, and found myself looking at eight members of the Wehrmacht. Every one of them was pointing a rifle at me. There was no time to fool around with the machine gun. I drew my .45, shot all eight Germans dead, and drove on." Haig said that at the time, he thought Holly was having a little fun with his audience of "hero-worshipping kids." However, he found out soon after from an eyewitness that the story was true.[14]

Holly was indeed looked up to by the cadets. One of them, H. Norman Schwarzkopf, who went on to four-star rank and the command of all forces in the first Gulf War, reflected in his memoir about his days as a West

Point cadet, recalling Holly as a "colorful character, profane as could be." Schwarzkopf remembered times when Holly would diverge from the lesson plan at hand and launch into war stories about combat in North Africa or Europe. Schwarzkopf wrote that Holly "described glorious scenes of victory and we loved every minute of it."[15]

Schwarzkopf wrote that Hollingsworth was a master at inspiring the cadets. He remembered one instance when he and his fellow cadets were being supervised by Hollingsworth on a 3.5-inch rocket launcher range. As the cadets fired the bazooka-like weapon at targets shaped like tank silhouettes 150 yards away, Holly ranged up and down the firing line urging on the cadets and making on-the-spot corrections as necessary. As Holly watched, Schwarzkopf fired his rocket. When it struck the target, Holly patted him on the back and said, "That's great, Mister! You're just the kind of killer we want to have in our Army!" Schwarzkopf later wrote of the incident in his autobiography, recalling, "I felt as if I'd been blessed by God."[16]

Although Hollingsworth greatly enjoyed working with the cadets, he was worried about how his career was progressing. He had received a number of encouraging letters while at West Point. One of them was from Brig. Gen. Hamilton H. Howze, assistant division commander of the 2nd Armored Division. Howze wrote, "I think you are especially qualified [for the position at West Point], particularly as I regard as an important part of your responsibility the inspiration of young officers which will lead the best of them to select armor as their branch."[17] Such communications, particularly from senior armor officers, were encouraging, but Holly continued chafing to get back to duty with troops. In a February 1953 letter to Brig. Gen. Einar B. Gjelsteen, Seventh Army chief of staff, he inquired about the possibility of being reassigned to Germany. He wrote, "I like very much being around the Cadets, but from a professional standpoint, I feel like I am in the midst of a retrograde movement (Army Hq, GS, C&GSC to teaching platoon, company, battalion and basic leadership)."[18] Despite his request to Gjelsteen, he was informed by Armor Career Branch that he would remain at West Point for three years and then go to the Army War College.

OCLL and "Revolt of the Colonels"

Prepared to stay at West Point for another year, Holly received a call in December 1953 from the Department of the Army saying that Gen. Matthew B. Ridgway had been appointed chief of staff of the army and that Holly was to report to him for duty. The Hollingsworths were sorry to leave West Point, but they departed for Washington nonetheless.

Holly was assigned to the Office of the Chief Legislative Liaison (OCLL) in the Pentagon. His role was to act as liaison between the army and the Senate and the House of Representatives in order to ensure the maintenance of proper relationships between the army and Congress.

In that capacity, he was responsible for, among other things, arranging for congressional visits to army installations across the United States and overseas, and answering congressional inquiries about army installations in their states, soldiers who needed compassionate reassignments or release from active duty for medical, and all manner of similar issues and complaints. Additionally, he traveled extensively with congressmen on overseas trips to the Far East, South Asia, and the Middle East.

One of Hollingsworth's major duties was to assist with legislation that improved the lot of the troops. He was particularly involved in obtaining favorable legislation concerning the serviceman's voting privileges and the soldier's absentee ballot, which provided a mechanism for soldiers to vote in state and national elections even while they were serving overseas.

Toward the end of Hollingsworth's time at the Pentagon, he became involved in controversy. The army was in a struggle with the Eisenhower administration, which, in the wake of the Korean War, wanted to increase US reliance on nuclear weapons for national defense and downsize conventional forces. Upon taking office, Eisenhower ordered a complete review of national security strategy. Once the review was completed, the president provided his new strategic guidance in National Security Memorandum 162/2 (October 1953). Called the "New Look," this strategy emphasized the use of strategic nuclear weapons to deter potential threats, both nuclear and conventional, from the Eastern bloc of nations headed by the Soviet Union. According to the new strategy, local wars of the Korean variety would be fought by America's allies, who would use their own ground forces, backed by American air and sea forces.[19] This signaled a shift in emphasis away from conventional ground forces and a large standing army. The resulting defense budget called for a drastic reduction in army troop strength, from 1,481,000 to 1,000,000, cutting the army from twenty divisions to fourteen. Under this concept, the army would transition to a strategic mobile reserve rather than a forward deployed force.

To many of the senior army officers, this was an obvious threat to the future of their service. Army general Lyman L. Lemnitzer spoke for many when he wrote in 1955 that "today it seems to me that the very survival of the Army . . . is at stake."[20] General Ridgway, the army chief of staff, apparently agreed with Lemnitzer. He was at odds with President Eisenhower, believing in the continued value of conventional forces and arguing that the army's end strength should not be cut in a haphazard manner.[21] He did not openly or directly go public with his opposition, but he continued to argue against the "New Look" and for a strong army capable of fighting and winning a limited war. His opposition to the "New Look" soon made him persona non grata to the Eisenhower administration, and particularly with Secretary of Defense Charles E. Wilson. Very vocal in his advocacy for the army, Ridgway was not asked to remain as army chief of staff when his first term was up in June 1955, so he retired.[22] However, on his way out, he sent a memorandum to Wilson on his views on the "New Look" and the administration's defense policy. There was nothing new in the memorandum, but Wilson directed Ridgway to classify the memo. Nevertheless, it was subsequently "leaked" to the *New York Times*.[23]

This was effectively the opening shot in a battle that would not go away between the administration and army leadership. Ridgway was succeeded by Gen. Maxwell D. Taylor, who shared Ridgway's views. Taylor and his deputy chief of staff for research and development, Lt. Gen. James M. Gavin, launched a campaign against the other services, the Department of Defense, and the White House for more army funding and an end to cuts in force. In several venues, they challenged the administration's assumption that the next war would be fought solely by nuclear forces and thus argued that there was a continued need for conventional ground forces.

Under the direction of Taylor and Gavin, the army staff began preparing a response to the "New Look." A group of army staff officers, among them some of the best and brightest young officers, many with advanced degrees and distinguished combat records, began to meet in private homes in the Washington area after duty hours to plot a way ahead in a campaign to discredit the "New Look."[24] The group leaked army position papers and other documents to congressmen and friendly journalists to gain support for the army position. Hollingsworth was part of this group and was responsible for contacts with members of Congress, including Rep. F. Edward Hebert (D, LA) and Sen. Henry "Scoop" Jackson (D, WA).

In January 1956, this group became known as the Coordination Group, but when the press became aware of what they were doing, their actions were dubbed by some as the "Colonels' Revolt." Once their doings became known, these officers were threatened with courts-martial. Hollingsworth was accused of passing classified documents to Congress, specifically to members of the House Armed Services Committee, House Appropriations Committee, Senate Foreign Relations Committee, and House Foreign Affairs Committee. However, the members of these committees all had high security clearances; the investigations into Hollingsworth's actions were terminated and no charges were filed.[25]

The situation seemed to come to a head on May 21 when a clearly agitated Secretary of Defense Wilson, joined by the military chiefs, including General Taylor, held a press conference. He assured the reporters present that the reports of interservice rivalry and dissent in the Pentagon were grossly overexaggerated.[26] The press was not placated and reported on a series of new leaks that came from colonels on the army staff attacking the other services, criticizing the "New Look," and advancing budget proposals at odds with the White House's strategic priorities.[27] General Taylor replied that he did not know who the colonels were, despite the fact that the revolt had been front-page news for several weeks; he further stated that the army was not out to make its own policies and strategies in defiance of national policy.[28] Meanwhile, Brig. Gen. William C. Westmoreland, secretary of the General Staff, was quietly preparing reassignment orders for the members of the Coordination Group. These orders sent them to career-enhancing assignments, like unit command or senior service schools. Hollingsworth received orders for the US Army War College (USAWC) at Carlisle Barracks, Pennsylvania.

In the end, the impact of the so-called Colonels' Revolt is debatable, but it is clear that the army's response to the "New Look" had some impact on changing the US defense policy. The debate that the revolt caused reversed the trend toward downsizing the army and tactical air force and returned the nation from dependence on strategic nuclear weapons to a sense of balance between nuclear and conventional forces in national defense.

The OCLL assignment proved to be very important for Hollingsworth's career. Not only did he become associated with those who were working to save the army in a time of peril, he also proved very adept at dealing with members of Congress and fostered several very close lifelong friendships with a number of influential representatives and senators such as Hebert and Jackson, as well as Mendel Rivers (D, SC) and Olin E. "Tiger" Teague (D, TX). A fellow army officer wrote in 1956 that "Holly has more personal friends and admirers in Congress than any other officer of his age and rank in the Army . . . a great many are ranking members on powerful committees including the Senate and House leadership and all members of the House Armed Services Committee."[29] Several of these friendships would serve him in good stead later in his military career.

USAWC and Pakistan

En route to the War College, Holly was promoted to colonel. The War College was a year-long course in which lieutenant colonels and colonels studied strategy and military policy. There, Holly and his fellow students examined and discussed a number of different scenarios, including Korea, Vietnam, and Pakistan as well as dealing with the Soviet Union. In one study, Holly chaired a student committee that war-gamed the situation in the Iran-Pakistan area. For six weeks, Holly acted as the Soviet commander responsible for the Persian Gulf area of operation. The studies that Holly participated in at Carlisle proved invaluable when, upon graduation, he was assigned as chief of the US Army Element of the Military Assistance Advisory Group in Pakistan.

Hollingsworth served there from 1957 to 1959. He was responsible for assisting in the training of five Pakistani Army divisions and equipping them with US weapons and equipment. Hollingsworth spent a lot of time in the remote tribal areas riding in a jeep with his Pakistani Army driver. In rugged areas around Khyber Pass, they were frequently shot at by members of unfriendly tribes. Holly liked the Pakistani soldiers but found that the Pakistani Army, as a rule, did not understand logistics and the management of things necessary to keep a fighting force sustainable in combat. Hollingsworth's assessment was borne out clearly in the fighting between the Pakistanis and the Indians after Holly departed Pakistan. The Pakistani tank battalions drove back the Indians until they ran out of fuel and ammunition.

In the course of his duties, Holly got to know Gen. Muhammad Ayub Khan, a Sandhurst-trained officer who had commanded a British Indian battalion during World War II in Italy. He and Holly became fast friends.

They both enjoyed the outdoors, particularly hunting. Mrs. Hollingsworth, at the same time, became very close to the general's wife and daughters.

At one point, General Ayub asked Hollingsworth, "How can you deny me the use of your military aid while at the same time your country gives the Indians $300 million grant aid to buy 106 millimeter recoilless rifles from you and Jaguar fighter planes from the British and they bring them here and use them against me?" Holly replied, "General Ayub, I'm a military man and a soldier, as you are, and I can't answer that question. That is a question that should be asked by your Prime Minister of our President."

One day in 1958, General Ayub visited Holly in his quarters. He began by saying, "Holly, I might as well get on with it. Have you ever thought about taking over a country?" Holly replied that he had not, but he had studied the principles involved in doing so at the War College. Ayub said that his government was trying to run a democracy in order to satisfy American foreign policy requirements and receive US aid. However, Ayub had a problem with the way the government was pursuing this goal. Therefore, he proposed to take over the government and run it himself.

After some discussion, Ayub told Holly that he could so inform Allen Dulles of the CIA. Holly did so, but the CIA said that a military takeover in Pakistan would never happen. Holly also shared this information with the defense attaché and the head of the Military Assistance Group, neither of whom believed that Ayub Khan would go ahead with his plans.

General Ayub had told Holly that he would know the coup was going down when the 13th Lancers moved out of Quetta to Multan. On the fifth of October, one of Holly's subordinates was supposed to visit the 13th Lancers in Quetta, but on the fourth, Holly received a message requesting that the Americans postpone their visit. On the fifth, the 13th Lancers moved out of Quetta for Multan. Holly notified the ambassador, a political appointee with little practical experience in Pakistan or any other embassy, that he thought the coup was going down; he thought the ambassador would notify the CIA, but the ambassador did not believe Hollingsworth and did not pass the word on to Washington.

The coup began in the early morning hours of 6 October. At 2:00 a.m., Ayub Khan called the ambassadors of the commonwealth and the United States together to inform them about the coup. The ambassadors from Great Britain, Canada, and New Zealand told Ayub Khan that he had their countries' support. The US ambassador demurred, virtually ignoring the coup and instead asking why Ayub Khan had not promoted one of his general officers whom the ambassador favored. According to Hollingsworth, Ayub Khan was incredulous, saying later, "Here we are at a time of crisis, and from one of the prime countries of the world all I get is why I didn't promote some general officer? This is unbelievable."[30]

Ayub Khan's coup was successful; he enjoyed the support of the people and the coup was virtually bloodless. The former prime minister and his family were sent to England. Ayub Khan served as president of Pakistan from 1958 until March 1969. Although he and Holly had no formal relationship after Ayub Khan became president, they remained friends until the Pakistani leader died in 1974.

Ayub Khan was not the only friend the Hollingsworths made in Pakistan. Holly traveled extensively throughout the country and was very well known in Pakistani military circles. The American colonel liked soldiers, and to Holly, Pakistani soldiers were just like American soldiers. He could relate to them and they to him. He was very outgoing and quickly won over everyone he met. He stayed in contact with a number of the Pakistani officers he met and worked with long after he departed Pakistan.

While Holly was assigned in Pakistan, his father passed away. The elder Hollingsworth died on 20 April 1958 after a long illness. He was buried in Valley View Cemetery in Cooke County, Texas. With his tour in Pakistan coming to an end, Hollingsworth received orders for Fort Hood, Texas.

Fort Hood and Tragedy

In August 1959, Holly was reassigned as the deputy commander, Combat Command A, 1st Armored Division. He, Nickie, and Jamie headed for Texas. They lived at Fort Hood, but Jamie entered high school in Killeen, the town adjacent to the base.

After nine months in the 1st Armored, Holly was reassigned as the chief of staff, 2nd Armored Division, also at Fort Hood. Hollingsworth was delighted to return to his old wartime unit. The division was scheduled to rotate to Germany and spent most of its time training for that deployment. Hollingsworth threw himself into the task of getting the division ready for Europe.

On the evening of 9 October 1960, tragedy struck the Hollingsworth family. Eighteen-year-old Jamie was involved in an automobile accident at Fort Hood. Jamie and William Keith Lain, both seniors at Killeen High School, were riding in Jamie's car with Lain driving. Military police reports said that the car was traveling toward North Fort Hood on East Range Road at 5:40 p.m. As the car topped a hill the driver lost control; the car ran off the road and into a deep ditch before flipping over and landing in dry Henson Creek.[31] The other boy was not injured seriously, but Jamie was hurt badly. Both boys were rushed to the Gatesville hospital, the closest medical facility. The lights of the local high school football stadium were turned on so that a Fort Hood helicopter transporting doctors and blood could land near the hospital. Young Hollingsworth had sustained a skull fracture, and despite all the best efforts of the doctors, he died in the hospital the next day. The funeral was held in Killeen, but Jamie was buried in the Sanger Cemetery.[32]

The loss of their only son was devastating to the Hollingsworths. In many ways, the general and his wife never got over it; they never had any more children. Overcome by grief but doing his best not to show it, Hollingsworth pushed himself even harder at work.

The Pentagon (Again)

In August 1961, after completing eighteen months at Fort Hood, Holly was again assigned to the Pentagon. He worked as a staff officer for a year, serving as deputy director and later director of the Reserve Affairs Division, Office of the Assistant Secretary of Defense (Manpower). In this job, Hollingsworth chaired a Department of Defense (DOD) working group that was chartered to study requirements for military participation in civil defense.

Largely because of his performance on the DOD working group, Hollingsworth attracted the attention of several powerful people. Ultimately, he received a political appointment as deputy assistant secretary of defense for Manpower (Reserve Affairs), a new office created by the secretary of defense to deal with reserve issues of all services. At the time, Rep. F. Edward Hebert, (D, LA), chairman of the House Armed Services subcommittee on reserve affairs, noted that the office was created without "fanfare" and was a direct result of a subcommittee recommendation to give reserve problems of all services "more recognition."

Hollingsworth served in this position from August 1962 to September 1965. It was quite unusual for a military officer to be appointed to a cabinet-level position, certainly not as a colonel. In his new appointment, he was directly responsible to Assistant Secretary of Defense Norman Paul. Hollingsworth was in a unique position; he had to give directives to generals who outranked him. He later said that during his tenure in this office, he "sent many memos to the Army, Navy, and Air Force that were directive in nature and that three and four star generals didn't like worth a damn."[33]

In the course of his job at the Pentagon, he had occasion to come to know Robert S. McNamara, the secretary of defense. He thought McNamara was "anti-people," someone who assumed that people were robots such that "if you pushed a button they would all fall out or line up." Still, Holly was impressed with McNamara and his intellect; he later called him "a phenomenal fellow." However, he did not have the same opinion of McNamara's "whiz kids," the group of experts with whom McNamara surrounded himself in order to turn around the management of the Department of Defense. Holly thought they were an "egotistical, anti-military lot." He got along with them but did not think they made a positive contribution; in fact, he thought "they probably contributed to the political loss of the Vietnam conflict."

Over the years, Hollingsworth had received a number of queries from various businesses discussing employment after his retirement. Perhaps unhappy that he was not on a recent brigadier general promotion list, he requested retirement effective 1 September 1962 for the purpose of joining the Reed A. Thursby Company, a civil engineering firm in Saint Petersburg, Florida. Because of his reputation and service in the Pentagon, it is not surprising that his request was denied and returned without action by the secretary of defense. Hollingsworth continued to soldier on in the Pentagon. At the same time, he continued his educational pursuits by seeking a master's degree in international affairs at George Washington University.

Shortly after his retirement request was turned down, the Cuban Missile Crisis erupted, almost plunging the United States and USSR into war. During the course of that situation, Holly and his boss slept in their offices. As the crisis unfolded and the tension grew, it appeared that the United States would have to commit combat troops to compel the removal of the Soviet missiles in Cuba. Holly opposed the call-up of the Reserve and National Guard units because he did not believe they were ready. He was overruled, and his office had begun planning for the mobilization of the Reserves and National Guard when the Soviets turned their ships around.

Although the new job called for someone of higher rank, Norm Paul was very satisfied with Hollingsworth and, in an 8 August 1963 letter to Army Chief of Staff Gen. Earle Wheeler, Paul requested that Hollingsworth be retained in his position instead of a general officer being assigned to replace him.[34] He also requested that Hollingsworth be given an early promotion. However, such was not to be the case.

In the aftermath of the Cuban Missile Crisis, Holly was also involved in the planning for the growing conflict in Vietnam. He was responsible for coming up with the manpower plan for supporting the US effort there. The plan was presented to McNamara, who in turn presented it to President Lyndon Johnson. Ultimately, the United States would commit ground troops in Vietnam in 1965.

In his position as the deputy assistant secretary of defense, Hollingsworth was very much involved in McNamara's controversial attempt to reorganize Reserve Components. McNamara wanted to merge the Army Reserve unit structure into the Army National Guard to increase combat effectiveness, improve the management system, and shorten the reaction time of Army Reserve forces; some were worried that this was an attempt by McNamara to abolish the Reserves. It was clear that McNamara felt that the Reserves and National Guard performed the same function, and he was not happy with the redundancy and inefficiency of both components. In the end, both the Reserves and the National Guard continued, but Hollingsworth played a vital role in revising and improving their personnel management systems.

During his tenure in the cabinet post, Hollingsworth was instrumental in the revitalization of the Reserve Officers' Training Corps (ROTC) program. A product of ROTC himself, he advocated for higher standards and better selection measures for senior ROTC cadets who would go on to army commissions. He played a major role in the passage of Public Law 88-647, the ROTC Revitalization Act of 1964, which provided for ROTC scholarships and an expansion of the Junior ROTC program.

He met a number of influential people during the course of his work in the Pentagon. Maj. Muhammad Zia-ul-Haq, a young officer from Pakistan, paid an office visit to Hollingsworth in 1964 after the young officer completed training at the Command and General Staff College at Fort Leavenworth, Kansas. Zia went on to a successful military career in Pakistan, ultimately achieving the rank of general before becoming the sixth president of Pakistan, in 1978.[35]

Norm Paul continued to be very impressed with Hollingsworth and the job he was doing. In a 9 June 1965 letter to Army Chief of Staff Harold K. Johnson, Paul requested that he be extended until June 1966 and be promoted early. He wrote, "I know of no officer in OSD [Office of the Secretary of Defense], irrespective of rank, who has devoted himself more selflessly to his job, who has demonstrated more guts on tough issues, or who has generally impressed me more as one hell of an officer—in every respect." Johnson replied two days later, but he was noncommittal, saying, "You can be sure that we want to reward brilliance as early as we can; but, at the same time, cannot reward one at a cost of discouraging several thousand others."[36]

While Hollingsworth felt that he was doing important work as the undersecretary, it is clear that he had begun to chafe in the position, primarily because it was away from the army. Additionally, the war in Vietnam was heating up, and he felt that he would serve the country better in combat than in continuing at the Pentagon. Accordingly, on 19 July 1965, he requested release and reassignment. Hollingsworth wrote, "My assignment as Deputy Assistant Secretary of Defense for Manpower (Reserve Affairs) has been very rich and satisfying and I appreciate the opportunity afforded me to continue in this assignment. However, during the time of crisis or emergency I prefer to serve with Army soldiers in the field. . . . Therefore, I respectfully request that I be released from duty in the Office of the Assistant Secretary of Defense (Manpower) not later than 30 September 1965 for the purpose of making myself available for service with the U.S. Army in South Viet-Nam."[37]

Paul was reluctant to see Hollingsworth go but understood his motivation; he approved the request the next day. However, in a 24 August memo to Secretary of the Army Cyrus Vance, he described Hollingsworth's departure as "an irreplaceable loss to this office." He continued, "His work for me has been outstanding in every respect. My views on the character of his performance have been expressed in efficiency reports, and last June, in a letter to General Johnson. I again expressed my opinion that Colonel Hollingsworth should be promoted at the earliest opportunity."[38]

Army Staff

Holly left his cabinet-level position in September 1965 after three years; upon his departure he was presented the Distinguished Service Medal by Norm Paul, citing "his dynamic leadership, diligent efforts, and devotion to duty, coupled with his willingness to assume responsibilities far greater than those normally expected."[39]

Upon Hollingsworth's release from OSD, he was reassigned to the Office of the Chief of Staff for Personnel, but after three months went to the Office of the Chief of Staff of the Army. In those capacities, he served on one promotion board and one selection board. The war in Vietnam was increasingly on his mind. In a letter to Lt. Col. Earl W. Bell in September 1965, he wrote, "I expect to go to Vietnam in early March. Abe Abrams [Army Vice Chief of Staff Creighton W. Abrams] told me today that I better hurry or the damn war may be over before I can get there. It does seem to be going a lot better and it may not be necessary to send over as many troops as we at one time planned for."[40] As it turned out, the war was not going that well in Vietnam, and Hollingsworth's concern about missing the war proved unfounded.

Although Hollingsworth was anxious to get back to the battlefield, he performed magnificently in the Pentagon and made many good contacts. In an October 1965 letter, Cyrus R. Vance, then deputy secretary of defense (Reserve Affairs) and later secretary of the army, wrote, "We will greatly miss your counsel and assistance. Your hard work, objectivity, and courageous proposals have demonstrated in a dozen different ways the finest qualities of the professional soldier."[41]

Hollingsworth was promoted to brigadier general in December 1965. The road to promotion had not been without drama. The first time he came up for promotion, he was number 66 on the list, but the Department of the Army promoted only through number 63. Long after his retirement, an interviewer asked him why he thought he had been number 66 on the first promotion list; in his usual fashion, he cracked, "I think that whoever was on the board liked 65 others better than they liked me."[42]

The next year that Holly was eligible for selection, the army threw out the list and did not promote any colonels to brigadier. Hollingsworth was getting concerned, because colonels were considered for promotion only four times. However, he was number 2 on the next list and was promoted almost immediately. He was very grateful to Norm Paul for Paul's efforts on his behalf. In an 8 December 1965 letter to Paul, he wrote, "Without your help it would have been impossible for me to attain General rank. This I shall never forget."[43]

Shortly after he was promoted, Hollingsworth received a letter from the army chief of public affairs. Along with his congratulations, Maj. Gen. G. V. Underwood outlined the ground rules for press interviews meant "to prevent misunderstanding of the use to be made by the correspondent of information obtained from the military source."[44] The letter was a thinly veiled admonition to be careful when dealing with the press. Hollingsworth's later difficulties with the media suggest that he should have paid more attention to the guidance provided in the letter.

Hollingsworth attended the army chief of staff's conference for newly nominated general officers in early March 1966. Among his fellow conference attendees were a number of senior officers with whom he would serve later in his career, to include Brig. Gen. Orwin C. Talbott, Col. William R. Desobry, Col. Harris W. Hollis, and Col. George S. Young. With the conference over, Hollingsworth prepared to depart for Vietnam in accordance with the orders he had just received.

5

Vietnam and the 1st Infantry Division

The Vietnam War

Hollingsworth's orders assigned him to the 1st Infantry Division, where he would become assistant division commander. The Big Red One, as it was known, was part of the initial US deployment of ground forces to Vietnam in 1965.

The United States had been involved in Vietnam since 1950. Initially, the United States supported France in the First Indochina War in an effort to stem the spread of Communism in Southeast Asia. The French were defeated at the Battle of Dien Bien Phu in 1954 and the Geneva Accords were subsequently signed, dividing Vietnam at the 17th parallel. From 1954 to 1956, the United States worked with France in support of the new government in South Vietnam in its struggle against the Viet Cong (VC) guerrillas and the Communist government in Hanoi. When the French forces departed Vietnam in 1956, the United States assumed the mission of support to the Saigon government.

In the beginning, American advisers worked to build the forces of South Vietnam to confront the Communists. However, those forces proved not up to the task and by 1964, the Saigon government and the Army of the Republic of Vietnam (ARVN) had lost control of large tracts of the country to the VC. In early 1965, in an attempt to stave off defeat and in response to VC attacks on American air bases in South Vietnam, the United States launched an air offensive against North Vietnam. This offensive did little to change the situation or lessen the will of the North Vietnamese leaders in Hanoi.

The war escalated in March 1965 when the VC attacked a US barracks in Qui Nhon, killing twenty-three American advisers. Shortly thereafter, President Lyndon Johnson ordered the deployment of the 9th Marines, who subsequently landed near Da Nang. The marines were initially deployed to protect US installations but very soon found themselves conducting offensive combat operations against the VC. Gen. William C. Westmoreland, commander of US forces in Vietnam, requested additional US combat troops. The president approved the request, and three brigades of US Army troops were alerted for deployment to Vietnam.

The first US Army combat brigade to arrive in Vietnam was the 173rd Airborne from Okinawa. The paratroopers arrived in early May and were given the mission to protect the Bien Hoa Air Base north of Saigon. Very soon after arrival, the 173rd was aggressively patrolling in its assigned area of responsibility. On 15 May, the brigade conducted its first heliborne combat assault, the first of the Vietnam War.[1]

The Big Red One

On 5 June, Westmoreland asked for a total of forty-four combat battalions to be deployed to Vietnam. Once again, the president approved the request, and the army alerted the 101st Airborne, 1st Cavalry, and 1st Infantry Divisions to provide one combat brigade each. Maj. Gen. Jonathan Seaman, commanding general of the 1st Infantry, ordered his 2nd Brigade to prepare for deployment from its home station at Fort Riley, Kansas, to Vietnam.

After completing preparations for the move, the 2nd Brigade and supporting units traveled by rail from Fort Riley to Oakland Army Terminal in California. There, the troops and their equipment were loaded onto transport ships. The embarked brigade aboard the *General W. H. Gordon* stopped first at Cam Ranh Bay, where the 1st Battalion, 18th Infantry, and one artillery battery were off-loaded to provide local security for the port facilities being built there. Then the *Gordon* made its way south with the rest of the brigade to the port of Vung Tau, arriving on 14 July. After unloading, the men and equipment of the brigade moved to set up the brigade base of operations about three kilometers southwest of Bien Hoa airfield in the III Corps Tactical Zone.

The brigade was put under the operational control of the 173rd Airborne Brigade and given the mission of establishing a fortified base camp to protect the airfield at Bien Hoa from enemy attacks from the southwest. The brigade commenced major combat operations on 8 September.

As the situation continued to develop in Vietnam, General Seaman received orders to deploy the rest of the division. The men and equipment went by rail to Oakland, where they were loaded onto twenty ships for the voyage to Vietnam. In October, the ships reached the ports at Vung Tau and Saigon and began to off-load the men and equipment. As the division arrived, it was separated and ordered to occupy four base areas: Division Headquarters and the Support Command went to Di An, fifteen kilometers north of Saigon; the 1st Brigade to Phuoc Vinh, forty kilometers farther north; the 3rd Brigade to Lai Khe, thirty kilometers northwest of Di An; and Division Artillery to Phu Loi. Initial combat operations were devoted to securing the immediate areas surrounding the base camps while also establishing the 1st Infantry Division's area of influence. By 1 November, the entire division, still under the command of Major General Seaman, was operational.

The division consisted of nine infantry battalions, two of which were mechanized, four artillery battalions, and an armored cavalry squadron. In addition, the division could call on several battalions of assault helicopters to ferry dismounted infantry to and from the battlefield.

The division's area of operations was in the III Corps Tactical Zone generally between Saigon and the Cambodian border, consisting primarily of Binh Duong and Binh Long Provinces. This area included the enemy-infested War Zones C and D and the infamous Iron Triangle, an area that was often described as "a dagger pointing at Saigon." The sparsely populated area of operations was characterized by thick jungle, rubber plantations, and rice paddies.

The mission of the 1st Infantry Division was twofold. First, it would provide protection for the local populace and support pacification programs meant to extend the influence of the Saigon government, and second, it was to find, fix, and destroy enemy forces within its assigned area of operations and at the same time block enemy infiltration toward Saigon from enemy sanctuaries in Cambodia.

Eleven days after becoming operational, the Big Red One fought its first major battle in Vietnam near Bau Bang on National Highway 13. There, elements of three divisional units overcame an estimated VC regiment. In the next big engagement, on 5 December, the 2nd Battalion, 2nd Infantry, defeated the Viet Cong in the Michelin Rubber Plantation northwest of the division's Lai Khe base camp. By the end of 1965 the division had participated in three major operations: HUMP, BUSHMASTER I, and BUSHMASTER II.

In early 1966, the enemy strength and activity in the III Corps Tactical Zone increased significantly. It had been known for some time that the Central Office for South Vietnam (COSVN), which controlled major operations in the region, was located somewhere along the Cambodian-Vietnamese border in or near War Zone C. This headquarters, under Gen. Nguyen Chi Thanh, controlled the efforts of three Communist divisions. The 5th and 9th VC Divisions continued to operate east and north of Saigon, respectively. Additionally, the 7th Division of the People's Army of Vietnam (PAVN) had recently come down the Ho Chi Minh Trail and moved into the area; the 7th was a division of North Vietnamese Army regulars that greatly strengthened COSVN capabilities in the area. The three divisions were supported by five

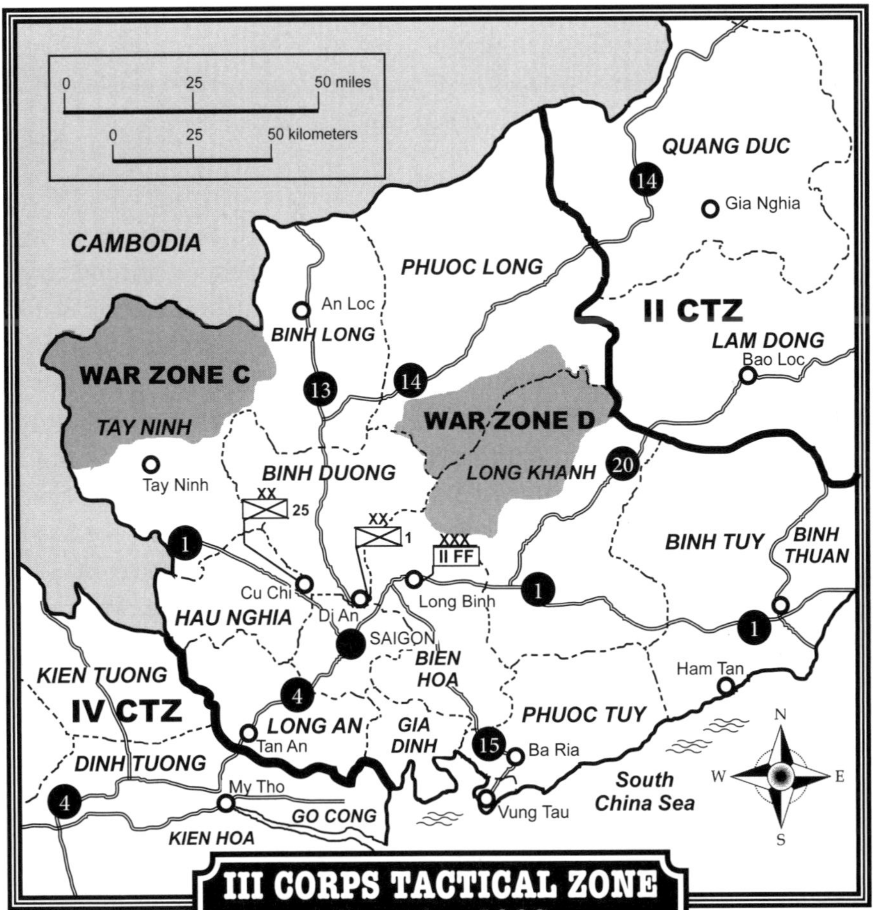

III CORPS TACTICAL ZONE
December 1966

battalions of artillery of various sizes and calibers. Lastly, the elite North Vietnamese 70th Guards Regiment provided security for COSVN headquarters.[2]

This was the situation when Hollingsworth joined the 1st Infantry Division in March 1966. He arrived at the division headquarters in Di An just two weeks before the division commander was to be promoted and elevated to command of II Field Force.[3] Upon General Seaman's departure on 1 April, Brig. Gen. William E. DePuy, who had been the chief of operations in J3 at Military Assistance Command, Vietnam (MACV), under General Westmoreland, assumed command of the division. The normal rank for a US Army division commander is major general; DePuy was on the promotion list and was promoted just after assuming command.

As Westmoreland's operations officer, DePuy had helped shape Westmoreland's theater strategy. Westmoreland saw the most dangerous threat to be the enemy main-force units, and that was where he and DePuy put their emphasis. They saw the mission of US forces to be one of closing with and destroying the main-force enemy. Pacification, winning hearts and minds, would largely be left to the South Vietnamese forces. Having helped formulate that strategy, DePuy would now be able to put it into action at the division level.

DePuy has been described as "intelligent, pragmatic, and forceful . . . with more energy than charisma."[4] Having previously served as corporal in the South Dakota National Guard, DePuy was commissioned into the infantry from the Reserve Officers' Training Corps (ROTC) at South Dakota State University in 1941. During World War II, DePuy served in the hard-luck 90th Infantry Division, taking command of a battalion during the Normandy campaign at age twenty-four. He led the 1st Battalion of the 357th Infantry in the fierce fighting from Utah Beach through the Battle of the Bulge. He saw firsthand the impact of poor senior leadership in the division and how it had resulted in extremely high casualties. As he recalled later, "We went to war with incompetents in charge. That incompetence trickled down and caused the tactical failures . . . and the incredible casualties. All this was indelibly stamped on my mind and attitude ever after for both good and bad."[5] As a result, DePuy was unflinching in his assessment of leaders, believing, based on his personal experience, that poor leaders meant more casualties; therefore he had absolutely no patience for those found wanting. His ideas about leadership and combat were grounded in his experience in the 90th Division, and those ideas provided the foundation for how he would command the 1st Infantry Division.

Hollingsworth and DePuy

Under the personnel system in place at the time, division commanders had little say in the assignment of officers as their assistant division commanders (ADCs), and DePuy did not know Hollingsworth before his arrival in Vietnam except by reputation. Upon meeting Holly, DePuy said, "General, I want only the best officers for my division. I don't want any softies, or behind-the-lines listeners, on my staff. If you can't hack it out here, just pack your bags and go back home." Hollingsworth was aware that he was suspect because to DePuy he was an unknown quantity, but, undaunted, Holly grinned and said, "I'll let you know if I can't handle the job, but don't bother looking for a replacement. You won't need one." DePuy stared at him in silence. Finally, he said, "Okay, we'll find out."[6]

From that somewhat testy beginning, Hollingsworth and DePuy would develop a close personal and professional relationship that made the 1st Infantry Division one of the most potent fighting forces in Vietnam. On the surface, they were an unlikely pair. DePuy was short in stature and did not waste a lot of words. Holly, on the other hand, as described by Henry Gole, author of a book about DePuy, was "a character right out of Hollywood's central casting version of a fighting general . . . profane, bombastic, brave, and the antithesis of a diplomat."[7] Lt. Gen. Phillip Davidson, who served as General Westmoreland's chief of intelligence from 1967 to 1969, described Holly as a "big, brash, tough, loud-mouthed Texan, given to excessive braggadocio," whose every utterance was "dogmatically delivered with supreme self-confidence to an accompaniment of profanity." There was no middle ground with Holly: one either admired and liked him immensely or disliked him just as intensely. This was just as true for Hollingsworth's peers as it was for his subordinates. Davidson pointed out that Holly's detractors accused him of consciously modeling himself after George Patton, but, as Davidson wrote, "what separated 'Holly' from most of the rest of the Patton imitators . . . is that when the bullets start to whine and the shells fall, 'Holly' always made good on his boasts."[8] The Big Red One was soon to see that firsthand.

As the assistant division commander, Hollingsworth was responsible for directing the employment of division units in combat against the enemy. He quickly made his presence known. As the 1st Brigade prepared for an operation in the area along the Cambodian border known as the Parrot's Beak, the general sat in on a briefing to the battalion commanders who would execute the operation. When the briefer concluded his discussion of the coming operation, Hollingsworth took the floor. If there was any doubt about where the new general was coming from, Holly quickly cleared that up. He moved to the front of the briefing tent and launched into an animated and profane discussion of what he expected from his commanders. Urging speed and firepower, he said, “We gotta keep going, like a good fighter, we keep going. These sonsa’bitches are going to be surprised all to hell. We don’t get ’em like that often. We will be in control, and goddamit I want to think we’re pushing a mean pointed stick out there against those sonsa’bitches. Get your men ready, get ’em mean. There are times to go slowly, and there are times to lock and load—kick ass. This is that time. Gotta get in there fast and move fast. Kill fast.” He paused for a breath and then said, “You’re good soldiers. Good luck. Remember: Kill ’em, kill ’em fast.”[9] This was vintage Hollingsworth: he was at war again, and to him there was only one way to go—as hard and as fast as possible.

Hollingsworth soon demonstrated that he was not all talk. DePuy reported to Hollingsworth that “Hanoi Hannah” had declared on the radio that the division’s cavalry squadron, the 1st Squadron of the 4th Cavalry, would not be able to use Route 13, which ran from Lai Khe to the Cambodian border, and that if they tried, the 271st VC Regiment would wipe out the Americans. Having passed on Hannah’s warning, DePuy told Hollingsworth that he wanted him to take the 4th Cavalry up the road.

Hollingsworth knew that DePuy was testing him, but he was not bothered in the least. Nor was he intimidated about the idea of a fight along Route 13. Hollingsworth called in the commanders from the 1st Squadron and told them that B and C Troops would move up the highway and conduct a reconnaissance along the way. He directed the troops to take separate routes to a rendezvous point on the highway and then move from that point up the highway toward the Cambodian border. The squadron commander asked where the rendezvous point was located. Hollingsworth replied, “Grid line seventy-nine. Same as my call-sign.” He added, “You won’t have to worry about locating it. You’ll know it when you get there.”

The young troop commanders were puzzled. How were they supposed to recognize grid line 79 on a highway? It was a mark on a map—nothing else. They left the meeting scratching their heads and wondering what kind of guy this new general was.

Hours later, as the two troops emerged from the jungle in the vicinity of grid line 79 on the map, one of the sergeants in the lead vehicle began to laugh. He pointed, yelling, "There's grid line seventy-nine!" There in the middle of the road was a large "79" in white paint. Over it was the crossed sabers symbol of the 4th Cavalry. Hollingsworth had made sure that the VC knew that the 4th Cavalry intended to use Route 13 whenever it pleased.[10]

From this beginning, Hollingsworth energetically began to build a reputation that would achieve almost mythic proportions. While Hollingsworth's approach could be bombastic, DePuy, although no less driven, was less dramatic. One might think that because the two had distinctly different personalities, there might have been conflict, but DePuy had found a kindred soul in Holly, and Hollingsworth flourished under his command. He was a fighter, and that was what DePuy wanted in his assistant division commanders. They soon formed a strong partnership. Only a few short months after Holly arrived, DePuy told Associated Press reporter Peter Arnett, "I have 1,000 per cent confidence in Hollingsworth. He is completely fearless [and] extremely aggressive."[11] Retired Brig. Gen. James E. Shelton, who served in the 1st Division under DePuy and Hollingsworth, observed after the war, "The 1st Division had not seen a more two-fisted approach to command of the division since the days of Terry de La Mesa Allen and his colorful assistant, Brigadier General Teddy Roosevelt Jr., in World War II."[12]

Holly was delighted to be in the division. He wrote Nickie on 14 March that "this is a fabulous assignment—a little bit of heaven. The men are the best I have ever seen."[13] It was soon clear that Holly and DePuy were kindred spirits when it came to fighting the division. Holly reported to his wife on 3 April that DePuy had gotten his second star, closing his letter by proclaiming that DePuy was "fabulous." Two days later, he reported, "General DePuy and I are having the times of our life." The generals shared many of the same ideas about how to fight the war. Under them, the 1st Infantry Division aggressively took the fight to the enemy.

DePuy was a firm believer in firepower; he wanted the division to find "the enemy with the fewest possible men, and . . . [then] destroy them with firepower."[14] He told all his battalion and brigade commanders, "I want you to remember that the United States of America is a very rich country. We have lots of ammunition. Use it on the enemy, and to hell with anybody who doesn't like it. The motto of this division is, 'Waste ordnance, not American lives.'"[15] DePuy later explained, "It was my idea to go after the Main Forces wherever they could be found and to go after them with as many battalions as I could get into the fight—what was later called 'pile-on.' . . . I took it as my main mission to defeat all the Vietcong Main Forces north of Saigon in the III Corps zone."[16]

In case there was any doubt in anyone's mind of DePuy's intentions, he gathered his officers together and told them, "I will never, ever hear again over the radio, 'I'm pinned down. I'm breaking contact.' [If] I hear it, that officer is relieved immediately. You're never pinned down. Period."[17] Holly was of like mind, often saying, "Grab the enemy by the balls and the hearts and minds will follow."[18]

When DePuy and Holly first arrived in the division, they were not happy with everything they found. Holly noted that the division headquarters had not moved since the division had arrived in-country. He thought the division was not aggressive enough in the field. DePuy, who had observed the division when he was General Westmoreland's G-3 operations officer, felt the same way; he believed that his predecessor had failed to exploit the division's potential for firepower and maneuver. He and Holly immediately set out to shake things up. This would ultimately cause bad blood between DePuy and Hollingsworth and their immediate boss. DePuy's predecessor, whom he and Holly deemed "not aggressive" enough, was Lieutenant General Seaman, commander of II Field Force, Vietnam, now DePuy's immediate headquarters, thus placing Seaman between DePuy and his former boss Westmoreland, with whom he still had a special relationship.[19] This was a situation that would cause difficulties for both DePuy and Hollingsworth later.

With a clear mandate from his new division commander, Holly threw himself into the job. Using the radio call sign "Danger 79er," which he would adopt for the rest of his military career, he was either in the air in his command helicopter over a battle or landing to participate in the fight directly.[20] He found the action exhilarating and seemingly could not get enough of it.

Hollingsworth's tactical philosophy was much like that of DePuy—find the enemy and pile on. After the war, he elaborated on this approach, saying, "It's always been my view that if one little patrol gets in trouble out there, we ought to give him the whole division, or we'll never get a patrol to go out 100 yards at night. The only way you're going to get patrols to go out is [for them to] know that they're going to be supported." And the only way you could know what was needed was to be on the spot; he was fond of saying, "The general's got to be there at the time of crisis, always. And if you are there, and you're talking to the little guys, and they know you're there, boy they will stick with you."[21] This approach won him the undying loyalty of his soldiers, who knew he would do everything in his power to provide the combat support they needed when they got in trouble.

Operation ABILENE

The first big operation under DePuy and Hollingsworth was Operation ABILENE, which commenced on 30 March. ABILENE was designed as a search-and-destroy mission in Phuoc Tuy Province, east of Saigon. The objective of the operation was to find and destroy the 274th and 275th Regiments of the 5th VC Division, which were thought to be operating in the region.[22] The operation involved two of DePuy's brigades in conjunction with the 1st Battalion of the Royal Australian Regiment and the 161st Battery of the Royal New Zealand Artillery. Initially, the US brigades reported light contact, as the VC largely avoided battle. DePuy moved the battalions around the area of operation, trying to find and fix the enemy; however, they never made contact with anything larger than a squad during this period. Although they found a number of supply caches, the enemy remained elusive.

On 11 April, as DePuy and Hollingsworth monitored the situation, 2nd Battalion, 16th Infantry, found an enemy base camp. Late in the afternoon, Company C, isolated in the thick jungle undergrowth, came under a heavy mortar barrage followed by a strong ground attack by elements of the D800 Battalion. The hastily dug-in US infantrymen held their position and beat back several attacks that continued throughout the night. Early the next morning, DePuy and Hollingsworth inserted two companies of reinforcements from two of the 2nd Battalion sister units that made their way cross-country through the thick jungle to join the beleaguered company. By the time they arrived at Company C's position, the VC had withdrawn, leaving forty-one of their own dead on the field. However, the battle had been costly for the 1st Division, too. According to an official account, thirty-five Americans died, primarily because effective firepower could not be brought to bear in such close-quarter fighting.[23] Another account tells a somewhat different story. According to Henry Gole, the outcome of the battle was the result of poor coordination, poor tactics, inability to provide timely fire support, friendly fire, and a stop-fire order that denied artillery support when it was most needed; Gole notes that Charlie Company went into battle with 134 men and came out with 28 effectives.[24] This battle would ultimately bring DePuy and Hollingsworth unwanted attention from above.

On 15 April, Operation ABILENE was terminated. The division reported 92 killed during the operation (bodies found on the battlefield) and estimated another 96 killed based on weapons and blood trails found after the operation was over. The division lost a total of 48 men killed (including those lost in the battle with the D800 Battalion) and 135 wounded. In the end analysis, Operation ABILENE had been less than conclusive, and the enemy likely reoccupied the area once the 1st Division troops were withdrawn. This would be a recurring theme for most US units, including the 1st Infantry Division. The US units were normally very effective in battle against the VC, but after a major engagement, they left to seek the enemy elsewhere and did not occupy any area for any length of time. That meant that the enemy was able to reoccupy those areas while the US units focused their attention on other areas.

Nevertheless, from DePuy's and Hollingsworth's point of view, the operation had been a success. The enemy had been brought to battle and serious casualties had been inflicted on him. If this could be done enough times, the enemy would eventually be routed. According to DePuy, "Operation ABILENE demonstrated conclusively that the 1st Infantry Division can move—and move rapidly—by airmobile operations . . . the Vietcong have suffered a tremendous loss of prestige in Phuoc Tuy Province."[25]

Trouble with the Army Chief of Staff

Not everyone agreed with DePuy's assessment of Operation ABILENE. Gen. Harold K. Johnson, army chief of staff, came to Vietnam shortly after the operation concluded. He visited General DePuy at his headquarters in Lai Khe. Speaking about the battle against the D800 Battalion, Johnson chastised DePuy, warning, "The American people won't support this war if we keep having the kind of casualties suffered by Charlie Company."[26] DePuy agreed to make the changes necessary to try to hold down casualties, but this was just the first in a series of incidents that would poison the relationship between the army chief of staff and DePuy.

It was during Operation ABILENE that Holly was decorated for saving a soldier's life. His command helicopter had crash-landed in a rice paddy because of mechanical problems, and the door gunner had been pinned under the aircraft. Hollingsworth had dug the soldier out of the muck with his helmet and comforted him until he could be evacuated by another helicopter. Shortly after the incident, Hollingsworth was featured in a report on *CBS Evening News with Walter Cronkite*. The report concluded the account of the incident by saying about Hollingsworth, "Clearly, this is no armchair general."[27]

DePuy followed Operation ABILENE with a succession of similar operations designed to find and bring the enemy to battle. The next large operation, BIRMINGHAM, was launched on 24 April northwest of Saigon in War Zone C in Tay Ninh Province. The objective of the operation was to find and destroy elements of the C230 and C320 VC Battalions. Additionally, it was thought that there were enemy base camps, rest areas, hospitals, and logistics facilities in the area. DePuy sent two brigades there and they were joined by an ARVN force of one infantry battalion, three ranger battalions, and three airborne battalions.

Initially, the operation resulted in only sporadic contact with the enemy. However, a battle broke out on 30 April when the 1st Battalion, 2nd Infantry started taking small-arms fire from the Cambodian side of the Rach Cai Bac River, which served as the border between South Vietnam and Cambodia. A major battle ensued when the American soldiers returned fire and called in artillery and air strikes. By the end of the day, 54 VC were killed on the eastern side of the river, plus another 75–100 probable on the western bank.[28]

Operation BIRMINGHAM was concluded on 16 May. In DePuy's estimation, the operation had been very successful. Afterward, 118 enemy bodies and 130 weapons were found. In addition, the 1st Infantry Division destroyed 3 hospitals, 66 base camps, 4 munitions factories, and 6 fuel dumps. In the course of their searches, the US soldiers found and destroyed 2,103 tons of rice, 323 tons of salt, and 35 tons of wheat. The Big Red One suffered 62 killed and 324 wounded.[29]

It was during Operation BIRMINGHAM that Holly first came under scrutiny from the press. After the operation, one reporter asked him whether it was true that he had called in artillery on targets across the Rach Cai Bac River, violating Cambodian neutrality. He quickly replied, "Sure, I am the guy that fired into Cambodia, but I'm going to protect our soldiers."[30] He implied he would do it again if necessary to save American lives. This would not be the last time that Holly would be brutally and often profanely candid, and this tendency did not always serve him well.

Building on the outcome of Operation BIRMINGHAM, DePuy launched a series of ever-larger search-and-destroy operations in the division's assigned area—LEXINGTON in April and May, EL PASO I in May, EL PASO II in June and July, AMARILLO in August, and TULSA and SHENANDOAH into October 1966.[31] DePuy and Hollingsworth pushed the division hard, always pressing the fight, urging their troops to find the enemy and "pile on."

The two generals were all over the battlefield. Not one to stay in his command post and listen to the action on the radio, DePuy was constantly in the air going to or orbiting over the battlefield, often landing to get an up-close feel for the battle. For Hollingsworth's part, he was the ideal complement to DePuy's style of command. Holly was "intimately engaged at battalion level and in frequent direct contact with soldiers on the ground in squads and platoons."[32] However, he did not, as some senior officers did, try to take over the squads and platoons. He joined the fight because he thought that was where generals should be—there with the troops in the middle of the battle where they could see you, providing inspiration and encouragement. He needed to get up close so he could determine what the commander and his troops needed to prevail in the battle; he was there to ensure that the needed support arrived when it was needed most. Mostly, though, he just relished being in the thick of the fighting; the idea that he would orbit at 1,500 feet and "monitor" the battle over the radio was anathema to him; he just was not made that way.

Trouble with the Media

Hollingsworth's colorful way of operating again gained the attention of the media. He was covered in several news stories from Vietnam and was featured in a report on *CBS Evening News with Walter Cronkite* on 5 May 1966. However, it was a report that appeared a month later in the *Sunday Times*, a weekly London paper, that caused Hollingsworth more than a little difficulty. Written by a reporter named Nicholas Tomalin, the story was titled "The General Goes Zapping Charlie Cong." Tomalin spent a day with Hollingsworth as he oversaw a search-and-destroy mission in the Iron Triangle. The story started out by describing the general and his "nonchalant" attitude toward killing the enemy. It portrayed Hollingsworth as an insensitive Texas redneck whose primary pleasure was shooting up the countryside from his personal helicopter and "killing cong." The reporter was struck by Hollingsworth's certainty and justification for fighting in what Tomalin saw as an indiscriminate manner.[33] Hollingsworth thought he was portrayed unfairly and later insisted that he was doing only "what I have done throughout my military career—saving as many lives as possible while destroying the enemy."[34] To Nickie, he wrote that "the article was lousy as hell and full of misquotes. If General Johnson sees that, my ass is out a mile." That proved to be a good prediction.

The article won Hollingsworth considerable notoriety in certain circles at home in the United States. Some government officials in Washington saw him as an "unguided missile" and a "hip shooter." This perspective was not limited to civilians in the government. Hollingsworth's style of command and approach to fighting the war were not always well received by more senior officers in the army. General DePuy received a letter from the chief of public affairs for the army suggesting that Hollingsworth had been less than judicious in his comments to the *Sunday Times* reporter; DePuy wrote back that "Holly is the best soldier in Vietnam" and, effectively, could say or do what he wanted as far as DePuy was concerned.[35]

The PAO was not the only senior officer to be concerned with Hollingsworth's portrayal in the media. The already strained relationship between General Johnson and DePuy and Hollingsworth became further agitated not long after the chief of staff's April visit to Vietnam. He wrote DePuy to comment on a news release that said that DePuy and Hollingsworth had been out chasing Viet Cong in their helicopters. "If I had wanted a lead scout in command of the 1st Division," Johnson wrote, "you would not have gotten the job. Your value and Holly's is proportional to the responsibility that you have for something over 15,000 men. Your job is not to shoot VC. Your job is to see that other people shoot VC. At least, that is the way I look at it."[36]

Hollingsworth's somewhat stormy relationship with the media would be a recurring theme in his career. He seemed incapable of filtering his language when talking with reporters. To more than a few, he came across as an insensitive, bloodthirsty braggart. To Holly's way of thinking, there was only one way to win a war and that was to kill the enemy; any moderation of that effort would be nothing less than criminal. In his mind, that was the only way he could minimize the loss of his own troops' lives; he had learned this lesson the hard way in the bitter battle in Europe, and he made no apologies for the way he went about taking the war to the Viet Cong.

Despite the chief of staff's admonition, both Holly and DePuy continued to run the division as they had since they had first arrived in the unit.

This was only the most recent incident in a growing confrontation that had been brewing between the chief of staff and the commanding general and the assistant division commander of the 1st Infantry Division. At the root of this situation was DePuy's approach to war, an approach that Hollingsworth supported wholeheartedly. One aspect of their approach was lavish use of artillery and air support. To DePuy and Hollingsworth, if they were limited in the amount of artillery they could shoot, they "would get more body bags."[37]

General Johnson had different ideas about the use of artillery and air support. He revealed his thoughts on the subject when he said, "It's very popular to say let's send a bullet instead of a boy [but] I think we overemphasize firepower."[38] While he did not mention DePuy and Hollingsworth by name, it is clear that there was a serious difference of opinion on how the war should be conducted.

DePuy and Hollingsworth nevertheless pushed forward with their operational approach to fighting the war, and under their leadership the 1st Infantry Division became very aggressive. The morale in the division rose as the brigades took the fight to the enemy. William J. Mullen III, who was a company commander under DePuy and Hollingsworth, said after the war, "Morale in the division was very high. We knew we were in a well-led, aggressive, fighting outfit. . . . We were in the Army's premier unit."[39]

Not everyone felt that way, particularly not those who dealt daily with the two generals. If DePuy and Hollingsworth were demanding of the units in the field, they were merciless on the division staff. Henry Gole describes the "Byzantine atmosphere" that pervaded DePuy's command as officers jockeyed for attention and favor, citing the "personal discomfort and fear" among staff officers that came with such a command climate.[40] However, one staff officer who went on to general officer rank recalled that Holly often provided an irreverent antidote to DePuy's intensity. According to this officer, Hollingsworth was a taskmaster, but he did not bully the staff officers and always had a humorous way to look at every situation, lightening the mood in division staff briefings.[41]

If DePuy was unforgiving of the division staff, he and Hollingsworth were draconian in their expectations of commanders and senior NCOs in the field. In his year as commander of the Big Red One, DePuy, who had vowed in World War II that he would never allow American leaders to kill American soldiers, was "ruthless in cutting loose commanders who were not worthy of the soldiers they commanded."[42] He would fire seven battalion commanders and many majors, captains, and sergeants major, for a total of fifty-six reliefs during his tenure in command.[43] Hollingsworth was just as ruthless as DePuy. They both believed that incompetent leaders got soldiers killed, and they were merciless in removing those who failed to measure up. They believed their troops deserved no less. The "midnight hook" became the expression for being relieved by DePuy and/or Hollingsworth. Reflecting on the issue after the war, DePuy said, "I can tell if a commander is competent. He is going to take care of his people or get them killed. I don't waste any time with that. I replaced them because no person's career is worth the sacrifice of soldiers."[44] Eventually, as the reliefs in the Big Red One piled up, they would contribute to the broadening gap between DePuy, Hollingsworth, and General Johnson, which would have serious consequences for both officers.

Hollingsworth could appear to be capricious, but he also knew when to back off. On one occasion when he was flying over one of his battalions, he observed something that did not make him happy. He immediately got on the radio and told the battalion commander, Lt. Col. Dick Prillaman, that one of his company commanders was all screwed up. "I want you to relieve him right now." Hollingsworth believed that the young company commander did not know what he was doing and risked getting his soldiers killed. However, that was not the case. Hollingsworth knew only what he saw from the air; he was not on the ground and did not know the whole situation. Prillaman, the battalion commander, responded instantly, "He's doing exactly what I want him to do. If you relieve anyone, it should be me." Hollingsworth could have done that, but instead he said, "Now dammit Dick, don't get your back up. It just looked screwed up to me from up here. Go down and check it out."[45] The captain was not relieved and Prillaman went on to a successful career, retiring as a lieutenant general.

While Holly was brutally demanding of company, battalion, and brigade commanders, he loved the "little fellers," as he called them—the soldiers who were down in the mud fighting the war nose to nose with the enemy. Holly went out of his way to recognize their bravery in battle. On his command helicopter, he carried a special box that contained Purple Hearts, Army Commendation Medals, Soldier's Medals, and Bronze Stars. It was his aide-de-camp's job to keep the box filled and make sure that the proper follow-up information was sent to the division G-1 personnel office so that the appropriate orders were prepared to substantiate the "impact" awards, as those awards and decorations that were given "on the spot" were known. In one week in July 1966, Hollingsworth pinned on 50 Silver Stars, 150 Bronze Stars for Valor, 200 Army Commendation Medals for Valor, 30 Distinguished Flying Crosses, and more than 300 Purple Hearts.

Hollingsworth wrote Nickie that week, "The soldiers are the bravest and most courageous I have ever seen." However, that bravery came at a high price. In another letter to Nickie, he wrote about one of his favorite company commanders, who was gunned down in the thick of battle when he personally charged a Viet Cong machine gun. He wrote, "He was one of the greatest captains I have ever known. Brave, courageous, loved his men and they loved him. He has two small sons three and four years old." He put the captain in for the Distinguished Service Cross and personally wrote the man's wife and parents to express his condolences for the loss of their loved one.

Such losses seemed only to motivate him more. In July 1966, he landed with the first lift of 1st Battalion, 28th Infantry, in a big battle that developed in the area between An Loc and Minh Thanh. Upon landing in the landing zone, the US troopers came under intense enemy fire. Moving forward with the infantry assault element, Holly came upon an eighteen-year-old soldier from A Company who was clearly frightened. Holly told the young soldier, "Son, you come with me and we'll kill every son of a bitch that we see." He later reported that the soldier "stuck to me like a leech." When a firefight broke out to the general's right, he moved through the five-foot-tall elephant grass to get closer to the fight. The young soldier followed close behind. During the course of the battle, three VC were killed in the immediate vicinity of the general's position. When the firing died down, the general and the soldier went forward. The soldier approached one of the dead VC, touched it with his boot, and said, "General, he is a dead son of a bitch. I would like to rejoin my squad and I am not afraid anymore." Holly replied, "I am not afraid either when I am with soldiers like you." He told Nickie, "They [the troops] are great and I love every one of them."

Holly was a soldier's general. They knew he would do everything in his power to support them in battle. They knew he was fearless and would never ask them to do anything he was not prepared to do himself. He loved his "little fellers" and always took time to provide a word of encouragement. During the course of one operation, Hollingsworth landed to talk with one of his battalion commanders. On the way to the battalion command post, Holly paused to say a good word to the troops manning fighting positions. One, Norman Ross, then a specialist fourth class and radio operator, remembers that Holly patted him on the back and made him feel that he was making a worthy contribution to the war effort.[46] Ross said it was one of the high points of his tour in Vietnam. During the course of researching this book, the author heard this kind of story repeated over and over again by former soldiers who served under the general. Holly had a remarkable way of connecting with the troops.

After Operation AMARILLO was over in September, Holly visited with the wounded at the hospital. In his usual boisterous manner, he was all over the wards, checking on the troops and providing encouragement. In a letter to Nickie about the visit, he said that the troops asked him, "General, did we win?" Holly said he told them, "You're damn right we won. You destroyed a VC battalion." Holly said they would smile and say, "General, we just didn't want to let you down." He had a connection with the troops; he was a fighter and he clearly appreciated their sacrifice. They in turn saw him as fearless and gave him both their love and loyalty. After the war, for example, former lieutenant Sam Floca, who served in the 1st Infantry Division, recalled how Holly had landed a helicopter to rescue him after he was injured in an armored personnel carrier accident; Floca said, "I would follow him right through the gates of hell even to this day."[47]

After the war, Hollingsworth was asked about the quality of the troops in the 1st Division; he replied, "They were all strong Americans looking for leadership. And where they had leadership, they were fantastic. Where they didn't have any leadership, they were mediocre."[48] He took it upon himself to make sure that his "little fellers" had the best leadership possible. This did not bode well for those who did not measure up. As he wrote Nickie in July, "We hang every medal we can on the good ones and kick the poor ones out." Some did not even make it to the division. At one point, the Department of the Army sent the names of twenty lieutenant colonels for prospective battalion command in the 1st Division. DePuy and Holly accepted only three; they wanted "the most professional division in the world" and went after only the best.

Those who "couldn't cut the mustard" made a fast exit. Between May and August 1966, DePuy and Hollingsworth relieved five battalion commanders and a brigade commander. Hollingsworth was unapologetic. He wrote Nickie, "They didn't have what it takes and men's lives were at stake. Bill and I couldn't care less about their careers. . . . The men deserve the best in leadership and that's what they are going to get in the Big Red One. . . . We put up with no horse shit, incompetence, inefficiency, slowness, blundering or stupidity. . . . They just weren't good enough for the Big Red One and the brave, courageous enlisted men of this division."

Hollingsworth was just as unforgiving with some of his peers. Writing to Nickie about one of his fellow general officers, who was not in the 1st Division, he said, "He doesn't have the stuff it takes to face the mad bullets . . . he is a fraud, phony, a liar and will play any game to get ahead . . . he is rather dumb about everything except being a crook and he's not smart there." He later recalled that he and DePuy "turned thumbs down" on fourteen different generals who wanted to come to the division.[49]

Hollingsworth pushed himself as hard as he did anyone else. He seemed to be everywhere. It took a toll on him, and he wrote Nickie on several occasions that he was very tired. However, he always bounced back and got back into the fight. There were a number of incidents in which he was very lucky. On 5 June, he was orbiting in his command helicopter at 2,000 feet over VC territory when the aircraft developed engine trouble. The pilot sighted a clearing and headed that direction, but at about 1,500 feet, the tail rotor and gearbox exploded. The aircraft began spinning, but the pilot was able to get it leveled out just before it hit the ground at seventy miles an hour, landing on its side in a rice paddy. Rescue helicopters arrived and Hollingsworth was offered the safety of immediate evacuation, but he chose to remain until the other wounded were evacuated. Holly got first-degree burns from raw fuel, but ultimately he and the crew were rescued. He reported to his wife in a letter that he "had had a bad day" but that he was "fine and OK."

Hollingsworth pushed himself so hard that he often did not have time to write to Nickie. On one occasion, she was clearly not happy with him for not writing more. He replied, "Life is short and I have so much to do for the good of these young men here, that I don't have time to worry about anybody but them. I am sorry, that's the way it is . . . please don't worry about me. God has already determined what will happen to me—and you and I will abide by His decision."

Still, Hollingsworth did his best to write to Nickie when he could. He was a gruff individual, but he often showed his softer side in these letters, particularly regarding the human toll the war was taking. A former enlisted subordinate from his time at West Point contacted him to see whether the general could help get him to Vietnam and land him an assignment with the Big Red One. The general did so, and while acting as the platoon leader of the reconnaissance platoon in the 1st Battalion, 18th Infantry, he stepped on a VC mine, losing his left leg and severely injuring his right. Holly went to see him in the hospital; the soldier was delighted to see the general and told him that it was a pleasure to serve with him. Holly was obviously very moved when he described the hospital visit to Nickie in his next letter.

Occasionally, Hollingsworth would let his guard down with someone other than Nickie. He helped a number of other men who had requested his assistance to get to Vietnam and the 1st Infantry Division only to die in combat. Recalling these fallen soldiers, he later told an interviewer, "I don't think if I had to go back tomorrow, I'd never allow anybody to talk me into letting him come along and be in a dangerous position."[50]

Hollingsworth clearly understood that men die in combat, but there were senseless deaths that he found especially tragic. After a particularly bad such occurrence, he wrote Nickie, "The fighting has been very successful, however some mishaps have occurred that tears your insides out. Two days ago, a 155mm artillery battery fired in the wrong direction. The volley of about 12 rounds fell on "A" Co, of 1/28 Inf[antry] killing one and wounding 34. These are the things that are hard to take—this tries your soul."

The loss of life no doubt took a toll on Hollingsworth, but if anything, it caused him to redouble his efforts to take the war to the enemy. This continually put him in harm's way. In November, his helicopter took ground fire and crash-landed. Again, he was not hurt seriously. He earned his second Distinguished Service award later that month for guiding close air support for three surrounded Special Forces units from his helicopter, flying repeated low-level maneuvers over the Viet Cong and taking heavy ground fire. In combat, he cut an imposing figure. In a story that appeared in the *San Francisco Examiner*, a reporter described Hollingsworth: "[He] wears tank goggles so he can peer out into the slipstream at enemy activity from his copter, and flies constantly over his division's battlefields, often with an M16 rifle cradled in his arms to answer enemy ground fire."[51]

Holly was famous throughout the division for calling in artillery or airstrikes on targets of opportunity from his helicopter. The artillery units knew to respond immediately to these calls for fire or they would soon get a visit from Danger 79er that would be an unpleasant encounter.[52]

On the battlefield, Hollingsworth could have an oddly calming effect on the troops. John Lesko, who as a young lieutenant served as a forward observer with the 1st Battalion, 28th Infantry, recalls accompanying his unit into a particularly hot landing zone (LZ). The Viet Cong had the unit in an effective cross fire. He remembers that he saw an "old man" land and get out of his helicopter; as it departed, the figure began walking across the LZ like he was "out for a stroll," despite a flurry of enemy tracers and mortars falling all around. The "old man" flopped beside him on the ground and asked what he needed. Lesko, without looking up, very excitedly said he "needed some fucking artillery." Then he turned and saw the single black star on Holly's helmet and immediately realized he had just cursed at the assistant division commander. Hollingsworth put an arm on his shoulder and said, "Son, calm down. I'll get you some artillery." Lesko later recalled how he knew that everything would be all right then. Nearly fifty years later, Lesko still marveled at the general's calmness under fire.[53]

Lt. Gen. (Ret.) Randy House relates a story told by his mentor, Gen. (Ret.) Dick Cavazos. Cavazos, at the time a lieutenant colonel commanding an infantry battalion in the Big Red One, was involved in a tough fight in a rubber tree plantation. Enemy shells were falling and the incoming rifle and machine gun fire was intense; at one point, as the unit ran low on small-arms ammunition, the order was given to fix bayonets. The American soldiers were all taking cover on the ground or behind trees as a heavy firefight raged. In the middle of the fight, Cavazos looked up only to see General Hollingsworth calmly walking around the area with no entourage and only a .45-caliber pistol stuck in his belt. Cavazos yelled for the general to get down, but Hollingsworth walked over to him, leaned over, and said, "This is a good one [firefight], Dick." Cavazos asked Hollingsworth how he had gotten there since he had not seen a helicopter land. Hollingsworth replied that he had been visiting a nearby battalion, but nothing was going on there. He said he heard the commotion going on in Cavazos's area, so he just hiked over to join the fight. Cavazos said the other battalion was some kilometers away; Hollingsworth replied, "Yes, it was, but it was mostly open terrain so I walked on over." General Cavazos, who had two Distinguished Service Crosses plus several Silver Stars and multiple Purple Hearts, later observed that Hollingsworth was "the only soldier I had ever met that really had no fear."[54]

It is clear that Hollingsworth was a taskmaster and at times could be capricious. However, he fostered a sense of intense loyalty among the troops and among the officers who met his high standards. He was not liked by those who ran afoul of him, but he had the respect and admiration of just about everyone else. By the time he left the division, he had achieved almost mythic proportions for his colorful way of commanding and his absolute fearlessness under fire.

In early November, during the conduct of Operation ATTLEBORO in War Zone C about sixty-five miles northwest of Saigon, Hollingsworth's aircraft was again shot down. However, he was not injured and was picked up by another helicopter. The incident had little impact on his approach to command; he continued to get as close as he could to the fighting.

Later that month, Holly wrote his wife an interesting letter. He told her, "Keep this to yourself. I may be leaving the Big Red One to take command of the 9th Infantry Division." The division was due in-country around the end of the year. General Westmoreland, MACV commander, had apparently mentioned to Hollingsworth that reassignment to the command of the 9th might be a possibility.

At about this time, Nickie received a letter from author, columnist, and commentator George Fielding Eliot that summed up the opinion of many at this point in Holly's career: "Your wonderful husband goes right ahead doing what he does best—giving the finest kind of front line leadership to his troops. He's one of a very special breed, a soldier's general. They're born, not made, and sometimes it seems as though the good Lord looks after them with a special care because he knows how badly their country needs them."[55] Eliot was right, but not everyone had the same opinion.

By the end of November, the possibility of taking command of the 9th Infantry Division appeared to be off the table. For whatever reason, Westmoreland had told him that it was not going to happen. In early December, it was announced that General Johnson, army chief of staff, would be making a visit to Vietnam. Holly wrote his wife that he was "anxiously waiting for Johnson to get here so I can find out what I am supposed to do [after leaving Vietnam]."

Johnson had been unhappy with DePuy and Hollingsworth over the earlier issues of heavy casualties, their style of forward command in battle, and the division's elaborate use of firepower. The issue this time was the growing number of officers being relieved in the 1st Division. Sometime before the trip to Vietnam was scheduled, a concerned Johnson complained to subordinates, "If every division commander relieved people like DePuy, I'd soon be out of lieutenant colonels and majors. . . . He just eats them up like peanuts."[56] Johnson wrote DePuy a letter admonishing him to slow down on the reliefs and give people a second chance. Part of the division commander's job, according to Johnson, was to train people.[57] Johnson was concerned that his message did not get through; on the scheduled Christmas Day trip to Vietnam in 1966, he met with DePuy and repeated his admonition in person.

When the chief of staff landed at the division headquarters near Di An, he, DePuy, and Hollingsworth went to DePuy's quarters for a private meeting. Some forty years later, Hollingsworth recalled what happened. "Johnson looked at me and said, 'You are relieving too many battalion commanders. You are supposed to train them.' Bill DePuy was sitting within three or four feet of me, and he said, 'I'll answer that.' I said, 'No, sir, he asked me.' And I said, 'General, I had the idea that you were going to train them and we were to fight them over here and save soldiers' lives.'" Holly later recalled, "Bill DePuy and I stressed on him that if you are going to clean up this country and get the enemy out, you have to get off your dead ass and get on with it. I will always remember that."[58]

After the somewhat heated discussion, the group went to lunch and Johnson departed, leaving DePuy concerned that he would be relieved over the incident.[59] According to Henry Gole, DePuy was sufficiently concerned about his clash with Johnson that he dejectedly told Col. Sid Berry, commander of the 1st Brigade, that he thought Johnson might relieve him. DePuy cited Johnson as saying, "I can't afford another Big Red One . . . I need division commanders who make the best of the human material they are assigned."[60]

Hollingsworth seemed unfazed by the confrontation. However, it is clear that the exchange did not do either of the officers any favors regarding their relationship with the army chief of staff, which would have an impact on both of their careers.

This situation was probably made worse by the fact that DePuy and his assistant division commander also did not have the best relationship with Lieutenant General Seaman, the II Field Force commander. Seaman was very critical of "them," meaning DePuy and Hollingsworth, but avoided using their names. On one occasion, he mentioned an assistant division commander who came in "shortly before I left the division," saying that "this particular individual [when he is selected for his second star] is going to get the Army in a hell of a mess one of these days." One of Seaman's staff officers later confirmed that Seaman was talking about Holly, for whom Seaman apparently had little professional regard.[61] Part of this ill will toward Hollingsworth may have been motivated by Hollingsworth's relief of Seaman's former aide, who had taken command of a troop in the 1st Squadron of the 4th Cavalry when he stumbled in an operation after about a month in command; after the incident, Seaman remarked, "I've never seen such a broken young man in my life." This, as Henry Gole observed, further illustrated that "the DePuy-Hollingsworth team was entirely focused on combat effectiveness, not with subordinates' feelings or career ambitions."[62]

If Hollingsworth was aware of Seaman's opinion, he did not let it bother him and he continued to do what he thought was right, fighting the war the only way he knew how—full out.[63] On 20 January, he wrote Nickie, "I killed some VC today without the press finding out! (I think) My best to those who can tolerate me; piss on the others!"

The fallout from the confrontation between DePuy, Hollingsworth, and the army chief of staff soon became apparent. DePuy wanted to be reassigned as the commandant of the US Army Infantry Center at Fort Benning, Georgia. It was there that he thought he could make his greatest contribution to the army. However, it appeared that Johnson did not want DePuy at Benning. Quoting General Westmoreland's aide, Henry Gole has written that Westmoreland "saved Bill DePuy's career" by calling Gen. Earle Wheeler, chairman of the Joint Chiefs of Staff, to put in a good word for DePuy, who would subsequently be reassigned to the Joint Staff.[64]

DePuy Departs

On 10 February 1967, DePuy turned over command of the division to Maj. Gen. John H. Hay. Holly wrote Nickie about the change of command, "[DePuy is the] best friend I have in this world. General Bill DePuy will depart Saigon tomorrow for Washington, D.C. This is the second most sad day in my life. I love him. He is the most magnificent and fabulous man I have ever known. God bless him forever." Thus, the partnership between DePuy and Hollingsworth came to an end; together they had forged the 1st Infantry Division into a very effective combat unit; now they would go their separate ways.

With DePuy gone, Hollingsworth did not slow down. On the night of 20 March, Troop A of the 5th US Cavalry was conducting a road clearance operation on Route 13 between Lai Khe and An Loc. They became involved in a large firefight with the 273rd VC Regiment in the vicinity of Bau Bang village along the road. The American cavalry unit actually belonged to the 9th Division, which had not fully arrived in-country yet, so they were attached to the 1st Infantry Division. Holly jumped in his helicopter and flew up the highway toward the action. As the enemy, which greatly outnumbered the cavalry troop, prepared for a final assault, Holly told the cavalrymen to put their M113 armored personnel carriers in a tight perimeter and when the VC attacked "to turn on all their vehicle lights." The squadron commander, now on the ground with his surrounded troop, protested that doing so would expose their position. Holly replied that this was exactly what he wanted. In the meantime, he had called in air support. When the VC launched their attack on the cavalry troopers, Holly skillfully employed fifteen fighter-bombers to inflict heavy casualties on the attackers and break up the attack. When the battle was over, the troopers from the 5th Cavalry had lost three killed in action and eleven wounded. The area around the troop's perimeter was littered with the bodies of nearly five hundred enemy dead.

This battle was emblematic of Holly's aggressiveness. He went where the action was and got right in the middle of it. His troops knew that when they got in trouble, Danger 79er would be there. One who had a ringside seat during this period was Warren Silva, then a captain who was Holly's command pilot from January to May 1967. In the first part of his tour, Silva had been the command pilot for Col. Sidney Berry, commander of the 1st Brigade. When Berry departed Vietnam, Silva was assigned to fly Hollingsworth. Silva had seen a lot of combat as Berry's pilot and was shot down twice during that period; he thought he was getting a softer job flying around the assistant division commander. However, Silva later recalled that he saw more combat during his first month with Danger 79er than in his previous six months with the 1st Brigade.

Silva remembers that DePuy, on several occasions before he departed, strongly chastised Hollingsworth for exposing himself to enemy fire the way he did. Silva said that Holly came away from these sessions appearing contrite, but "that would only last until the next fire fight [and] then we would be right back in the middle of it again." Silva said that Hollingsworth had "absolutely no fear of anything."[65]

The soldiers in the division, who called him "our Patton," adored the general, and he returned the affection. Silva remembers that on one occasion, Hollingsworth was wearing new boots that had rubbed a blister on his heel. When visiting one of his battalions, he sought out one of the unit medics to take care of the blister. A young medic from Stone Mountain, Georgia, came over and lanced the blister. The medic was an interesting fellow named William Kendregan. He had been assigned in Alaska but hated the cold, so he went AWOL (absent without leave) and returned to Georgia. When the military police caught up with him, he was given two choices: Vietnam or the Disciplinary Barracks at Fort Leavenworth, Kansas. He chose Vietnam and ended up in the Big Red One, where by all accounts he was a superb medic.

Before Kendregan applied the bandage to the general's blistered heel, he needed to apply some disinfectant to the wound. The medic, who was chewing tobacco, spit in his hand and applied the tobacco juice to Holly's blister. Holly got a kick out of that, making a big "to do" of the medic's home remedy, and from that point forward the medic was known as "Plug" in honor of his "special" medicine. Kendregan's company commander, William Schreiber, remembered that Holly never failed to check on Plug when he was in his unit's area and would even ask to speak to him on the radio to see how the soldier was doing.[66] The general stayed in touch with Plug over the years and sent him money when Plug fell on hard times. Many years later, Plug visited Holly the day he died, paying him back and visiting with him on his deathbed. The former medic was one of the many Big Red One soldiers who attended Holly's funeral in Arlington Cemetery; he spoke eloquently about the general at the reception that followed the burial.

In another instance, Holly joined a unit on the ground after a firefight. Checking on the troops, he asked a slightly built young Hispanic soldier, who was carrying a radio, how he was doing. The lad said that he was doing fine but that he could use some jungle fatigues that fit. The soldier was short in stature and when he rolled down his shirt sleeves, they hung down more than a foot. During the course of Holly's travels in the next few days, he made a special trip to pick up six sets of very small jungle fatigues and then flew back to drop them off at the young man's unit. Acts such as this won the undying loyalty and admiration of the men in the division.[67]

It is not surprising that Holly won the loyalty and admiration of his soldiers, but he was also popular with the division chaplains. The general was a devout Episcopalian and went to services every Sunday he got a chance. The late chaplain Wesley Geary remembered a time when the II Field Force chaplain was invited to preach at the Division Headquarters at Di An. According to Geary, the visiting chaplain gave a long-winded, boring sermon. After the service, Holly called for a meeting with Geary and the other chaplains in attendance. Holly told Geary never to invite that chaplain back; the general "wanted to hear the Gospel," not some uninspiring recitation by an "outsider."[68] Geary was full of stories about Holly, who became a lifelong friend.

Reassignment

Hollingsworth kept up his frenetic pace, seemingly all over the division area wherever the troops were in contact, but he was soon to be disappointed about what was to follow. He would not be getting command of the 9th Infantry Division as he had hoped; he learned that he would be reassigned to be deputy commanding general, Test and Evaluation Command at Aberdeen, Maryland. Westmoreland wanted Holly to remain in Vietnam for another year, but in the end the army chief of staff decided that Hollingsworth would not be given the opportunity to command a division in combat. It is likely that Hollingsworth's reputation had been damaged by the unflattering news reports that plagued him during his tour in combination with the often contentious relationship between Johnson and the leadership of the Big Red One.

He received orders to report to Aberdeen on 15 June. However, in March, Westmoreland visited the 1st Division and inexplicably again mentioned the possibility of Holly assuming command of the 9th Infantry Division. Hollingsworth wrote his wife, "My orders may be changed [to remain in Vietnam to command the 9th Division]. God only knows." By April, the situation had apparently changed again, and it became clear that Hollingsworth was indeed leaving Vietnam for Aberdeen. It is safe to say that Hollingsworth's poor relationships with the army chief of staff and the II Field Force commander had some part to play in the determination of his ultimate assignment.[69] Holly left for home in late May 1967.

During his fifteen months with the 1st Infantry Division, Hollingsworth achieved almost legendary status among the men of the division. He became known as a "soldier's soldier" who was fearless in combat and compassionate about his troops. As far as the more senior members of the command, he and DePuy mentored a long list of officers who would go on to lead the army in the years after Vietnam—men such as Paul Gorman, Dick Cavazos, Carl Vuono, George Joulwan, Al Haig, Dick Prillaman, Rich Keller, and many others.[70] The Big Red One would occupy a special place in Hollingsworth's heart for the rest of his life.

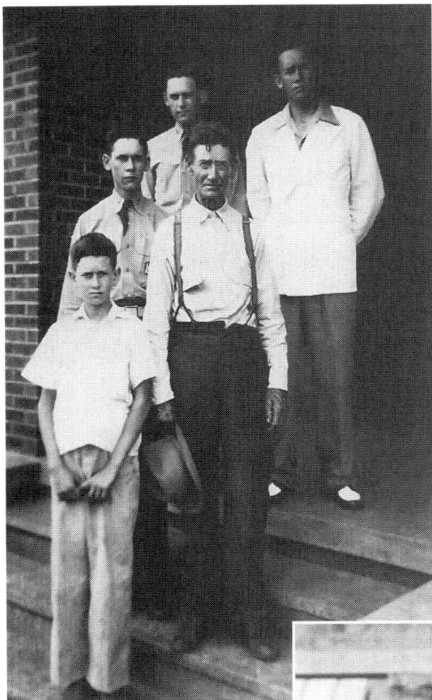

James Hollingsworth with his father, James, and three brothers (Gerald, Ross, and Cecil) (author's photo).

Jamie Hollingsworth, the Hollingsworth's only child, was mortally injured in a car accident near Fort Hood, Texas, and died on 10 October 1960 (author's photo).

James Hollingsworth as a cadet at Texas A&M in 1939 (Texas A&M University photo).

Norm S. Paul, assistant secretary of defense for Force Management Policy (on the right) presents Colonel Hollingsworth with a Distinguished Service Medal for his time as deputy assistant secretary of defense for Manpower (Reserve Affairs) in the Pentagon (US Army photo, Hollingsworth Papers, Cushing Library, Texas A&M University).

Brigadier General Hollingsworth confers with Maj. Gen. William E. DePuy, commander, 1st Infantry Division, and Col. William Broadbeck, commander, 3rd Brigade, near Loc Ninh, May 1966 (US Army photo, courtesy of 1st Division Museum).

Grid line 79, which Brigadier General Hollingsworth painted on Highway 13 in Binh Long Province to provide a guide for the advance of the 4th Cavalry (US Army photo, Hollingsworth Papers, Cushing Library, Texas A&M University).

Brigadier General Hollingsworth visits with Maj. Gen. John Hay and troops from the 1st Infantry Division in Vietnam (US Army photo, Hollingsworth Papers, Cushing Library, Texas A&M University).

The crew of Brigadier General Hollingsworth's helicopter present him with a plaque denoting his call sign, "Danger 79er" (US Army photo, Hollingsworth Papers, Cushing Library, Texas A&M University).

General Hollingsworth presents an award to Chaplain (Capt.) Wesley Geary at 1st Division Headquarters in Vietnam (US Army photo, courtesy of 1st Division Museum).

Between Vietnam tours, Brigadier General Hollingsworth and his wife, Nickie, enjoyed the roses he was so fond of growing (author's photo).

Brigadier General Hollingsworth reviews the troops at Aberdeen Proving Ground in Maryland (US Army photo, Hollingsworth Papers, Cushing Library, Texas A&M University).

Brigadier General Hollingsworth visits with Alaskan Scout in the field (US Army photo, Hollingsworth Papers, Cushing Library, Texas A&M University).

Major General Hollingsworth presents Silver Star to Capt. John B. Whitehead of the 3rd Brigade, 1st Cavalry Division, for his daring helicopter rescue of three American advisers and four Vietnamese soldiers surrounded by the enemy near An Loc (US Army photo, courtesy of US Army Heritage and Education Center, Carlisle Barracks, PA).

T-54 tank killed during the Battle of An Loc; Major General Hollingsworth was instrumental in coordinating the massive US air support that enabled the South Vietnamese defenders to hold An Loc against repeated enemy attacks (US Army photo, Hollingsworth Papers, Cushing Library, Texas A&M University).

Madonna survived the battle of An Loc, but the Catholic church behind her was destroyed in the fighting (author's photo).

Major General Hollingsworth with Col. Walter Ulmer, senior adviser to 5th ARVN Division, in An Loc, July 1972 (photo courtesy of Ron Skrupa).

Lieutenant General Hollingsworth with his I Corps (ROK/US) Group staff, which included both US and South Korean staff members (US Army photo, Hollingsworth Papers, Cushing Library, Texas A&M University).

Lieutenant General Hollingsworth speaks with South Korean soldiers near the DMZ (US Army photo, Hollingsworth Papers, Cushing Library, Texas A&M University).

Lieutenant General Hollingsworth greets President Gerald Ford upon his visit to South Korea, November 1974; the president is wearing a sweater presented to him by the 2nd Infantry Division (White House photo, courtesy of Gerald R. Ford Presidential Library, Ann Arbor, MI).

Texas governor and Mrs. Bill Clements congratulate Lieutenant General (Retired) Hollingsworth and the former Janie Harris after their wedding on 24 March 1990 (family photo, Hollingsworth Papers, Cushing Library, Texas A&M University).

Lieutenant General Hollingsworth reviews the troops at his outgoing change of command in Korea, June 1976 (US Army photo, Hollingsworth Papers, Cushing Library, Texas A&M University).

Lieutenant General (Retired) and Mrs. Hollingsworth review the Corps of Cadets at Texas A&M following the dedication of the statue in honor in the corps area (*Texas Aggie*).

Lieutenant General (Retired) and Mrs. Hollingsworth with fellow veterans who served under him in 1972 on the day the statue of the general was dedicated at Texas A&M University. From left to right: Lt. Gen. (Ret.) John McGiffert, Frank Muller, Maj. Gen. (Ret.) Niles Fulwyler, and the author (author's photo).

Poster at the "From Texas to Bastogne" exhibit at the Bastogne Museum in Belgium; Hollingsworth (on the left) was one of five Aggies highlighted in the exhibit (author's photo).

6

Between Vietnam Tours

The Pentagon

By this time, a number of equipment problems had arisen in Vietnam. There were severe problems with the M16 rifle, and there were also difficulties with multifuel engines in cargo trucks. About eleven thousand multifuel engines made by Continental Motors had performed so poorly that many were still in depots awaiting salvage. Congress had been very vocal about these problems and demanded that the army do something.

Upon Hollingsworth's arrival at the Pentagon, the army chief of the staff told him that he was reassigning him to Aberdeen Proving Ground in Maryland to see whether he could remedy the army's equipment problems. Reassigned as deputy commanding general, US Army Test and Evaluation Command, Hollingsworth went to Aberdeen as ordered. Six months after he arrived, Hollingsworth sent the chief of staff a report that said it was not flawed testing that was causing the equipment problems in Vietnam, but rather the insistence on getting the new equipment to the field before it was ready. He recommended that the new equipment be more thoroughly tested before it was committed to the field.

Also during this period, there had been riots in Washington, Detroit, and Newark. The government tried to use the National Guard, but in every case, the Guard's performance was substandard and federal troops had to be called in to quell the riots. As a result, in August 1967, Hollingsworth was personally selected by Secretary of the Army Stanley R. Resor to conduct a study of the National Guard failures during the riots, and more specifically to look into the leadership of both the Guard and the Army Reserve. Additionally, he was to examine the Army Reserve Component promotion and appointment program. He put together a team of twenty officers and over the course of the next year, the Hollingsworth Board, as it became known, conducted an exhaustive study, visiting 90 percent of the states but focusing its efforts on the performance of the Guard in the riots in Washington, Detroit, and Newark.

The result of this study became known as the Hollingsworth Report, which was very critical of the inadequacies of the National Guard and the Reserves. In the course of the study, the Hollingsworth Board acknowledged that "the great majority [of National Guard officers] . . . are highly competent and dedicated professionals" but found that some who ought to have been relieved had in fact been retained because of favorable efficiency reports. The report included some fifty recommendations on how to remedy the situation; chief among these was that promotion standards and methods of identifying and eliminating unfit officers needed to be revised and sharpened along with state programs of instruction for Army National Guard officer candidates. The report tasked both the National Guard and the Reserves to get rid of "dead wood" in the officer ranks by conducting periodic reviews of all officer files to spot those who should be eliminated or retired because of "poor qualification, non-participation, maximum age or failure to meet mobilization requirements."[1]

The impact of the Hollingsworth Report was a much-needed tightening up of the selection, appointment, promotion, and retention of Army Reserve Forces—both Army National Guard and Army Reserve. Most of the board's recommendations were accepted by the secretary of the army and implemented immediately or phased in over the next three years.

While Hollingsworth had been toiling away in the Pentagon, the war in Vietnam had increased in intensity. In January 1968, the Communists launched a massive countrywide offensive in South Vietnam. This followed in the wake of public statements by Gen. William Westmoreland that the United States was making progress in the war and that there was "light at the end of the tunnel." The scope and violence of the Tet Offensive surprised the US and South Vietnamese forces and stunned Americans on the home front, making them skeptical about reports from Vietnam.

After recovering from the initial surprise of the widespread attacks, US and South Vietnamese forces fought back and inflicted heavy casualties on the attackers. However, the offensive ended up being a psychological victory for the Communists when a dejected President Lyndon Johnson announced that he would not run for reelection. Shortly thereafter, it was announced that General Westmoreland would be reassigned as army chief of staff and that Gen. Creighton Abrams would succeed him as commander of US troops in South Vietnam.

From Washington, Hollingsworth watched the Tet Offensive unfold. He desperately wanted to get back to the war. He wrote in a letter to Lt. Gen. Bruce Palmer, commander of II Field Force in Vietnam, "I talked with General Dick Stilwell [commander of US XXIV Corps] just prior to his departure for Vietnam and advised him of my desire to return to Vietnam as soon as possible. I know there must be a lot of changes in the wind, however, as soon as Westy gets back [to the Pentagon], I am going to get in touch with him. I would give my right arm to command a division in Vietnam or anything else as far as that goes."[2] In another letter in August 1968, Holly wrote, "With Westy in the saddle . . . I hope to be back in Vietnam in command of the 1st or 4th Division as early as March."[3]

Such was not to be the case. In May 1968, Hollingsworth was assigned as deputy commander of the US Army Training Center at Fort Jackson, South Carolina. He was told that the commander there was "practicing on-the-job retirement" and that he was to go down there as the commander's deputy but was to be prepared to take over, which he would when the previous commander departed Jackson shortly after Hollingsworth arrived on post.

General Palmer, who was returning to the United States to become vice chief of staff of the army, said in a response to Holly's earlier letter, "I realize that you are dying to get back to Vietnam again, I have mentioned this to Abe [Abrams]. However, we also badly need tough, experienced combat commanders like yourself in our training centers."[4]

Fort Jackson

Fort Jackson, located in the Midlands of South Carolina, was created in 1917 to prepare American troops for World War I. After the war ended, Camp Jackson was shut down, but it was reactivated for World War II. The post was supposed to be closed again after the war, but the outbreak of the Korean War caused it to remain open. As the United States ramped up for the war in Vietnam, Camp Jackson was redesignated Fort Jackson and again became a major basic training base responsible for training soldiers for the war in Southeast Asia.

When Hollingsworth arrived, Fort Jackson trained about 125,000 to 150,000 combat infantrymen a year. The base encompassed more than 52,000 acres, including more than a hundred firing ranges and field training sites. As a former assistant division commander in Vietnam, Hollingsworth knew the demands of the war intimately and was infinitely qualified to oversee the training of replacements for Vietnam. However, the general was appalled at some of the recruits who showed up for training. They were mostly draftees, a cross section of the eastern part of the United States including Ohio, West Virginia, and Tennessee (mostly from east of the Mississippi River). Having been in Vietnam with the Big Red One, he took the training mission and the preparation of these soldiers for Vietnam very seriously. Believing implicitly in the base's motto, "Victory Starts Here," Hollingsworth set about improving training and turning out a better product who was more ready for combat.

At the change of command ceremony, Hollingsworth told the audience that the most important person in the army was the combat infantryman. He pledged to produce a training environment at Fort Jackson that was conducive to preparing new soldiers for combat. As soon as the ceremony was over, he immediately set out to do just that. Hollingsworth began by concentrating on improving the orientation and preparation for Vietnam. He immediately directed improvements to Bau Bang, the training center's simulated Vietnam village. He also increased emphasis on rifle marksmanship and first aid training. He made sure that the training focused on readying the trainees for combat duty in the jungles of Vietnam.

Hollingsworth assumed command of Fort Jackson during turbulent times, and he soon learned that improving training was not his only problem. The army was beginning to pay the bills for the Vietnam War. As a draftee force, it represented the society from which it was drawn. As that society became deeply divided over the war, the army, dependent on the draft to sustain operations in Vietnam, drew in more and more recruits who did not support the war. The number of dissident elements within the ranks of the army grew. In this situation, it is not surprising that there were a growing number of disturbances at various army installations overseas and in the United States. The dissidents, often aided by civilian radicals, wanted to "stop the war machine," end the war in Vietnam, bring all the troops home, and democratize the army.[5]

Fort Jackson had already played an important role in the dissident movement even before Hollingsworth was reassigned there. It was at Jackson in 1967 that Capt. Howard Levy, a young army dermatologist from Brooklyn, took a stand against the war. Special Forces medics from Fort Bragg, North Carolina, were sent to the Fort Jackson Hospital to receive training on the various rashes and other skin disorders they would encounter in Southeast Asia. Levy, who considered the Special Forces nothing but "killers of peasants and murderers of women and children," refused to train the Green Beret medics; when he was given a direct order by the hospital commander, he again refused. Levy was court-martialed and charged with disobeying a lawful order, promoting disloyalty and disaffection by his statements at the hospital, and conduct unbecoming an officer and a gentleman. Levy was ultimately convicted by a panel of five officers, sentenced to three years in prison, given a dishonorable discharge, and stripped of all pay and allowances.[6]

The Levy trial was only the most prominent indication of the disaffection of a small group of troops at Fort Jackson. In January 1968, a group of civilian activists opened the "UFO Coffeyhouse" in nearby Columbia. The UFO became a meeting place for both disaffected soldiers and students from the University of South Carolina. The UFO, like the Oleo Strut, which operated just off post near Fort Hood, Texas, was just the latest in a series of these types of establishments that were opened outside army installations. The UFO Coffeyhouse became a thorn in the side of senior officials in both Columbia and Fort Jackson.

It was also at Fort Jackson that the G.I.'s United Against the War in Vietnam was formed in 1968. The group attracted considerable media attention when nine of its members were arrested following a mass on-base meeting on 20 March 1969. They were charged with breach of peace, disrespect toward an officer, failure to obey an order, and agitation against the Vietnam War. They became known as the "Fort Jackson Eight" when one of their members was revealed as an informant and released. Eventually, the charges were dropped when peace activists rallied behind the soldiers and challenged the army's violation of their civil rights. The eight soldiers were subsequently discharged as undesirables.[7]

This was the environment at Fort Jackson when Hollingsworth arrived to take command. Shortly after he arrived, there was a disturbance in one of the training brigades caused by five soldiers who wanted to disrupt training. Later described by Hollingsworth as "Socialist Worker Party types," they were in advanced infantry training and were trying to sow dissent among their peers, calling for revolution and speaking against the war in Vietnam. Hollingsworth responded swiftly and threw all five in jail. He made it known that he would not tolerate any indiscipline in the ranks, particularly any that might be politically motivated.

When Hollingsworth announced that he would try the five in closed court, he ran afoul of both the American Civil Liberties Union (ACLU) and the *New York Times*, but he stood his ground. The reporters and the ACLU went to the secretary of defense, Melvin Laird, and placed a formal complaint, demanding that the accused be tried in open court. The army general counsel contacted Hollingsworth and said that the formal complaint had been lodged and that the secretary of defense and assistant secretary of defense for public affairs thought that Hollingsworth should open the trial to the public. Hollingsworth refused and told the general counsel that if the army wanted the trial open, it would have to get a new commander of Fort Jackson. Hollingsworth had called their bluff, and he remained in command.

The "Fort Jackson 5" were subsequently tried in closed court. There were eight to ten charges, which included defiance of regulations and standing orders, as well as misconduct. All five were found guilty and given discharges, which were either undesirable or dishonorable, depending on the seriousness of the charges on each individual.

The defendants sued Hollingsworth and the secretary of the army in federal court for denying their rights under the First Amendment. Hollingsworth took a lot of heat from several members of Congress, but he again stood his ground. He told the *New York Times*, "I'll take action against anybody that I am convinced is working against the interests of the United States Government, because that's the oath I took—to defend our country against all enemies, foreign or domestic. That's what I understood at the time, and that's exactly what I understand today."[8]

The federal court ruled that military organizations could not be run as civilian organizations from the standpoint of discipline and the authority of the commander, upholding Hollingsworth's decision as a commander to hold the trial in closed court. The defendants appealed, but Hollingsworth and the secretary of the army prevailed in a two-to-one vote in the circuit court in Richmond, Virginia. A vindicated Hollingsworth declared that he would not be intimidated by anyone while he was in the performance of his official duties.

In a speech before the South Carolina Law Enforcement Officers' Association, Hollingsworth explained his view on the recent conflict with his soldiers. He said, "I am sure you have questioned the validity of my statements toward individual freedom, and rightly so. The problem, however, is a problem of semantics. Let me clarify: The Army is respectful of the individual's right to dissent. We do not, however, hesitate to separate dissent from anarchy. Dissent is disagreement. I fought and bled over many countries so you gentlemen could practice dissent. But dissent is different, much different, from destroying buildings and property and defying the laws of this country and usurping and destroying the rights of the people in this great country—that is anarchy."[9] These would not be his final words on the topic.

Despite the political turmoil at Jackson and throughout the army, Hollingsworth soldiered on. He did the best he could to improve training in order to better prepare those soldiers in his charge to survive in Vietnam. He also focused on improving the living conditions of the soldiers and expanded recreational facilities on post. An avid outdoorsman, he placed new emphasis on conservation of wildlife and beautification of outdoor areas.

Hollingsworth believed that outreach to the local civilian community was important. Accordingly, he devoted much time to speaking engagements in Columbia and around the state. He was also on the board of directors of the Columbia Chamber of Commerce and participated in a number of different community forums. In the process, he met a number of important men and women who remained friends for the rest of his life.

As Hollingsworth went about his daily work of preparing young men for war, he was always on the lookout for talented officers and NCOs. One young officer at Fort Jackson demonstrated how Hollingsworth could take people under his wing. On a previous assignment, Hollingsworth had befriended a young African American officer named Porcher Taylor. Over the years, he had stayed in touch with Taylor, one of a group of young up-and-coming African American officers who were beginning to make their mark in the army. When Hollingsworth got to Fort Jackson, Taylor was already there; the general made Taylor his deputy chief of staff for personnel and community affairs (G-1). Later that year, Hollingsworth, whom Taylor called his "mentor," helped Taylor enroll in the doctoral program at the University of South Carolina in Columbia to study counselor education and personnel work. Taylor would become one of the first African Americans to earn a PhD there. At about the same time, Taylor was promoted to colonel, making him the highest-ranking African American officer to have been assigned to Fort Jackson at that time.[10]

Hollingsworth's outlook was simple: "We are obligated to bring the best out of everyone and if their best isn't good enough, dispose of them rapidly."[11] He was a demanding taskmaster, but he found a place in his heart for those who measured up to his high standards. He demonstrated this loyalty to his subordinates wherever he went, whether it was Vietnam, the Pentagon, or any of his other various assignments in the latter years of his career.

In the summer of 1970, Hollingsworth was promoted to major general and was subsequently notified that he was to be reassigned to Alaska. He believed for the rest of his years that he might have been too controversial at Jackson, leading to his reassignment from the training base there. He and Nickie had grown very comfortable in South Carolina and were sad to leave Fort Jackson, but once again they prepared to pack up everything and move to a new assignment.

The change of command ceremony was held at Fort Jackson on 11 July 1970 on the parade ground adjacent to the Post Headquarters. A list of attendees indicates the contacts that Hollingsworth had made over the years and the influence he had; among those in attendance were South Carolina senators Strom Thurmond and Ernest Hollings, Rep. L. Mendel Rivers, and South Carolina governor Robert E. McNair. Hollingsworth relinquished command to Brig. Gen. William Coleman. Having passed the flag, Holly and Nickie set off for the long drive overland to his new command in Fort Richardson, Alaska.

Alaska

On 12 August 1970, Hollingsworth arrived in Fort Richardson to assume command of all army forces in Alaska. There he was responsible for the training of a division of Arctic soldiers and Eskimo Scouts. An avid outdoorsman, hunter, and fisherman, Hollingsworth was excited about being in Alaska. It was a unique command in an environment that was different from anywhere he had ever been before.

Hollingsworth threw himself into his new job with his usual fervor. He was in his element—with soldiers in training. He really enjoyed visiting with the Eskimo Scouts, who spent part of their time hunting seal and walrus on Saint Lawrence Island; he joined in the local customs, which included eating clams from the belly of a freshly killed walrus. He thought the Scouts were excellent soldiers and visited them as often as he could.

He spent a lot of time out with other soldiers as well. On one particular exercise, the Arctic Ranger Company parachuted onto the polar ice cap, about 130 miles north of Point Barrow, Alaska. It was the first time a unit of that size had made a mass jump in that region. Hollingsworth joined them during the exercise, during which the temperature was -70 degrees Fahrenheit. This exercise demonstrated only too clearly the demands of combat operations in the Arctic.

One of the unique aspects of the new command was the opportunity to work with the Canadian armed forces. He found the Canadian officers and soldiers to be of very high quality. They were very capable in reconnaissance, operations behind the lines, and internal security. They were not prepared to conduct operations on the scale of the US Army, but what they did they did very well, and Hollingsworth had great admiration and respect for the Canadian Army. He was fond of saying that he would fight alongside them, under their command, at any place and time in the world.

He organized and conducted a combined exercise with the Canadian military involving experiments with the use of helicopters in extreme cold conditions. In temperatures that ranged between -50 and -75 degrees Fahrenheit, they learned much about the effect of such weather on troops and equipment.

In training, Hollingsworth found that in combat at such temperature extremes, 10 percent of the effort is spent in fighting and 90 percent in just surviving the environment. The general designed his own cold-weather gear. It was a two-piece garment with form-fitting goose-down underwear and zippers "all over the place." The outer garment, developed by Natick Laboratories (now called Gore-Tex), was wind resistant and waterproof. It formed a one-piece coverall lined with goose down. This proved very effective in the harsh Arctic climate.

Despite the demands of training, Hollingsworth was also very active in the local Alaskan community. Always colorful and gregarious, he was in great demand as a speaker. H. A. Boucher, then lieutenant governor of Alaska, remarked in a letter to General Westmoreland, army chief of staff, that Hollingsworth "is such a dynamic speaker I hate to be on the same platform with him—thank God I'm not running against him in the political arena."[12]

As commander in Alaska, Hollingsworth had to deal with a number of issues besides training and interacting with the local community. In October, just a few months after arriving in the command, the general uncovered a grand larceny ring. What he called the "civilian mafia" had penetrated the aviation supply company at Fairbanks. According to Hollingsworth, they were stealing, with the assistance of military personnel, thousands and thousands of dollars' worth of supplies. This became apparent when some of the supplies from Alaska began showing up in other parts of the Lower 48.

With the Pentagon's approval, Hollingsworth called in fifteen special army auditors and about the same number of trained agents (from both the Federal Bureau of Investigation and the army's Criminal Investigation Division) to investigate the situation. In the end, some two hundred military personnel and civilians were implicated in the theft of more than $100,000 in government property that dated back to 1966.

When Hollingsworth arrived in Alaska, he found the officers and noncommissioned officers clubs throughout the command in deplorable condition. Although he decreed that the situation would be remedied, after several months he saw no signs of improvement. He charged the inspector general to investigate the club systems. The investigators determined that the clubs had lost so much money in the previous two years that "they were damn near out of business." The general findings of the investigation revealed gross mismanagement, lack of supervision on the part of post commanders and their staffs, theft, and misconduct. Hollingsworth preferred charges on a number of individuals for specific crimes and misconduct. He had little patience with dishonesty or incompetence.

While in command in Alaska, Hollingsworth again became involved in a political battle with one of his soldiers. In the late spring of 1971, Pvt. Ed Jurenas, a self-proclaimed member of the Socialist Workers Party and the Young Socialist Alliance, was court-martialed at Fort Greely for having distributed an underground newspaper called "Arctic Arsenal." The newspaper was found "to contain material designated to promote disloyalty or conduct prejudicial to good discipline and morale within the services." Hollingsworth subsequently received a letter from Rep. Herman Badillo from the 21st Congressional District in New York, who said he would call for a House Armed Services Committee investigation if the charges against Jurenas were not dropped. On 27 June 1971, Hollingsworth wrote the congressman, "I wish to advise you that I have no intention of being threatened or intimidated by you or anyone else who presumes to interfere with my official duties and the orderly process of military justice."[13] Nothing ever came of the congressman's threat, and Jurenas was found guilty as charged.

In response to a letter from a lady in Fort Richardson, Alaska, Hollingsworth acknowledged that he was "often the object of close scrutiny by many different thinking people," but he hoped that his motives were clear because "as always, my aim is to do what I consider best for the United States Army in its role as a key instrument of our great nation."[14]

One thing that concerned Hollingsworth during this time was the deterioration of the army in the wake of its long commitment to the war in Vietnam. Because of the unpopularity of the war and the demands the war had made on it as an institution, the army had initiated the Modern Volunteer Army Program to assist in reducing reliance on the draft by attracting and increasing the enlistment of able men and women, raising the quality of army life, and improving professionalism throughout the rank and file. An important part of the program was Project VOLAR, a field experiment conducted at selected army installations from 1970 to 1972 to develop the methods and procedures for achieving the program's objectives.[15] Many in the army were concerned about the "country club atmosphere" that was perceived as part of the VOLAR experiment. In a letter to Mr. J. R. Blandford, chief counsel for the House Armed Services Committee, Hollingsworth said he was "distressed and concerned" about some of the attitudes evidenced in the VOLAR literature. Hollingsworth agreed that the army needed to "clean itself up," but he believed that the best way to do that was through "a higher degree of discipline and . . . higher standards of performance." He was "sorry that the Department of the Army has waited so long to attempt to clean itself up and then, when it came, it used the Volunteer Army tag." In Hollingsworth's estimation, the only way forward was to raise standards while at the same time cleaning out the deadwood among officers and NCOs; then, and only then, in his opinion, would the army create an image that would inspire good people to join and stay.[16]

Hollingsworth felt so strongly about the situation that on 27 January 1971 he wrote General Westmoreland, army chief of staff, "I am concerned that a credibility gap may soon be staring us in the face. On one hand, we speak of enhancing the quality of the soldier coming into the Modern Volunteer Army while on the other hand we continue to accept marginal personnel in the Army."[17] Hollingsworth doubted the efficacy of the all-volunteer army and remained concerned with the direction the army was headed.

Hollingsworth would have ample opportunity to see the current state of the army in Vietnam firsthand. He received a message from the army chief of staff saying that Gen. Creighton Abrams, now commander of US forces in Vietnam, had requested Hollingsworth's reassignment there, and he had seven days to get there. Hollingsworth was elated to be going back to Vietnam, but he was not happy about leaving Alaska before the entire aviation supply debacle could be cleaned up once and for all. Nevertheless, the Hollingsworths had to rush to meet the chief of staff's deadline. Hollingsworth got his wife resettled in Washington, DC, and departed for Vietnam. He had enjoyed his sojourns in Fort Jackson and Alaska, but he was anxious to get back to the war.

7

Second Vietnam Tour and the War He Came to Fight

XXIV Corps

General Abrams, commander of the US Military Assistance Command, Vietnam (MACV), needed Holly in-country to help deal with a situation in Military Region I, the area formally known as I Corps Tactical Zone. There had been several disasters in the region south of the Demilitarized Zone (DMZ). The 5th Mechanized Division had sustained a large number of casualties when a North Vietnamese rocket struck the mess hall where soldiers were taking their meal. In another incident, at Firebase Mary Ann, the guards went to sleep and allowed the Viet Cong to overrun the base and kill many of the sleeping soldiers. By this time in the war, drugs were rampant in US units in Vietnam, and there was a strong suspicion that drugs had been involved in both incidents in I Corps.

Abrams wanted a "mean son of a bitch" to come in and shake up the command. When Holly arrived in Saigon, Abrams told him, "I want you to get up there and get it sorted out." Holly replied, "I'll look at it." Abrams said, "I don't want you looking at it, I want you to sort it out."

Holly went north as ordered, but this was not a great time for him. He was a man born for war; during his first tour, he had reveled in taking the fight to the enemy. Now he had arrived in Vietnam to find an army in disarray making preparations to leave. He seemed ill disposed to deal with the situation. However, as events unfolded in early 1972, Hollingsworth would find himself involved in a battle for the survival of South Vietnam; it would become "the war he came to fight."[1] However, first he had to deal with the situation in Military Region I.

By the time Hollingsworth arrived in Military Region I, the area was occupied by elements of the 23rd "Americal" Division, the 101st Airborne Division, and a separate brigade from the 5th Mechanized Infantry. There were also scattered artillery units and several support units in the area. Holly became the deputy commander of XXIV Corps, the senior US Army headquarters in Military Region I, the old I Corps Tactical Zone. The commander of XXIV Corps was Lt. Gen. Welborn G. Dolvin. Holly later described him as a "nice guy," but apparently Abrams thought that what the command needed was someone who would not take no for an answer. Holly was that man. General Dolvin told Holly, "I know why you are here" and turned him loose.

Hollingsworth was all over the place, ruthlessly imposing his will on an army that, in his opinion, was clearly more interested in going home than in fighting a war. He inspected an artillery battery that was "so hopped up on drugs" that he deactivated them in place. He visited a unit in the 101st Airborne Division and found rusty weapons. He returned to his headquarters and called in the division, brigade, and battalion commanders; when they reported, he read them the riot act.

Hollingsworth was incensed at the state of the army in Vietnam.[2] The depth of his disgust with the situation, not just in XXIV Corps but throughout the army, is revealed in a letter to Col. Eugene M. Perry on 25 November 1971. He wrote, "When I arrived here on 30 August, it took only about two days to see that little interest had been displayed on the behalf of the soldier for apparently some time. . . . When I left here in late May 1967, our Army in Vietnam, less a few commanders, was probably the greatest army that had ever been put in the field. Four years later it was hard for me to believe the deterioration. In my opinion our problem is one of leadership at all levels. . . . The failure on the part of the Army to clean itself up leadership-wise is a major factor in the problems that we are confronted with today. Our inability to recognize those who have the capability to lead and set high standards and to promote leadership continues to be of deep concern to me."[3]

In another letter to a former subordinate later that month, Hollingsworth wrote, "In the final analysis, drug abuse, undisciplined acts, and dissent are a direct result of poor leadership and failure on the part of officers and NCOs to know their jobs, to set high standards, to clean out the dead wood, and to display interest in the soldiers. The Army has no one to blame but itself."[4]

Hollingsworth set out to correct the situation in Military Region I. He planned to do everything he could to right the ship in his area of responsibility. At the same time that he was concerned about the situation in the US Army, he was also concerned with the progress of Vietnamization. By this time in the war, President Nixon had instituted his program to gradually turn over the conduct of the war to South Vietnamese forces. The ultimate objective of this program, first announced in 1969, was to increase South Vietnamese military capabilities and bolster President Nguyen Van Thieu's government such that the South Vietnamese forces could stand on their own against the Communists from North Vietnam after all US forces were withdrawn.

Hollingsworth privately doubted that the South Vietnamese forces could ever be sufficiently prepared to stand against the North Vietnamese Army, but he threw himself into the task. He stressed development of the Regional Forces and Popular Forces throughout Military Region I and took measures to secure modern equipment and weapons for them. He also focused on increasing the capabilities of the National Police in the area, personally directing the upgrades and improvements to facilities at the National Police Training Center in Da Nang.

Hollingsworth was busy supervising all these activities when he received a call from General Abrams telling him to stop what he was doing and get to Military Region III (the area formally known as III Corps Tactical Zone) as soon as possible. He was to assume the role of senior adviser to the ARVN III Corps commander. Hollingsworth was delighted with the new assignment. He wrote Brig. Gen. Sam Walker that "the 5th, 18th, and 25th ARVN divisions [the three divisions assigned to III Corps] are not as good as the ARVN up here [in I Corps], however, I can assure you that they will get better damned fast . . . they haven't seen anything yet."[5]

Intelligence reports indicated that the North Vietnamese Army was beginning a buildup of its forces in Cambodia, and it appeared that it was planning something for the coming year. Hollingsworth was excited about the opportunity to meet this challenge. On 15 December, he departed Da Nang for Third Regional Assistance Command (TRAC) headquarters near Long Binh.

TRAC and the Easter Offensive

As one of the most critical aspects of Nixon's Vietnamization program, MACV increased the advisory effort to assist in improving the quality of the Republic of Vietnam Armed Forces (RVNAF). This was not a new program; US advisers had been serving with South Vietnamese units since 1955.[6] However, the emphasis on the advisory effort had been lessened with the arrival of US ground combat troops beginning in 1965. When Nixon announced the new Vietnamization policy and the subsequent phased US troop withdrawal, the advisory effort then became a priority again. The importance of the advisory program had only increased as the number of American combat units dwindled. By 1972, most US ground combat forces had been withdrawn, and the only Americans on the ground in combat roles were advisers who served with ARVN forces in the field.[7] There were US advisers at corps, division, and regimental levels; additionally, in the elite airborne, ranger, and marine units there were American advisers with each battalion. There were also advisers with each South Vietnamese province and district headquarters as part of the Civil Operations and Rural Development Support (CORDS) program.[8]

Vietnamization had received its first big test in early 1971 before Hollingsworth returned to Vietnam for his second tour. In that operation, called LAM SON 719, South Vietnamese forces attacked into Laos to cut North Vietnamese supply lines and take out enemy base areas in Laos along Highway 9. Because of US congressional legislation, the advisers assigned to the attacking South Vietnamese forces were forbidden to cross the border into Laos. The attack across the border went reasonably well in the beginning as the ARVN advanced west along Highway 9 toward Tchepone, a key transportation hub along the Ho Chi Minh Trail. However, the South Vietnamese forces soon became bogged down as the North Vietnamese Army 70B Corps responded by rushing three divisions to the area to block the South Vietnamese advance. In the heavy fighting that ensued, the South Vietnamese forces sustained heavy casualties and withdrew in disarray back into South Vietnam.[9]

Operation LAM SON 719 revealed many shortcomings that continued to haunt the South Vietnamese forces. Additionally, the outcome of the fighting in Laos had badly shaken their confidence. It was also a setback to the Vietnamization program, and many senior American military leaders in Vietnam were seriously concerned about the ability of the South Vietnamese to deal with the North Vietnamese Army once all US troops were withdrawn. General Abrams, MACV commander, intensified efforts to address the critical South Vietnamese weaknesses revealed by the debacle in Laos. No doubt, Holly's assignment to TRAC was part of Abrams's effort to pull out all the stops to improve the South Vietnamese forces.

Holly's new job at TRAC entailed command of the US advisory structure in Military Region III. MR III, as it was known, was the new designation for III Corps Tactical Zone, where Holly had served in his first tour with the Big Red One. The region, comprising the eleven provinces that surrounded Saigon, was located between the Central Highlands and the Mekong Delta. The senior US headquarters in the region had previously been II Field Force, a corps-level headquarters that had been responsible for controlling the tactical operations of subordinate US forces in Military Region III. With most of the US combat troops having departed and II Field Force deactivated, Hollingsworth's job was to serve as the senior adviser to the ARVN III Corps commander, providing military advice and logistical assistance. His counterpart, Lt. Gen. Nguyen Van Minh, commanded all the ARVN troops in Military Region III. Minh had at his disposal three infantry divisions; the 5th, headquartered at Lai Khe, was responsible for Binh Duong, Binh Long, and Phuoc Long Provinces; the 18th, headquartered at Xuan Loc, was responsible for Bien Hoa, Long Khanh, Phuoc Tuy, and Binh Tuy Provinces; and the 25th was responsible for the area encompassing the provinces of Tay Ninh, Hau Nghia, and Long An. Hollingsworth would supervise and direct the US advisory teams with each of those divisions. He would also supervise the provincial advisory teams that supported the province chiefs in each of the eleven provinces in Military Region III.

Hollingsworth arrived on the scene at his new headquarters at the "Plantation" near Long Binh in typical fashion. Don Gregg, from the Central Intelligence Agency, who would meet frequently with the general at TRAC, remembers Hollingsworth as "tall, muscular, and leathery-faced, and his glare was like a fist in your face. His smile, rare as it was, seemed almost a benediction."[10] Hollingsworth immediately took charge and began to set about the business of preparing III Corps for carrying on the war after all US troops were withdrawn. The years had not mellowed the general. He had been given a job that was more to his liking and he was raring to go.

The urgency of the situation would soon become apparent. Intelligence reports in the latter part of December 1971 revealed that North Vietnamese troops were moving down the Ho Chi Minh Trail in force. Another report indicated that there was major buildup in Laos adjacent to Military Region I (the area immediately south of the DMZ). Yet another report identified an enemy tank park in southern North Vietnam. General Abrams at MACV sensed that the North Vietnamese were making preparations for a new major offensive.[11] The general's sensing was reinforced when a revised intelligence estimate predicted a North Vietnamese offensive in early 1972. Some analysts thought the new offensive would come during the Tet Lunar New Year celebration in February, but others believed it would be later in March. Regardless of the timing, most analysts agreed that the North Vietnamese main effort would come in Military Regions I and II (the area south of the DMZ and the Central Highlands), with only limited supporting attacks in Military Region III.[12] They would be proven wrong very quickly once the offensive began.

While the intelligence analysts at MACV tried to discern what the enemy was planning, the North Vietnamese leaders in Hanoi had already made up their minds. They had been considering a new major offensive since 1970, but there was disagreement in the Party Central Committee of the Politburo about the wisdom of doing so. The proponents of the offensive received a setback in the spring of 1970 when US and South Vietnamese forces attacked into Cambodia, severely damaging the logistic apparatus that supported Communist troops in the southern half of South Vietnam. However, encouraged by the outcome of Operation LAM SON 719, Le Duan, party first secretary, and his supporters convinced the rest of the Central Committee in Hanoi that with the preponderance of US forces having already departed Vietnam, the time was propitious for a final, decisive, all-out offensive designed to win the war once and for all. Le Duan and his supporters agreed that there was an element of risk involved but argued that a victory, or even partial success, would fatally damage the government in Saigon, defeat the Vietnamization effort, and humiliate Nixon and his war politics.[13] This was an important part of the argument because a successful offensive would no doubt have a negative impact on Nixon's bid for reelection later in 1972.

The Party Central Committee approved the decision to begin preparations for a new general offensive in the coming spring. While the military planners devised a plan to strike a knockout blow against the South Vietnamese forces, Le Duan went to Moscow to make a plea for assistance in the form of new equipment and weapons. Subsequently, North Vietnam received massive quantities of war matériel and modern weapons systems from both Moscow and Beijing. When this equipment arrived in North Vietnam, it was transported to the frontline troops that would participate in the offensive as preparations intensified for the coming campaign.

The plan for the offensive called for a massive, three-pronged invasion of South Vietnam aimed at three critical areas. The first thrust would be made in the north against the provincial capital of Quang Tri in Military Region I; the second at Kontum in the Central Highlands (Military Region II); and the third at An Loc in Binh Long Province in Military Region III. A total of fourteen North Vietnamese Army (NVA) divisions and twenty-six separate regiments, numbering more than 130,000 troops and approximately 1,200 tanks and other armored vehicles, would participate in this offensive.[14] The offensive was to be known as the Nguyen Hue Campaign in honor of Nguyen Hue, the birth name of Emperor Quang Trung, who in 1789 dealt invading Chinese troops a resounding defeat just outside Hanoi.

The Nguyen Hue plan was somewhat risky, but the North Vietnamese counted on the simultaneous attack on three major fronts to disorganize the South Vietnamese forces and thus prevent Saigon from mounting an effective defense. Any of the three prongs, if successful, could have a major impact on the course of the war. The northern prong could sever the two northern provinces from the rest of South Vietnam and capture the old imperial capital at Hue, which would have a crippling effect on the morale of both the military and the civilian populace of South Vietnam. A successful attack in the Central Highlands had the potential to cut South Vietnam in two, a blow from which the government in Saigon would probably not recover. The attack in the south had the greatest potential payoff. The objective, An Loc, was only sixty-five miles north of Saigon, and a victory there would put South Vietnam's capital city at great risk. Success on any of the three fronts would have repercussions for the staying power of President Thieu and his forces; if all three prongs were successful, the South Vietnamese would be decisively defeated and the war would be over.[15]

The Easter Offensive, as the Nguyen Hue Campaign became known in the American press, began on Good Friday, 30 March 1972, when three NVA divisions attacked south across the DMZ toward Quang Tri and Hue. Additional North Vietnamese divisions began to close on Kontum in the Central Highlands.

The coordinated enemy thrusts, employing conventional tactics and introducing weaponry not used in any previous Communist offensive in South Vietnam, were characterized by a ferocity the South Vietnamese forces had never experienced before. Initially the attackers were successful, particularly in the north. There, the NVA troops quickly overran Quang Tri, threatened Hue, and virtually routed a large part of the defending South Vietnamese forces. One *Newsweek* journalist described the offensive in the following manner: "It was a classic World War II-style assault with Russian-made arms—long-range artillery that rained thousands of screaming shells on the Army of South Vietnam (ARVN) and Soviet tanks that churned through the hastily abandoned fire bases and country-side."[16]

With the North Vietnamese forces fully engaged in Military Region I and preparing for a major attack in the Central Highlands, the focus of the North Vietnamese attack in Military Region III would be Binh Long ("Peaceful Dragon") Province, located in the northwestern portion of the region and bordered on the west by Cambodia. The capital of the province, An Loc was a city of fifteen thousand in 1972 and lay only sixty-five miles north of Saigon. It was surrounded by vast rubber plantations totaling seventy-five thousand acres and sat astride QL-13, a paved highway leading directly from the Cambodian border to the South Vietnamese capital. Because of its proximity to Communist base areas in Cambodia, the city had endured the rigors of war since the early 1960s. Because of its strategic location on the main attack axis between Cambodia and Saigon, An Loc figured prominently in the North Vietnamese strategy in 1972. Hollingsworth was very familiar with An Loc and the surrounding territory because the region had been part of the 1st Infantry Division's assigned area of operations during his first tour in 1966 and 1967.

When the NVA offensive began, the 5th ARVN Infantry Division, commanded by Brig. Gen. Le Van Hung, was the only South Vietnamese division operating in Binh Long Province, but it had been reinforced with a two-battalion task force from the 18th ARVN Division, normally stationed at Xuan Loc in Long Khanh Province. Hung and his division were supported by a small advisory team led by Col. William H. Miller, a veteran of both World War II and Korea.

During the coming battle, Hollingsworth would work very closely with Lt. Gen. Nguyen Van Minh, III Corps commander. Minh had been a very good regimental and division commander, but Holly found him to be unprepared to be a corps commander. The South Vietnamese general had been fighting for twenty years and had been wounded "seven or eight" times. According to Hollingsworth, he was tired and sick; during the coming desperate battles in Binh Long Province, Holly would virtually command III Corps when Minh was overwhelmed with the task. It was something Hollingsworth had been preparing for all his life.

The Battle of Loc Ninh

When the Nguyen Hue Campaign began in Military Region III, most divisional elements of the 5th ARVN were dispersed throughout Binh Long Province. Most of the 9th Regiment and the divisional cavalry squadron were located at Loc Ninh, a small town north of An Loc on Highway 13 fourteen kilometers from the Cambodian border. The 7th Regiment was operating to the west of An Loc. The 8th Regiment, the remaining regiment from the 5th Division, was operating in Binh Duong Province. Additionally, Task Force 52, attached to the 5th from the 18th ARVN Division, was operating from two small firebases at Hung Tam, ten kilometers north of An Loc. The 5th Division headquarters was at Lai Khe but had a light advance command post at An Loc.

The North Vietnamese campaign in Military Region III would be directed by Lt. Gen. Tran Van Tra, commander of the B-2 Front, whose headquarters was probably somewhere in the vicinity of Snuol in Cambodia. For the attack, Tra had at his disposal more than thirty-three battalions organized into three divisions and several separate regiments.[17]

General Tra's plan in Binh Long Province focused on the capture of the provincial capital at An Loc. However, prior to launching the preliminary attack into Loc Ninh, which would facilitate the follow-on main attack on An Loc, two independent NVA regiments would attack outposts in Tay Ninh Province to the southwest of Binh Long. This was the traditional Communist attack route out of Cambodia toward Saigon. These attacks were meant to focus the allies' attention in that direction, while additional NVA forces maneuvered to assume assault positions for the main attack to be conducted against An Loc. The NVA planned to roll over Loc Ninh, encircle An Loc, cut QL-13 south of the city to preclude its reinforcement, destroy the ARVN forces in the city, and use it as a base for a follow-on direct attack toward Saigon.

The offensive in Military Region III began on 2 April with attacks by the 24th and 271st NVA Regiments against 25th ARVN Division firebases along the border with Cambodia in Tay Ninh Province. Although there

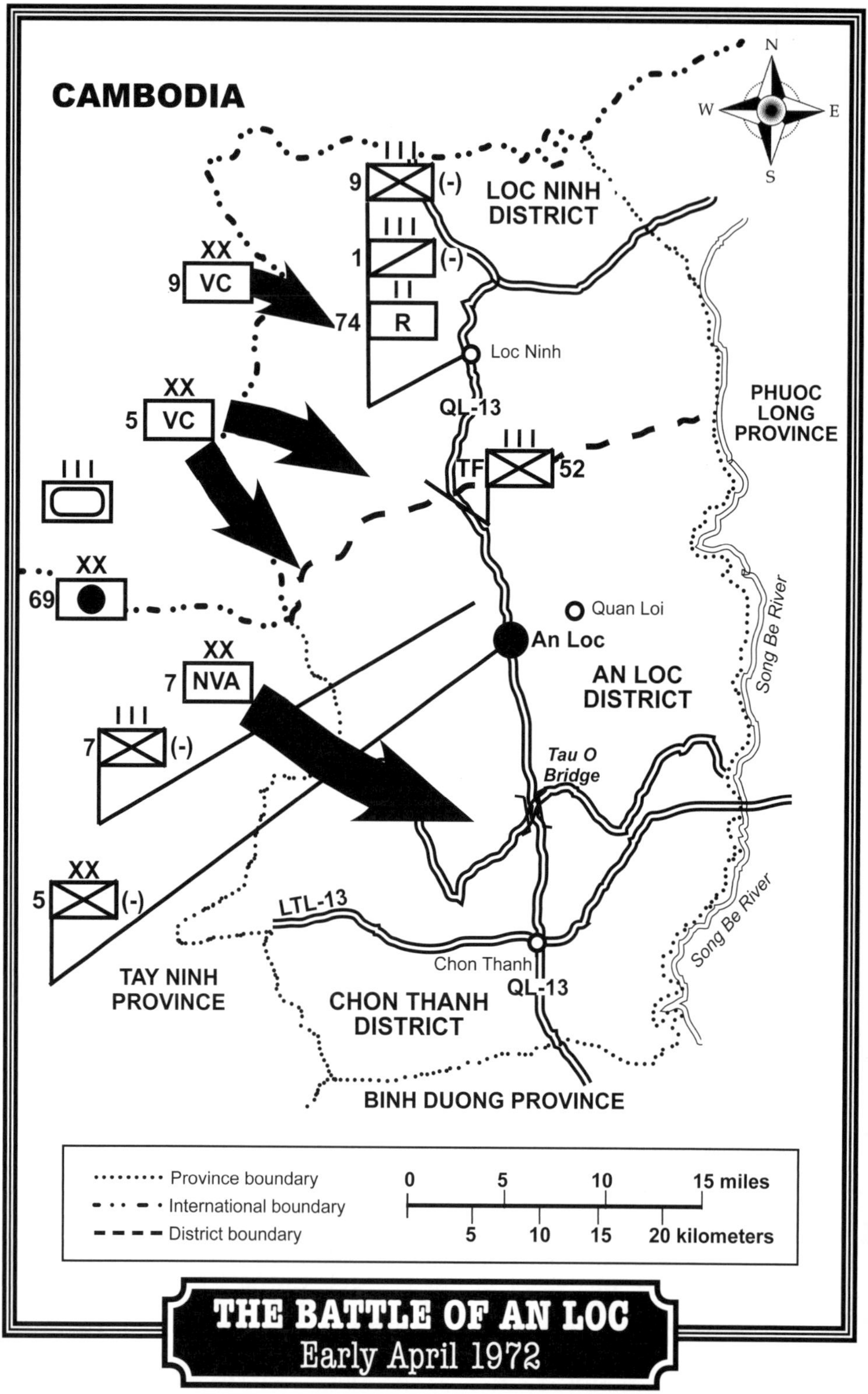

THE BATTLE OF AN LOC
Early April 1972

had been earlier intelligence reports that the North Vietnamese were making preparations for offensive operations in MR III, there was little indication that there would be any action on the scale of what had occurred in Quang Tri in MR I. To Generals Hollingsworth and Minh, the attacks in Tay Ninh, supported by tanks, rockets, and heavy mortar fire, seemed to confirm earlier intelligence that the main North Vietnamese effort in the region would come in that province. Thus, while the South Vietnamese were surprised at the ferocity of the enemy attacks and the use of tanks, the attacks themselves coincided with expectations that any significant attacks in MR III would come in Tay Ninh.[18]

For three days after the North Vietnamese attacks in Tay Ninh, Binh Long Province was relatively quiet. Senior US advisers with the 5th ARVN Division picked up indications of increased enemy activity in the area, but Hollingsworth and Minh, as well as the analysts at TRAC and their counterparts at MACV in Saigon, continued to believe that the main attack would come in Tay Ninh. Holly and the rest would soon be proven wrong. In reality, the attacks in Tay Ninh effectively masked the movements of three NVA divisions that were preparing to launch the main attack on Binh Long.

In the early morning hours of 5 April, the war came to Binh Long Province when the enemy opened up on Loc Ninh with a heavy barrage of artillery, rockets, and mortars. The intense shelling was followed by ground attacks on several points in the town. By this time, the defenders were in two compounds—one on the northeast corner of the Loc Ninh airstrip, manned by two companies of RF/PF soldiers with their two US advisers, and one on the southern end of the airstrip, which was occupied by the 2nd Battalion of the 9th Regiment and their five American advisers.[19]

With both compounds at Loc Ninh under heavy attack, Hollingsworth and Minh, from the III Corps tactical operations center in Bien Hoa, quickly realized the seriousness of the situation. The increasing intensity of the fighting convinced Hollingsworth that he had been wrong; the attacks in Tay Ninh had been a diversion and it was clear that Binh Long, not Tay Ninh, would be the focus of the NVA main effort. Accordingly, he ordered all available tactical air support north to Loc Ninh. More aircraft began arriving in the area almost immediately—USAF A-37s from the 8th Special Operations Squadron, naval attack aircraft from the carrier *Constellation*, Vietnamese Air Force F-5s and A-1s, and USAF F-4s and AC-130 gunships from US bases in Thailand. These aircraft provided continuous air cover as the desperate battle unfolded. The volume of wellplaced airstrikes and AC130 fire would enable the advisers and a rapidly dwindling number of South Vietnamese defenders to hold the NVA at bay for two days, fighting off at least three massed attacks in the process.

On the sixth, Hollingsworth flew to the Loc Ninh area to make an assessment of the situation. On arrival over the ARVN compound in the southern part of the town, the general's aircraft came under intense antiaircraft fire. As his pilots tried to avoid the enemy fire, Hollingsworth counted seven tanks attacking the compound. Meanwhile, an American adviser in the northern compound reported that they were under attack by twelve more tanks. Tactical air support helped turn away these attacks initially, but then there was an unfortunate half-hour window during the battle when there were no supporting aircraft on station. Holly could do nothing except orbit overhead and encourage the advisers on the ground as the NVA pummeled their positions.[20]

The North Vietnamese attacks against the small Loc Ninh garrison were relentless, employing tanks and large volumes of artillery, mortar, and rocket fire. As the battle intensified, Hollingsworth directed even more air support to the area, including AH-1G Cobra gunships from F Troop, 9th Cavalry, and from F Battery, 79th Aerial Rocket Artillery; skillful coordination by the American advisers in Loc Ninh inflicted heavy casualties on the attackers, but one Cobra was shot down and exploded on impact, killing both American pilots.[21]

At about noon on the sixth, the North Vietnamese made another push to take the southern compound, but timely fire from an orbiting AC-130 caught the enemy in the wire; the aircraft armed with 7.62 miniguns and one 105-mm gun stopped the attackers in their tracks. Another airstrike caught enemy soldiers attacking across the airstrip with well-placed CBUs (cluster bomb units consisting of more than two hundred bomblets that were devastating against personnel targets). Holly was very pleased with the advisers and their use of the airpower. In his daily situation report to General Abrams, he said, "I estimate that the better part of a regiment operating southwest and west of Loc Ninh have been blown away by tac air strikes."[22] He singled out Captain "Zippo" Smith, one of the US advisers on the ground in Loc Ninh, for his direction of close air support that helped turn back repeated enemy attempts to breach the ARVN perimeter.[23]

By the morning of 7 November, however, the enemy attacks had taken their toll. The strength of the northern compound was down to about forty soldiers; the strength of the southern compound was estimated to be about fifty soldiers. Hollingsworth could see that the ARVN did not have sufficient strength to hold off the attackers for much longer.

Despite the general's best efforts to keep the air support flowing and its skillful use by the advisers on the ground, sheer numbers ultimately overwhelmed the defenders. Hollingsworth observed enemy tanks in groups of seven and eight being beaten back on five separate occasions, but the enemy was just too strong for the defenders. By late afternoon, repeated human-wave attacks supported by tanks and heavy artillery fire resulted in the NVA overrunning both ARVN positions. As this happened, Hollingsworth tried to extract the American advisers, but the NVA antiaircraft fire was so intense that helicopters could not get through. Hollingsworth lost contact with the advisers in both compounds about 6:30 in the evening.

While some of the ARVN soldiers and one adviser managed to escape, the fate of the rest of the advisers was unknown and they were listed as missing in action.[24] Hollingsworth was devastated by the loss of the advisers. He reported to Abrams, "Those on the ground at Loc Ninh fought valiantly against insurmountable odds. . . . Dauntless and remarkable courage kept them going," but "the camp appears to be have been overrun. Some fighting continues, I have no estimate of friendly casualties within the Loc Ninh complex. I feel it must be heavy."[25]

The general did not have time to grieve for the losses at Loc Ninh, because the enemy was making final preparations to attack An Loc, the main prize. The plan for taking the town involved the use of three NVA divisions and supporting forces. By this time in the war, although some Communist formations still carried the traditional Viet Cong designations, these divisions were organized and equipped as main-force North Vietnamese Army units manned primarily by North Vietnamese soldiers who had come down the Ho Chi Minh Trail from the north. These divisions ranged in size from 7,000 to 9,000 soldiers; additionally, 10,000 other NVA troops in various types of support units would participate in the battle for An Loc.[26] According to the North Vietnamese plan, the 9th VC Division, considered one of the elite NVA divisions, was targeted against An Loc itself. The 7th NVA Division was tasked to interdict supplies and reinforcements from reaching An Loc from Saigon by cutting QL-13 south of An Loc, between Chon Thanh and Lai Khe. The 5th VC Division, which initiated the offensive campaign in Binh Long by capturing Loc Ninh, was to join the 9th VC Division in its assault on An Loc after the Loc Ninh area had been secured.

As the battle unfolded in Loc Ninh, the NVA also attacked an ARVN regiment-sized task force (TF-52) from the 18th ARVN Division that had been under the operational control of the 5th ARVN Division commander since mid-March.[27] The task force had been conducting operations from two small firebases located along Route 17 between Loc Ninh and An Loc. When the situation began to deteriorate at Loc Ninh, Hollingsworth tried to get Brigadier General Hung and Colonel Miller to order TF-52 to reinforce the Loc Ninh garrison, but Hung was at first reluctant to do so. However, on 6 April, Hung acceded and ordered TF-52 to reinforce An Loc with one battalion.

When the battalion began to move north, it immediately ran into a stubborn enemy force in the vicinity of the junction of Routes 13 and 17. The ARVN troops came under intense direct and indirect fire from both mortars and artillery. It was clear that the North Vietnamese were trying to isolate Loc Ninh and planned to block any attempt to reinforce from the south.

Early the next morning, the task force was subjected to intense shelling and there were ground probes from the west, southwest, and north. It appeared that TF-52 was now surrounded. The shelling and ground attacks continued throughout the day and into the night. The next day, with the task force under attack by the 272nd VC Regiment, General Hung ordered Lt. Col. Nguyen Ba Thinh, the task force commander, to withdraw to An Loc by road. As the first convoy departed to make its way to Route 13, it was stopped short of the road by a strongly entrenched NVA force and could go no farther. General Hung, realizing he was about to lose the task force, ordered Thinh to destroy all equipment and withdraw cross-county on foot to An Loc. Still in heavy contact, the South Vietnamese troops broke out and began to withdraw to the south. The retreating ARVN troops were under so much pressure that they were unable to destroy several artillery pieces; General Hollingsworth later ordered an air strike to destroy the weapons and equipment so the enemy could not use them.

During the course of the withdrawal, the ARVN column ran into an ambush, taking fire from three directions. Eventually, the ARVN managed to break through and continue southward but ran into another ambush. During the intense fighting that followed, one of the three American advisers with the task force was seriously wounded. Along with fifteen wounded

ARVN soldiers, the advisers remained at the ambush site and called for extraction. They were surrounded by the enemy, and several attempts to rescue them by helicopter failed, resulting in the first two aircraft being damaged by ground fire and the third being shot down. Finally, an OH-6 helicopter flown by Capt. John Whitehead landed amid withering enemy fire to pick up the advisers and several other wounded ARVN. Hollingsworth later awarded Whitehead the Silver Star.[28] With Loc Ninh falling and Task Force 52 pushed off its position, Hollingsworth landed at An Loc to make an assessment of the defenses there and confer with General Hung and Colonel Miller, who had moved the 5th ARVN command post to the city.

An ARVN officer who had been captured by the North Vietnamese at Loc Ninh and then managed to escape and make his way to An Loc told General Hung that the North Vietnamese were going to take An Loc at "any cost." Hollingsworth promised Hung that he would make available all air support that he could muster and would do everything he could to support the city.[29] Unfortunately, the general did not get to spend much time on the ground, because the NVA began to fire 82-mm and 120-mm mortars into the city. It was clear to all that the situation there was about to get worse.

If that was not enough, during the night of 7–8 April, the US communications relay station on top of Nui Ba Den Mountain was destroyed by enemy sapper attacks, followed by a ground assault by an NVA rifle company. The mountaintop base was a critical allied communications node, and Hollingsworth turned his attention to routing out the enemy soldiers and reestablishing security for the relay station. Three US soldiers had been killed in the battle and six were wounded, but with the help of an AC-130 Spectre gunship and several close air support sorties, security was reestablished by 4:00 p.m. Apparently, the NVA had hoped to set up its own communications equipment on the mountaintop to support its ongoing attacks. It was clear to Hollingsworth that he was witnessing the opening rounds in a new major enemy offensive.

The Battle of An Loc

Shortly after the fall of Loc Ninh, the 9th VC Division made its opening move against An Loc by seizing the airstrip and helicopter rearming and refueling point at Quan Loi, just three kilometers northeast of the city.

The fall of Quan Loi was significant because it left the enemy in possession of high ground that dominated the city from the northeast. From this position, they were able to observe the city clearly and shell it freely.

Meanwhile, south of the city, the 1st ARVN Airborne Brigade, which had been moved to Binh Long from Saigon, was directed to move north up QL-13 from Lai Khe to reinforce the An Loc garrison. The paratroopers immediately ran into heavy contact with elements of the 7th NVA Division entrenched along the highway. It was apparent that the North Vietnamese were determined to interdict any attempt to reinforce or resupply An Loc by road.

Hollingsworth reported to Abrams that with the fall of Loc Ninh and the subsequent pummeling of Task Force 52, the "situation in Binh Long has taken a turn for the worse."[30] He predicted that the enemy would continue its momentum south astride Highway 13 and eventually threaten Saigon. Having provided an update to MACV, he immediately put all US elements and military personnel in Military Region III on alert and ordered them to be prepared to defend against enemy tanks.

It had become imperative to open Highway 13 south of An Loc. Accordingly, Holly went forward to see how the airborne brigade was doing. Capt. Mike McDermott, an American adviser with the 8th Airborne Battalion, later described the situation when Holly arrived at his unit. McDermott reported that a jeep arrived in a cloud of dust and out bounded "an aging but slim and energetic American wearing a helmet sporting two stars." McDermott noted that the general had an oversized pearl-handled pistol strapped around the waist of his starched jungle fatigues. The general was a "bundle of energy" who waved his arms and "demanded to know what was going on, who was doing it, where it was happening, how well it was being done, and what kinds of problems needed his attention." Shortly after the general arrived, a caravan of civilian cars arrived and out poured a number of reporters; they appeared to have been chasing the general up the highway.

"In response to the very first barrage of their questions," according to McDermott, "General Hollingsworth turned on his audience and launched into a fantastic harangue [of his own]." He refused to answer their demands but cut loose with a tirade built around "damning the communist enemy to an everlasting and painful level of Hades." He felt that the enemy, by blocking Highway 13, had provided him with a great opportunity, and he planned to "take advantage of their [the NVA's] impertinence by administering a beating that he described in a dramatically obscene and bloodcurdling fashion." McDermott said that this went on for some time, "heavily flavored with the most creative, graphic, and instructive profanity I had enjoyed in years." When the reporters asked whether they could quote the general verbatim, Holly laughed and told them in a fairly earthy way that they were free to do so. When it became clear that the impromptu press conference was over, the reporters, knowing that the front line was not too far from where they stood, decided that discretion was the better part of valor and jumped in their cars, fleeing the scene back toward Saigon as the battle began to unfold. McDermott observed that the departure of the reporters was like turning a light switch; Hollingsworth "switched personas and became the engaging and professional leader that marked him as a real warrior." The general spent some time with the ARVN paratroopers and their leaders, asking questions and encouraging them. To McDermott, it was clear that Holly "understood and loved being with combat soldiers."[31]

Despite Hollingsworth's encouragement, the airborne brigade was not able to break through the NVA roadblocks to reach An Loc. The blocking of QL-13 and the loss of the Quan Loi airstrip meant that An Loc was surrounded and cut off from the outside. Thus began a siege that would last for more than two months.

After the seizure of Quan Loi, a brief lull in the battle occurred while the NVA prepared for the main attack on An Loc itself. However, artillery had begun to fall on the city on 5 April and had continued intermittently as the North Vietnamese forces maneuvered to their new attack positions in the rubber plantations surrounding An Loc. As the enemy units arrived in the area, they launched small probing attacks against the South Vietnamese positions along the city's outer defensive perimeter as artillery, mortars, and rockets continued to rain down on the defenders.

With the situation heating up in An Loc, Hollingsworth urged Lieutenant General Minh to move the airborne brigade to the city immediately to help defend against the coming attack. Minh did not order the airborne brigade into the city at this time; he had just sent two battalions from the 3rd Ranger Group the day before. He may have been worried that the airborne brigade was the only thing standing between the North Vietnamese surrounding An Loc and Saigon to the south. Hollingsworth understood but warned General Abrams that the situation was becoming dire and that "An Loc will fall and it will be clear sailing [southward from there] into Lai Khe."[32]

On the eleventh and twelfth, additional reinforcements were airlifted into An Loc. The 1st and 2nd Battalions of the 8th ARVN Regiment were flown to the city by helicopters from the 1st Cavalry Division.[33] By the afternoon of 12 April, ARVN forces in and immediately around the city had grown to a total of nine infantry battalions, consisting of regular infantrymen from elements of the 5th and 18th ARVN Divisions, as well as airborne, ranger, and territorial forces.[34] General Hung, 5th ARVN Division commander, was given operational control of all South Vietnamese units in the city, approximately 3,500 soldiers, who were outnumbered six to one by the NVA forces surrounding An Loc.

With An Loc encircled by enemy troops, South Vietnamese president Nguyen Van Thieu radioed the senior ARVN officers in the city that it would be defended to the death.[35] This had a psychological impact on the enemy, as well as the defenders. Colonel Miller later commented that for Thieu, An Loc was "a Bastogne, a place where a stand or die defense would decide the fate of the enemy offensive closest to the national capital."[36] By directing that the city be held "at all costs," Thieu all but challenged the North Vietnamese to take it. In the weeks that followed, they became virtually obsessed with the desire to overrun An Loc, even long after it had ceased to hold any real military significance.

The American advisers in An Loc were about to get some orders of their own. When the enemy offensive had started in Military Region I, some advisers had been pulled out of Quang Tri, and this had had disastrous effects on the morale of the South Vietnamese defenders there. The ARVN defense subsequently fell apart in the face of the NVA attack. General Hollingsworth determined that the stakes were too high in An Loc to risk a reoccurrence so close to Saigon; he believed the withdrawal of the American advisers in An Loc would result in the collapse of the South Vietnamese defense in the city. After directing the evacuation of all nonessential US personnel, Holly notified the remaining advisers that they would stand or fall with their counterparts.[37] Thus, the American advisers stayed in place and prepared to share the fate of their ARVN counterparts in the coming battle. The presence of the advisers during the bitter fighting proved to be a crucial factor in convincing the South Vietnamese defenders that they would not be abandoned to face the repeated North Vietnamese attacks alone; moreover, the presence of the advisers meant that the South Vietnamese defenders would have access to US air support in all its forms.

On 12 April, about a thousand soldiers from the 7th Regiment withdrew from their earlier positions into An Loc. As the North Vietnamese prepared to launch their attack on the city, the defenders included a mixture of regular ARVN infantrymen from elements of two different divisions, border rangers, sector artillery, and Binh Long Territorial Forces.

Refugees streaming into An Loc along Highway 13 from the north reported sighting tanks, artillery, and other heavy equipment between Loc Ninh and the city. An ARVN officer who had been captured by the NVA and escaped to An Loc reported that his captors had told him that they were going to capture An Loc at "any" cost.[38] A feeling of panic seemed to lurk just under the surface among the soldiers and civilians in the town; everyone on the ground realized that the North Vietnamese were going to hit An Loc with everything they had. It became clear that this would be a fight to the finish.

At TRAC headquarters, Hollingsworth and his advisers realized that the enemy's main attack on An Loc was about to begin. They met with air force representatives at Lai Khe to plan B-52 missions and tactical air strikes on suspected enemy positions around the city for the next day. Hollingsworth was concerned that there might not be enough air support once the battle was joined. Accordingly, he flew to Saigon to confer with General Abrams. Holly made the case that the NVA was massing for an all-out push at An Loc and requested additional B-52 sorties. Abrams agreed and gave the order to divert B-52 missions from I and II Corps for the next day.[39]

The preparations for the initial NVA direct attack on An Loc began in the early morning hours of 13 April, when North Vietnamese gunners brought a wide range of guns, rockets, and mortars to bear on the city. A total of seven thousand shells and rockets would fall on An Loc in the next fifteen hours.

With the shelling growing in intensity, security forces posted to the west and southwest on the ARVN defensive perimeter reported sizable enemy forces moving toward their attack positions around the city. Three hours later, new reports revealed that tanks and other enemy vehicles were moving to the northwest of the city. At the same time, on the eastern side of the perimeter, a company from 3rd Ranger Battalion reported that tanks could be heard moving in front of their positions. The North Vietnamese had the city surrounded and were preparing to launch an attack.

Shortly after dawn, the NVA forces began a coordinated tank and infantry assault on the city from the west and northeast. Soviet-made T-54 and PT-76 tanks attacked down the main north-south street into the city. Panic ensued among the ARVN defenders, who had never encountered enemy tanks before. Several units broke and ran. The situation stabilized somewhat when one of the Binh Long RF/PF soldiers knocked out the lead tank with an M72 Light Antitank Weapon (LAW), thus demonstrating that infantry soldiers could stop tanks. Capt. Harold Moffett, an adviser with the rangers, said after the battle, "Once the word [of the destruction of the tank by the RF/PF soldier] spread it was just like wild fire. . . . Everyone wanted to see how many tanks they could kill."[40]

The battle raged for three days as the NVA advanced house to house. While the ARVN and Binh Long Province troops tried to hold on, Cobra gunships engaged the enemy tanks. At the same time, Hollingsworth coordinated the seemingly unending flow of close air support and B-52 strikes, which repeatedly struck the attackers despite intense NVA antiaircraft fire.

During the battle, Holly was in constant contact with Colonel Miller and the other advisers on the ground in An Loc—pushing, encouraging, and more importantly, ensuring that the critical air support continued without letup. The tenacity of the defenders and the continual air strikes prevented the enemy from expanding its initial foothold in the northern part of the city. Lt. Col. Ed Benedit, Miller's deputy, later recalled, "The enemy pounded and pounded. He'd hit and take a house, then reinforce at night, and next day the next house and the next."[41]

Casualties were heavy on both sides. The ARVN situation was tenuous at best. After three days of combat, the NVA had lost twenty-three tanks but had forced the ARVN defenders into a small redoubt in the southern part of the city, measuring only 1,000 by 1,500 meters. The NVA forces held the northern part of the city; in many cases the opposing forces were separated only by the width of a city street. On several occasions, the attackers almost succeeded in taking General Hung's 5th ARVN Division command bunker.

The critical factor in thwarting the initial North Vietnamese attack was American air support, coordinated by the US advisers with the ARVN units on the ground in An Loc. While air force, navy, and marine fighters and fighter-bombers, AC-130 gunships, and army attack helicopters worked to support the South Vietnamese defenders in close contact with the attacking NVA forces, General Hollingsworth directed B-52 strikes against North Vietnamese staging areas in the rubber plantations around the city; each strike included three aircraft, each carrying 108 bombs of 500 and 750 pounds. The devastation wreaked by these strikes was horrendous; a Viet Cong described the impact of such a strike after the war: "From a kilometer, the shock waves knocked their victims senseless. . . . It was not just that things were destroyed; in some awesome way they had ceased to exist."[42] This air support made the difference in the pitched battles that raged for the first three days, saving the ARVN from almost certain defeat.

After three days, the intensity of the fighting in the city abated somewhat as the NVA attacks lost momentum as a result of the continuous airstrikes. Nevertheless, the North Vietnamese tightened their stranglehold on An Loc, completely encircling the city. They continued to shell the city heavily; 25,000 artillery rounds and rockets fell during the first three days of the NVA attack. They continued to fire between 1,200 and 2,000 rounds per day into the city for the next week as they regrouped for a renewed assault.

At the same time, the North Vietnamese increased the coverage of their available air defense weapons, attempting to cleave away the air support that had proved so devastating. Hollingsworth noted that increased ground fire made flying into and out of An Loc "most gamey."[43] Nevertheless, he was constantly over the battlefield so he could see what was going on himself and provide guidance and encouragement to his advisers on the ground in the city.

On the evening of 16 April, Hollingsworth reported to Abrams that "there was a great battle at An Loc yesterday, perhaps the greatest of this campaign. The enemy hit us with everything he could muster—and we threw it right back at him. The forces in An Loc realized that they had to fight and they fought well."[44] In truth, the fighting by the South Vietnamese forces had been uneven at best, but the South Vietnamese nevertheless held the city in the end.

That same day, Lieutenant General Minh, at Holly's urging, directed the 1st Airborne Brigade to disengage along QL-13 and mount a helicopter assault into the high ground just to the southeast of An Loc to reinforce the city. General Minh was able to do this because he had just received operational control of the 21st ARVN Division, which had been operating previously in the Mekong Delta area. Minh ordered the 21st to move to Lai Khe and assume the previous mission of the airborne brigade to open QL-13 to relieve An Loc.

Although the ARVN continued to hold An Loc, the situation inside the city was growing pretty grim by this time. Colonel Miller, senior adviser to the 5th ARVN, reported, "The division is tired and worn out; supplies minimal, casualties continue to mount, medical supplies are low; wounded a major problem, mass burials for military and civilians, morale at a low ebb. In spite of incurring heavy losses from US air strikes, the enemy continues to persist." In a subsequent report, an exhausted Miller said, "I believe the enemy can take An Loc anytime."[45] Hollingsworth did not like hearing that and redoubled his efforts to boost the morale of Miller and his advisers.

The original plan for NVA forces to overrun and occupy An Loc no later than 20 April had failed. Some of the difficulties that the enemy incurred were revealed when the 92nd Border Ranger Battalion killed an individual who was identified as a high political officer from the Central Office for South Vietnam (COSVN). He was carrying a six-page handwritten letter from the political officer of the 9th VC Division to COSVN headquarters.[46] This letter divulged the plans for the coming second attack on An Loc. Additionally, it explained to COSVN the serious problems incurred in the first attack on the city. The letter stated that the tac air and B-52 strikes had been unbelievably devastating. Nevertheless, the 9th VC Division would be reinforced with the 203rd Tank Regiment and the 69th Artillery Regiment for the next major attack on the city, which would come on the nineteenth.

In accordance with the revised plan, the North Vietnamese repositioned forces for another attempt to take the city; they hoped to attack from multiple directions and force the ARVN to withdraw into a smaller perimeter. The 271st Regiment would make the main attack from the west, the 272nd Regiment would attack from the north, and the 95C Regiment from the northeast. At the same time, the 275th Regiment from the 5th Division and the 141st Regiment from the 7th Division would attack the 1st Airborne Brigade positions southeast of An Loc. In order to counter the American air support, the NVA moved up additional antiaircraft weapons, including Soviet-made SA-7 Strela heat-seeking antiaircraft missiles to provide cover for the new attack.

The second major attempt to take An Loc began in the predawn hours of 19 April with a massive artillery bombardment of both the city and the 1st Airborne Brigade positions southeast of An Loc. The subsequent ground attacks against the airborne forces were successful, overrunning one battalion and driving the other two battalions out of their positions and into the city.

The main NVA attack against the city was less successful. The ARVN defenders and their advisers continued to fight off repeated ground assaults and employed close air support to bring devastating fire against the human-wave attacks. The fighting was intense, but the air support permitted the defenders to beat back the attackers again.

By the twentieth of April, the North Vietnamese attacks had abated somewhat. However, conditions inside the city had continued to deteriorate. Colonel Miller reported to Hollingsworth that the NVA continued to pour 100-mm tank gunfire, rockets, and artillery and mortar rounds into the city "almost to the point of bombardment."[47] It was estimated that enemy indirect fire continued to strike the city at a rate of about one thousand rounds a day. The defenders and the unfortunate civilians who were unable to leave before the NVA attacked lived underground because moving around aboveground invited near-certain death. Most buildings in the city had been destroyed by the repeated ground attacks, shelling, and air strikes. The city was strewn with mounds of rubble, shattered trees, garbage, and dead domestic animals. One adviser described the scene as "looking like Berlin at the end of World War II."[48]

The human toll inside the city was ghastly; the streets and rubble were littered with bodies, both military and civilian; the smell of death permeated the air. One adviser reported that "the bodies of men, women, and children are everywhere."[49] A South Vietnamese soldier, writing after the war, recalled the "dead bodies scattered like weeds. . . . All humanity died in An Loc."[50] Under these conditions, innumerable diseases, including cholera, soon ran rampant through both the civilian and soldier ranks. To avoid a full-fledged epidemic, bodies were buried in mass graves, some containing 300–500 corpses, by soldiers operating bulldozers during the infrequent lulls in the shelling. Many bodies had to be reburied after exploding shells churned up the original graves.

Antiaircraft fire had increased to the level that it became almost impossible to resupply the defenders by air. Air force C-130s braved intense fire in an attempt to drop supplies to the defenders, but during the month of April, more than 85 percent of the C-130 high-altitude drops landed in the hands of the enemy.[51]

Inside the city, medical supplies were exhausted and little could be done for the increasing number of casualties; at one point, the single South Vietnamese Army doctor was boiling strings from nylon sandbags to use for sutures to sew up his wounded comrades. The food and ammunition status was not much better. Virtually nothing could get into the city; consequently, there was no way out for the wounded. These facts, coupled with the continual artillery bombardment, had a demoralizing effect on ARVN resolve, and morale plummeted. The advisers were afraid that the South Vietnamese troops would break if the NVA attacked in force again, and they redoubled their efforts to bolster the confidence of their ARVN counterparts. Under these bleak conditions, the defenders, now numbering approximately 4,500 troops with the arrival of the two airborne battalions, prepared themselves for the next North Vietnamese onslaught.

This situation had an impact on the US advisers as well. The sheer destruction of the constant shelling wore on them, just as it did on the South Vietnamese. The Americans fully realized what a tenuous position they were in, but they had to put on a good face for their counterparts; they could not allow the South Vietnamese to see their concern. That was a difficult proposition. The advisers, many of whom had never before experienced this level of combat, worked around the clock with little rest and were exhausted.

With the situation still very much in doubt, Holly told a reporter from *Pacific Stars and Stripes*, "The enemy isn't going to give up easy on An Loc. They've already announced they want it for one of their liberation capitals."[52] He knew that there was more to come in this desperate fight so close to the national capital. Hollingsworth did everything in his power to shore up the morale and confidence of both the South Vietnamese forces and their American advisers.

The general's omnipresence over the city, even in the thickest of the fighting, was one of the major factors that helped sustain the advisers throughout the battle. Even when things looked the worst, he was in the air over the city encouraging the advisers and their counterparts. He would be on the radio for long periods in detailed conversations with the advisers on the ground. One might have wondered whether these conversations gave the enemy too much information, but the old warrior knew that the men on the ground needed his personal encouragement, and he exposed himself repeatedly in the deadly airspace over the city to give it. Even when the advisers were convinced that the defenders could not hold out and were about to be overrun, the gruff voice of "Danger 79er" convinced them that he would give them all the support they needed if they could just convince their counterparts to hold on. This may not seem like a lot to some readers, but it meant everything to those on the ground in An Loc.

Trouble with the Media (Again)

Hollingsworth was naturally concerned about the fate of his advisers on the ground in the city, but he was excited about the opportunity to get the NVA to stand and fight. If he could get the South Vietnamese and their advisers to hold out against the attackers, he could bring maximum firepower to bear to destroy the North Vietnamese troops. He told the advisers, "Hold them and I'll kill them with airpower; give me something to bomb and I'll win."[53]

Not surprisingly, the reporters present at Hollingsworth's headquarters picked up on this statement. During a subsequent interview with a *Newsweek* reporter, Hollingsworth declared that he intended to "kill every one of these [NVA] bastards before they can get back into Cambodia. . . . I'm movin' to the north and I'm exploiting the success we had at An Loc." To many observers, it was clear that Hollingsworth considered himself the commander at An Loc even though the South Vietnamese commander was technically in charge. The remark contradicted US claims that the South Vietnamese were in total control of their own affairs and cast doubt on the Nixon administration claims that Vietnamization was succeeding.

When Holly's remarks appeared in the press, an angry General Abrams rebuked Hollingsworth, telling him to "shut his mouth." Abrams was incensed because he thought Holly had given the impression that he had taken over what should have been a South Vietnamese–run show.[54] In fact, Hollingsworth, in his remarks to the reporters, had pointed out that he was "only an adviser" to General Minh, and the men doing the fighting were under the Vietnamese general's command. However, this remark was omitted from most of the subsequent news reports, which focused on the more controversial aspects of Hollingsworth's pronouncements.[55]

Holly's bellicose comments drew fire from another quarter as well. After the article appeared in the US press, the general received a letter from Msgr. Marvin Bordelon of the United States Conference of Catholic Bishops. The monsignor castigated Hollingsworth, saying, "I was very upset by the direct quotes attributed to you. While Judeo-Christian theology has tolerated under very stringent provisos the evil of war, this is always done with much reluctance. If you had said that you were happy to achieve victory, and quite saddened about the necessary killing, this might have made some sense. As it is, I can reach no other conclusion but that you have helped dishonor the name and reputation of the United States."[56]

Hollingsworth was undeterred. To him, his mission was all about destroying the enemy. There was no room for compassion in war. Moreover, in Hollingsworth's private opinion, the ARVN corps commander was not prepared to handle a battle of this magnitude, and it was just what Holly had prepared for his whole life. He had the enemy right where he wanted it and was prepared to do whatever was necessary to hold An Loc.

Meanwhile, the ARVN and its advisers in An Loc continued to hang on, but just barely. Nevertheless, Hollingsworth was greatly encouraged. On 23 April, an optimistic Holly told a reporter from *Pacific Stars and Stripes* newspaper, "They [air support] did a magnificent job. They have done magnificently all the way, just tremendous." However, he added, "the real credit goes to the little ARVN soldier. He is tremendous, just magnificent. He stood in there, took all that fire and gave it back."[57]

However, it soon became clear that the battle for An Loc was not over. On 5 May, an enemy soldier from the 5th VC Division headquarters turned himself in at An Loc to an RF patrol operating just a short distance from their perimeter. When the soldier was interrogated by Col. Tran Van Nhut, the Binh Long Province chief, he revealed that the 9th VC commander had been severely reprimanded for failing to take the city in the first two attempts by his division. He further stated that the 5th VC Division commander had been assigned responsibility for the next attack on An Loc and that he would be supported by reinforcements from both the 7th NVA and 9th VC Divisions.[58]

As the North Vietnamese made preparations and maneuvered their forces to their new attack positions, Hollingsworth and his intelligence analysts determined that the enemy was preparing for the new push. When he shared this information with the advisers on the ground in the city, they told the general that they doubted the weakened ARVN forces could hold against another determined attack. By this time, the defenders had been under almost constant attack for the better part of a month. They had turned back two major assaults, but they were both physically and mentally exhausted; more than a thousand had been wounded. The failure of the Vietnamese Air Force to evacuate seriously wounded casualties, the continual incoming rocket, artillery, and mortar fire, and the resultant low morale of the remaining forces had brought the troops to a point where they evidenced all the signs of battle fatigue. The troops were "afraid to move, shoot, or expose themselves," and the advisers were afraid that they would break if the NVA attacked in force.[59]

North Vietnamese High Tide

Realizing that the situation inside the city was reaching a dangerous stage, General Hollingsworth took to the air once again in a renewed attempt to encourage the division commander, the province chief, and the advisers to hold their positions, but it was clear to all concerned that the outlook was dire at best, and in the minds of many, beyond hope. Concerned with the deteriorating morale among the South Vietnamese in An Loc, Hollingsworth made it a point to speak by radio with the American advisers daily to get a sense of what was really going on in and around the city on the ground. The advisers confirmed that the situation inside the city was desperate and getting worse as they waited for the next fight to unfold. They did not have long to wait.

A worried Hollingsworth reported to Abrams that "my attempts to belittle the capability of the enemy and to strengthen friendly forces' morale seemed almost hopeless. Enemy positions and movements, intensity of antiaircraft fire, and the increase in enemy artillery and rockets against An Loc point to an imminent all-out attack."[60]

At TRAC headquarters in Long Binh, all intelligence reports seemed to confirm that the enemy was preparing to make another big push to take An Loc. More frequent reports of enemy movements and a tremendous increase in shelling indicated that the time of the attack was near.

At 5:30 a.m. on 9 May, the enemy began strong probes all around the ARVN perimeter in An Loc, but particularly in the south and southeast. Additionally, the incoming artillery and rockets increased drastically. Based on the patterns he had observed in the previous two attacks, General Hollingsworth correctly guessed that the main enemy effort would come on the morning of 11 May.[61] Accordingly, he planned eighteen B52 boxes (target sets for threeship missions) and almost two hundred tactical air strikes to support the besieged defenders. Armed with his air support plan and intelligence reports, Hollingsworth again flew to Saigon to speak with General Abrams at MACV headquarters. He convinced Abrams that the enemy main attack on An Loc was coming and that the ARVN could not hold without maximum air support. General Abrams agreed and promised to send him everything he needed for the battle when the next assault began.[62]

On 10 May, the enemy continued the pattern from the previous day, with heavy shelling and limited ground probes throughout the day. Hollingsworth chose this time to send Colonel Miller out. Miller had been fighting the battle night and day since early April and was near exhaustion. Since he was slated to assume command of a brigade in the 101st Airborne Division at Fort Campbell, Kentucky, Hollingsworth replaced him with Col. Walter Ulmer, a West Pointer who had arrived at Lai Khe in early May. After a flurry of briefings at TRAC, at 5:30 a.m. on the tenth, Ulmer was flown into An Loc by helicopter; as he got off, Colonel Miller got on. Ulmer arrived just as things started to go badly for the defenders.

With the increase in artillery and ground probes, Hollingsworth became more convinced that the enemy's main attack would come the next day. Accordingly, he readjusted the eighteen B-52 boxes he had already planned and added seven more. That afternoon he once again called Abrams, advising him that the main attack would start the next morning and requesting that he be allocated one B52 strike every 55 minutes for the next 25 hours beginning at 5:30 a.m., 11 May. The MACV commander agreed, and Hollingsworth's planners quickly drew up plans for their use and transmitted them through channels to the 7th Air Force planners at Tan Son Nhut Air Base in Saigon.

Just as Hollingsworth had predicted, the attack began at 5:00 a.m. on 11 May with an opening NVA artillery barrage. During the next twelve hours, the city was struck by ten thousand rounds of enemy indirect fire. Under this artillery cover, the NVA attacked from the north and northwest. The North Vietnamese attacks, supported by tanks, were successful in forging two salients in the ARVN lines, almost bisecting the ARVN defensive perimeter. The fighting was intense and the ARVN defenders were close to the breaking point on several occasions.

Seeing that the situation in An Loc was going sour quickly, Hollingsworth declared a tactical emergency and put out the call for all available air support. Everything in the air headed for An Loc. Air force, navy, and marine aircraft made rapid turnarounds after expending their ordnance to get back to their bases, where aircraft handlers loaded all available ordnance to allow them to rush back to the An Loc area to support the defenders. The airspace over the city was extremely crowded as fighter-bombers, AC-130 gunships, Cobra attack helicopters, and B-52s vied for position to place ordnance on the attackers. Skillful coordination by the advisers working with the air force forward air controllers made maximum use of all available air assets.

The most effective weapons in Holly's arsenal were the B-52s. Wave after wave of the big bombers struck the area surrounding the city; they were a tremendous morale booster for the defenders, who could readily see the effects of the strikes. The American advisers requested that the strikes be brought closer to the South Vietnamese perimeter, and several of them were moved to as close as eight hundred meters to the ARVN positions.[63] This air support, flown in the face of some of the most severe antiaircraft fire ever encountered in South Vietnam, broke the NVA attack, enabling the ARVN forces to stabilize their lines and eventually to reduce both of the salients the North Vietnamese had formed in the ARVN defenses.

In one instance, South Vietnamese forces captured an NVA soldier who said that his regiment had been ordered into the craters of an earlier B-52 strike, thinking that lightning would not strike twice in the same place. The results of the interrogation were called in to Hollingsworth, who called for a strike on the original target. Later, he said, "I'm so proud of that strategic air force. . . . That crew diverted the strike in 20 minutes, put it in . . . and destroyed that whole damn regiment, right in the same holes where they had gone to reorganize when I'd missed them in the morning."[64] This might seem a bit bloodthirsty, but Hollingsworth was exultant that the enemy had been stopped just sixty-five miles from Saigon. He was in his element, leading men in desperate battle against an enemy that was finally out in the open. It was indeed the war he came to fight.

At a commander's conference in Saigon on 12 May, he told General Abrams, "I can't think of a better place to destroy the enemy outfits than right here [An Loc], if we can maintain enough strength in there to keep them out so that they can be killed by firepower. I like to think that in this type of conflict the answer to the problem is instant decisions by the man with all the resources who is sitting looking at the battle, followed by creation of all the violence that can be created instantaneously and maintain it continuously until the battle subsides to where you can get by with less."[65] In this case, Hollingsworth was that man.

The heavy shelling of An Loc would continue unabated for the next three days, but the ground attacks decreased in frequency, intensity, and duration. There were only two more significant attempts to breach the ARVN perimeter between the eleventh and the fifteenth, and both efforts were blunted by the everpresent B52 strikes; the most significant activity was at 1:45 a.m. on 14 May when the South Vietnamese observed troop movement to the west and southwest; at the same time, tank fire was received from the west. The enemy may have been preparing for another go at the ARVN perimeter, but three timely B-52 strikes eliminated this threat.

By nightfall on 15 May, it appeared that the NVA forces had called off their attack and had withdrawn farther into the surrounding rubber plantations. Hollingsworth concluded that the South Vietnamese had weathered what turned out to be the North Vietnamese high tide during the fight for An Loc. A triumphant Hollingsworth reported to Abrams that "the enemy had lost his capability for further offensive actions in Binh Long Province."[66] The shelling continued, but there were no more large-scale attacks against the An Loc defensive perimeter.

By the end of May, although the battle of An Loc was not over, the tide had turned in favor of the defenders. Hollingsworth had employed 297 sorties of tactical air support on 11 May and approximately 260 sorties on each of the following four days. The around-the-clock air strikes had taken a horrendous toll on the NVA forces; ARVN intelligence later estimated that the NVA forces attacking An Loc sustained ten thousand casualties in April and May.[67] The North Vietnamese had reached their culminating point and they were not able to mount another large-scale attack on An Loc in 1972.

In early June, the ARVN cleared the center of the city of most enemy resistance and began to expand the area controlled by friendly units. Lieutenant General Minh was able to send reinforcements into An Loc and started to withdraw the much-battered 5th ARVN Division. In mid-June, Hollingsworth flew into An Loc, accompanied by Sir Robert Thompson, a British counterinsurgency expert who served as special adviser to President Nixon. When Col. Tran Van Nhut, the Binh Long Province chief, showed him the NVA tanks that had been destroyed in the city, Thompson replied that An Loc was the biggest victory in the post–World War II era, far exceeding the battle of Dien Bien Phu.[68] That may have been hyperbole, but it was clear that the ARVN had won a great victory. Holly told a reporter that day, "I would think the enemy is fully aware of their total disaster. Two and two-thirds division [of enemy troops] is one helluva rent to pay for twenty-five percent of a small inconsequential province capital for less than thirty days' occupancy."[69]

On the sixteenth of June, Hollingsworth again flew into the city, this time accompanied by Lieutenant General Minh. On the way to the 5th ARVN Division headquarters to talk with General Hung, Hollingsworth stopped in front of the 1st Airborne Brigade headquarters. There he pinned Silver Stars on Lt. Col. Art Taylor, senior adviser to the airborne, and Col. Tran Van Nhut, the inspirational Binh Long Province chief. Both Taylor and Nhut were overcome with emotion; it was a moving moment shared by the warriors who had played such key roles in the defense of An Loc.

Breaking the Siege

Two days later, South Vietnamese president Nguyen Van Thieu declared the siege of An Loc broken. The battle for the city was over. The continuous shelling, estimated at more than 78,000 rounds during the two-month period, had reduced the city to almost total ruins.[70] The ARVN defenders had sustained 5,400 casualties, 2,300 of whom were either dead or missing. As one adviser later described it, "The graves, burned out vehicles, and the rubble were mute testimony to the intensity of the battle that had been fought there."[71] Nevertheless, the city of An Loc remained in ARVN hands. In spite of the costs, the defenders and their advisers, with the help of American tactical airpower, had decisively defeated three of the finest divisions in the North Vietnamese Army and held the city against overwhelming odds.

No one who fought at An Loc will disagree that Hollingsworth made the difference in the outcome of the desperate fighting. As the battle developed, Hollingsworth orbited over the battlefield in constant communication with all the advisers on the ground, encouraging both them and their South Vietnamese counterparts.

In a letter to Hollingsworth on 17 July 1972, Lt. Col. Art Taylor, senior adviser to the airborne brigade, said, "Your daily contacts, dispensing combat assets and reports on the big picture . . . boosting our morale by your presence, were often the only bright spot during many otherwise gloomy days."[72] These sentiments were echoed by Capt. Mike McDermott, another airborne adviser, whose experience with the general during the battle was shared by all the advisers who took part in the battle on the ground. Hollingsworth, McDermott wrote, "seemed to be where the fighting was the heaviest, encouraging and guiding, pumping up and promising the air support that was essential to survive in that terrible place. He was the man who kept the show together . . . I am absolutely sure General Hollingsworth made the difference between life and death for me personally. I, and every other American advisor that I knew, respected and loved him."[73] McDermott was not wrong; Hollingsworth was the difference between victory and defeat. As Gen. Phillip B. Davidson observed, "A lot of people deserve credit for saving An Loc, but Jim Hollingsworth stands at the head of the list."[74] Had Holly not encouraged the defenders during the darkest hours and made sure that the massive volume of airpower, particularly B-52s, essential for the survival of the garrison kept coming and that it was delivered when and where it was most needed, the city would have fallen to the North Vietnamese Army. It was Holly's finest hour.

On 9 July, the euphoria over the victory at An Loc evaporated when Brig. Gen. John Tallman, Holly's deputy, and three of his staff officers landed in An Loc by helicopter. The helicopter lifted off and the party ran for the cover of the nearest bunker. However, an NVA artillery shell landed in the middle of the group, killing three Americans and one Vietnamese, and mortally wounding General Tallman. Two advisers (the author included), who had met the general's party when it landed, were also wounded. The general and the two other wounded officers on the ground were evacuated by helicopter to 3rd Field Hospital in Saigon, where the general died on the operating table.[75]

Hollingsworth was devastated by the loss of his deputy and the others. General Hollingsworth had just promoted General Tallman a week before the tragic incident. Holly had to call Tallman's wife and give the devastating news. Lt. Col. Stanley Kuick was the TRAC chief of staff and was due for promotion to colonel. Maj. Peter Bentson was assistant chief of staff for operations, and 1st Lt. John Todd was aide to General Tallman and the son of Col. John Todd, deputy commander of the 1st Aviation Brigade at Long Binh, twelve miles north of Saigon. General Hollingsworth was very close to all these men and this was a heavy blow, coming on the heels of the great victory at An Loc.

Despite the tragic loss of Tallman and the others, Hollingsworth had found the "war he came to fight." The reputation that had been somewhat tarnished by reports in the media during his first tour in Vietnam was rebuilt. He had taken an army no one thought could fight and taught it to hold out against all the North Vietnamese regulars in some of the bloodiest fighting of the war. He had performed magnificently and stopped the enemy on the approach to Saigon.

Aftermath

After the battle, it was discovered that Hollingsworth had been in considerable pain as he carried out his duties at TRAC. During the course of the fight in Binh Long, Holly had sustained damage to his right eye. He kept his own counsel, refusing to make any concessions to his injury while the battle still raged in An Loc. However, with the battle over, he went to see an army ophthalmologist in Saigon. The doctor determined that he had a 90 percent detached retina, more than likely from the concussion of one of the many near-miss antiaircraft shells that exploded around him as he was orbiting over the battle. The doctor made arrangements for Holly to be admitted to Walter Reed immediately. That was on the afternoon of 31 August. The next morning the South Vietnamese presented Hollingsworth with their third-highest award, and that afternoon he boarded a plane for the United States. Upon arrival at Andersen Air Force Base outside Washington, DC, he was transported to Walter Reed, where he was immediately admitted. He stayed at Walter Reed until 22 December. He underwent three operations, which left him with limited sight in his right eye. The old warrior knew that his career was most likely over.

While he was in the hospital convalescing, Holly was visited by General Abrams, who had returned to the United States in June 1972 to become the army chief of staff. Abrams told Hollingsworth that he was going to send him to Fort Sam Houston (Texas) to rest up for a few months. Holly replied that he would probably lose his eye and was thinking about retiring. Abrams told him, "I'll tell you what to do. You don't tell me. I'd rather have you with one eye than most people with two. You keep your mouth shut, you son of a bitch, because I am going to give you that tactical army command in Korea and promote you to lieutenant general. Now you go down there and get rested up, you sorry bastard."[76] The two old soldiers parted company. An ecstatic Hollingsworth went to Fort Sam Houston in March 1973 as ordered, and eventually his eye healed. While under the doctor's care at Fort Sam Houston, he was initially assigned as special assistant to the commander at Headquarters Fifth Army at Fort Sam Houston. Then he was named deputy commanding general of Fifth Army and deputy commander for reserve forces for the southern area until he received orders for Korea. On 1 July 1973, he was promoted to lieutenant general and shortly thereafter departed Fort Sam Houston for his new assignment.

8

Command in Korea

Korea

The United States had long been involved on the Korean Peninsula, dating back to World War II. When that war was over, the Japanese in Korea surrendered to US forces in the south and to Soviet forces in the north. The 1943 Cairo Declaration had provided for a reunified Korea, but the Cold War that quickly developed in the postwar years resulted in the establishment of two separate governments in Korea. In the South, US-backed Syngman Rhee, a staunch anti-Communist, won the first presidential election of the newly proclaimed Republic of Korea (ROK) in May 1948. That same year, a former anti-Japanese guerrilla and Communist activist, Kim Il-Sung, was appointed premier of the Democratic People's Republic of Korea in September. Both sides began campaigns for unification of Korea under their control.

On 25 June 1950, Kim Il-Sung's forces invaded South Korea, resulting in a bitter three-year war. The Soviet Union and China backed the regime in Pyongyang, which hoped to reunify the country by force of arms. The US rushed troops to support the South Koreans and barely avoided disaster in the early days of fighting. When the Soviets boycotted the United Nations, resolutions were passed authorizing an international intervention in the civil war. Under US leadership, UN forces from fifteen nations and South Korea pushed the North Koreans back and attacked to the Yalu

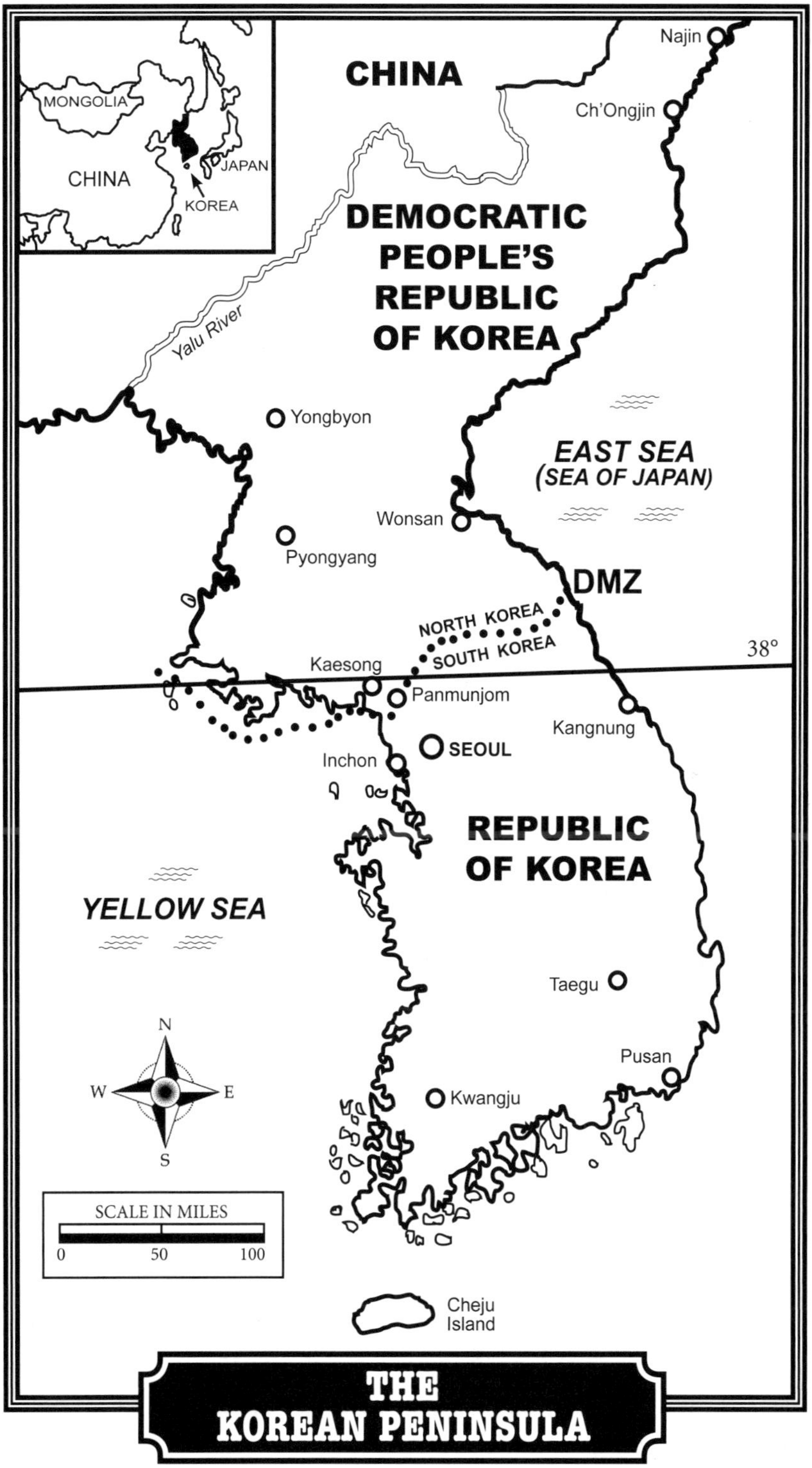

THE KOREAN PENINSULA

River, which resulted in the commitment of Chinese ground troops that forced the US forces to withdraw toward the south. Eventually, the war resulted in a bloody stalemate along the 38th parallel. The armistice in 1953 effectively split Korea along the original demarcation line, forming a Demilitarized Zone (DMZ) meant to separate the two forces. However, there was no formal peace treaty and the two Koreas remained technically at war from that point forward.

As Don Oberdorfer points out, "The battle for Korea firmly established the cold war and brought the Korean peninsula to the center of global attention."[1] As the years went by, Korea continued to be one of the most important fronts in the Cold War, and the United States stationed troops there to support the Seoul government and ensure that North Korea did not attack the South.

In 1960, a student uprising resulted in the ouster of President Rhee. What followed was a period of political instability in Seoul. In May, Gen. Park Chung-Hee seized power and took over as president. Park was criticized for his ironhanded rule, but under his tenure, the South Korean economy prospered.

Meanwhile, tensions remained high between North Korea and South Korea. The United States remained committed to providing support for South Korea to defend against any attack by North Korea. With the withdrawal of US troops from Vietnam in 1973, Korea became the main focus for US anti-Communist efforts in the Pacific region.

I Corps Group

This was the situation in July 1973 when Hollingsworth assumed command of the I Corps (ROK/US) Group, which at the time was the largest combined field army in the world. Consisting of some 185,000 Korean and American soldiers, it was organized into thirteen divisions. Hollingsworth's new command was deployed along 151 miles of highly volatile frontier between North and South Korea and included the most critical terrain leading to the heartland of South Korea and its capital city of Seoul.

The command that Hollingsworth was taking over was a unique headquarters. It was a totally integrated staff with somewhere between 60 and 80 percent Korean personnel. His deputy was a Korean major general. His chief of staff was an American brigadier general. His deputy chief of staff was a Korean colonel. His chief of operations was a Korean brigadier general. His chief of intelligence was an American colonel. His chief of supply and logistics was an American with a Korean deputy. Wherever there was a Korean in a key slot, the deputy was an American; wherever there was an American in a key slot, the deputy was Korean. Hollingsworth's assigned forces in the corps group included one US division, the 2nd Infantry Division, and twelve South Korean divisions.

As Holly prepared to take command, the situation on the peninsula was very tense; two tunnels had just been discovered under the DMZ, and Kim Il-Sung of North Korea was making a visit to China amid speculation that he was seeking support for another invasion south.

Shortly after assuming command, South Korean president Park Chung-Hee visited Hollingsworth at his quarters and asked, "Are you going to do the same thing here that you did in Vietnam?" After signing the Paris Peace Accords in January 1973, the United States had withdrawn all troops from South Vietnam. Park was insinuating that the United States had abandoned its ally in Saigon, and by his question, Park was wondering whether it would do the same thing to South Korea. Holly, fully understanding Park's implication, emphatically responded, "I'm here to fight and die to save your country. That's what I'm going to do."[2]

Hollingsworth very quickly established a close relationship with President Park. In retrospect, this seems a bit strange since there was a US ambassador and an army four-star general in charge of all US troops in Korea. Perhaps the South Korean president appreciated the energy that the new commander brought to his mission to assist the South Koreans in the defense of their nation.

At the time, it appeared that the departure of US forces from Vietnam earlier in 1973 had emboldened the North Koreans, who were making noises about launching an attack south. At least one journalist opined, "That may have been the only reason that he [Hollingsworth] got the job. They [the leadership in Washington] finally realized that they needed someone who'd fight."[3] Whether that was true or not, Hollingsworth was there and he was prepared to fight if necessary to save South Korea.

Making good on his promise to defend Korea proved more difficult than Hollingsworth had anticipated. When he arrived in-country, Hollingsworth found a situation not much to his liking. The US Army, just coming out of Vietnam, was in poor shape; more than ten years of war in Southeast Asia had effectively broken it. This was particularly true in Korea, where the American troops were demoralized, did not appear to be that well trained, and seemed ill prepared to prevent any North Korean attack.

Hollingsworth traveled all over the country trying to get a feel for the state of his new command. He visited an army ammunition depot shortly after his arrival and found some 3,000 8-inch artillery shells, but only about 100 fuses. A closer look at the ammunition in the Corps Group revealed a shortage of 156,000 fuses for 155-mm and 8-inch artillery shells throughout the command. Shells without fuses are virtually worthless in combat. Elsewhere, he found Honest John rockets with corroded tail fins that rendered the weapons unserviceable and inoperable. In general, Hollingsworth observed what he thought was a general state of unreadiness.

However, what stunned Hollingsworth more than the poor status of weapons and equipment was what he saw as a completely inadequate defense plan. The mission of the US Army in Korea was to defend the nation and its thirty-seven million citizens from any North Korean invasion. This problem was exacerbated by the location of the nation's capital, with its population of nine million, which was just twenty-five miles south of the DMZ.

For three years, the North Koreans had been increasing their strength near the DMZ, while moving air bases farther south and increasing the southern operations of their sea patrols into areas that were previously the domain of the Korean Navy. They had also dug in hardened artillery positions close to the DMZ. To Hollingsworth, these actions were indicators that at some point the North Koreans planned to attack South Korea.

By this time, the North Korean Army had grown to more than 408,000 troops, the fourth-largest among the world's Communist armies; it was an efficient, well-trained, highly disciplined force that was undergoing modernization. It had twenty-three infantry divisions, fourteen of which were positioned from east to west along the DMZ. This was a formidable enemy that confronted Hollingsworth as he surveyed the war plans he inherited when he assumed command.

Changing the Plan

The defensive plan in place when Hollingsworth arrived in Korea called for US and ROK forces to fall back on successive delay lines to the Han River, which bisects the capital city of Seoul. There, the final line of defense was to be held against any further North Korean advance to the south. To Hollingsworth, this approach was nonsense—a classic no-win situation. He believed that even if the North Koreans could not physically attack Seoul, they would destroy it by long-range fires. With the acquiescence and assistance of President Park, Hollingsworth, borrowing an old football adage that "the best defense is a good offense," developed a plan for the defense of Seoul and the rest of Korea by going on the offensive.

Holly put his planners to work to develop the plan in detail. They started with an extensive study of weather, terrain, rates of fire, and reinforcement times. Staff planners studied the weather for decades back to estimate the chances of cloud cover that might hinder air support. Intelligence analysts focused on Kim Il-Sung's philosophy, tactics, and capabilities.

The plan that evolved was very offensive in nature. Upon receiving warning that the North Koreans were moving south, Hollingsworth planned to strike them preemptively as they massed on the plains for an attack south. The new plan called for a forward defense that focused on destroying the attackers as far forward as possible using massed firepower from artillery and airpower. Accordingly, Hollingsworth moved the bulk of his artillery forward to just short of the southern edge of the DMZ. He moved two brigades of the US 2nd Division with orders to seize Kaesong, the most important city in the southern part of North Korea, in case of attack from the north.

Prior to Holly's arrival, it was thought that the main enemy avenue of approach would be the Chorwon-Uijongbu corridor in the central sector of the country; Holly thought the enemy main attack would come in the Kaesong-Munsan corridor farther west, and that was where he planned to destroy the North Korean attack before it could gain any momentum. The plan was built around strong, fortified positions that could withstand enemy indirect fire and that would "force the enemy to fight where we want him to fight, then [we can destroy] his offensive capability with massive firepower—artillery, tactical air and B52s."

Hollingsworth had thirty-three artillery battalions at his disposal to provide massed fires on any attacking army. When a reporter asked Holly why he had thirty-three battalions, he replied that he "had to do one better than I did in WWII some 25 years ago when I laid 32 battalions on 22 Tiger Royals [tanks]." He planned to have all thirty-three battalions fire a time on target (TOT, an artillery technique in which multiple artillery units are targeted to land on one target at exactly the same time) on the North Koreans as they crossed the DMZ.

Once the massive use of US and ROK long-range firepower stopped the North Korean advance north of Seoul, then US and ROK forces would launch a powerful offensive counterpunch to finish off the enemy. Hollingsworth was crystal clear about what he planned to do; he wanted to make sure that the North Koreans knew what was planned for them so they did not "miscalculate" and start a new war. Explaining the plan to South Korean president Park, Hollingsworth reassured him that "we're not going to give up one inch of your precious land."[4]

While Park was pleased with Hollingsworth's new plan, it was not as popular in many quarters within the administration back in Washington. Hollingsworth's superior, Gen. Richard Stilwell, had long been constrained by political considerations imposed by the White House. The administration was more interested in restraining the South Koreans from attacking north than it was worried about the North Koreans attacking south. The prevailing policy regarding planning for the defense of the peninsula was not to give the South Koreans any plan that was offensive in nature. The State Department was concerned that Holly and his offensive outlook might entice the South Koreans into attacking north. For example, when a tunnel under the DMZ was discovered, there was some talk in the State Department as to whether it might have been built by the South Koreans at Hollingsworth's urging. The State Department wanted to downplay the North Korean threat. The fear was that the South Koreans would get over-adventuresome and involve the United States in a war. Part of this effort was to keep certain information about the true capabilities of North Korea from the South Koreans. The thinking was that if the South Koreans were privy to all the intelligence on the North Koreans, they would press the United States for more weapons and equipment. Hollingsworth did not see it this way; he was fully committed to total cooperation with the South Koreans in defense of their homeland.

Implementing the New Plan

Hollingsworth did not let the State Department outlook bother him and threw himself into the task at hand. His sense of urgency was felt throughout his command. He was very demanding of his US and ROK commanders down to the battalion level, never allowing them more than two nights a month with their families, and never on weekends. He was just as hard on himself as on his commanders, taking only eight days of leave in two and a half years; his wife lived in Seoul but got to see him only a few hours a week because he spent every night in his forward command post.

Hollingsworth seemed to be everywhere at once as he flew around the country at top speed, usually at treetop level, overseeing training and unit redeployments to conform to the new plans. He spent a lot of time with the US 2nd Infantry Division. Its flamboyant commander, Maj. Gen. Henry "Hank" Emerson—the "Gunfighter," as he was known—and Hollingsworth were kindred spirits and formed a strong bond. Together, Hollingsworth and Emerson developed a demanding training program, including maneuvers in which the US troops focused on operating at night. They also placed an emphasis on cold-weather maneuvers.

Since most of the troops in I Corps were Korean, Hollingsworth was very active in visiting Korean units. He made frequent inspection trips and visited with as many troops as possible. Addressing groups of Korean soldiers, he stressed his short-war strategy and exhorted the Korean troops, saying that they would have to be fit in order to be able to turn back the North Koreans if they attacked. He always closed by saying, "Those that can do it will enjoy destroying the enemy while those who aren't fit will regret that they couldn't savor the victory."[5]

Holly was very impressed with his South Korean troops. He was fond of saying that a Korean division was equal to a US light infantry division and could hold off three Soviet infantry divisions. He said the Korean soldiers were "the toughest little guys you've ever seen in your life."

Despite their capabilities as fighters, the South Korean units had some deficiencies: they needed more secure communications equipment, more air defense weapons, newer artillery and more modern ammunition, and better tank ammunition. However, as far as physical fitness, alertness, readiness, and leadership, Hollingsworth thought they were "tops."

As he traveled around Korea, he developed great relations with the South Korean people. When he visited Korean units, he made a point of meeting with local dignitaries and factory owners in the area. Hollingsworth was too difficult for the Koreans to pronounce, so they called him "Ho Lim Su," which roughly translates to "Dignified Tiger in the Forest."

As Hollingsworth implemented his new plan, it proved to have an unexpected impact. Because the US and Korean forces now planned to defend far forward as close to the DMZ as possible, this opened up thousands of acres of previously unused land that had been reserved for military use. President Park directed the Korean Department of Agriculture to come up with a plan to cultivate these lands. In twelve months, that land was under cultivation. Additionally, a reforestation program was started that resulted in the planting of fifteen million to twenty million pine trees in a former fallow area that had been denuded for firewood.

The new plan also called for a number of new roads meant to increase the mobility of the US and South Korean troops. These roads were a boon to the economies of the areas in which they were built. Additionally, Hollingsworth made friends with Korean farmers, planting trees and lending them soldiers to help with the annual harvest. Vietnam had taught him that you do not win a war in a foreign country if you do not win the support of the people. A Korean official remarked, "Hollingsworth tells us he'll die for us and we believe him."[6]

In September 1974, fully engrossed in his duties in Korea, Hollingsworth had to deal with two personal losses. First, his beloved mother passed away, and shortly thereafter so did Army Chief of Staff Gen. Creighton Abrams, who died of cancer. Holly returned to the United States for the funerals. He was asked to serve as one of the honorary pallbearers at the funeral of his old friend Abrams.[7]

Hollingsworth returned to Korea and renewed his breakneck work schedule, which continued without letup. As 1974 came to an end, the general watched helplessly as the situation in South Vietnam rapidly deteriorated. The South Vietnamese forces had acquitted themselves very well against the North Vietnamese troops in the year after US forces departed in March 1973. However, when the North Vietnamese launched a multidivision attack against Phuoc Long, the South Vietnamese forces fought poorly and were routed. Seizing the moment, the North Vietnamese launched a major large-scale offensive, with the initial target of Ban Me Thuot in Darlac Province. As a result of poor leadership and a number of other factors, the entire province fell in a matter of days. The North Vietnamese stepped up their timetable, and after wiping out the better part of a South Vietnamese corps in central Vietnam, they launched a major attack from Quang Tri in the north toward Da Nang, South Vietnam's second-largest city. The South Vietnamese forces fell apart, and fifty-five days after the initiation of the new offensive, South Vietnam unconditionally surrendered.

In April 1975, on a television in his office in Korea, Hollingsworth watched with helpless anger as the North Vietnamese tanks crashed through the gates of the Presidential Palace. Holly had helped halt the enemy's Easter Offensive, and he thought the South Vietnamese forces could have prevailed in 1975 if the United States had provided the support that President Richard Nixon had promised South Vietnamese president Nguyen Van

Thieu. He believed that the United States had sold out our allies and was disgusted at the outcome of a war in which we had lost 58,000 lives only to abandon our allies when they needed us most. Hollingsworth, in his usual blunt fashion, remarked to one reporter when asked about the fall of Saigon, "We should have blown the living shit out of them [the North Vietnamese] until they quit."[8]

President Park also watched the fall of Saigon. He again asked Hollingsworth whether the United States was going to abandon Korea as it did Vietnam. Hollingsworth replied that the United States had a mutual security pact with South Korea and would honor the agreement. Park said that the United States also had a treaty with South Vietnam and asked whether the United States would treat South Korea as it had done South Vietnam. Hollingsworth replied that he had come to Korea to help the South Koreans defend themselves and that he would fight and die with the South Korean people if he had to. He told Park, "I just want you to know that I am totally convinced that we will live up to our treaty in the case of Korea."[9] Park was reassured by Hollingsworth's words.

That the United States would not withdraw as it had in Vietnam was a continual theme in his talks with the Koreans. The fall of Indochina to the Communists led to increased fear of hostilities in Korea, and Hollingsworth tried to rally Korean morale with his continued promise to destroy any North Korean attack in "nine days of violence." He told one group of ROK Marines, "Every American here is going to fight and die with his counterpart." He pledged, "If anything happens out here, I am, by God, going to bring you all the ammo and all the firepower you need."[10]

At the same time he was encouraging and reassuring the South Koreans, Hollingsworth continued his efforts to get influential senior officers back in the States to understand what he was trying to do in Korea. In a March 1975 letter to Maj. Gen. Donn A. Starry, commander of the Armor Center at Fort Knox, Kentucky, Hollingsworth wrote, "Here in Korea, we are faced with the problem . . . : how to win decisively and quickly though outnumbered. My answer is to defeat the cheap part of communism—his manpower—with the cheap part of the free world—our munitions. I intend to obliterate him before he can close with the friendly front line elements." He acknowledged that "there are skeptics who seem to accept the fact that we are outnumbered. To them, attempts to redress unfavorable balances in combat power need not be taken seriously and our being outnumbered, outgunned and under supported is the natural order of things."

He closed by saying, "We have got to turn that line of thinking around. If we do that, we can win."[11]

Hollingsworth invited Secretary of Defense James Schlesinger to visit Korea. While the secretary was there, the general briefed him on the new plan. Schlesinger was impressed and said that Hollingsworth could have two weeks to get the war over if the North Koreans attacked. Hollingsworth later recalled that he "told him [the Secretary] that I didn't need the extra time, but it was nice to have a cushion."[12]

Throughout 1975, Hollingsworth continued to push his staff on the refinement of the Korean defense plan. He also continued to talk to the press. He told one reporter, "I frankly feel that Kim Il Sung [the North Korean president] knows our capability and he's not likely to want any of what I have laid out for him. But if he does, it will be an honor and a privilege to deliver some of it."[13] He told another reporter that he did not know what the North Koreans planned to do, but "whatever they do, I hope they do it while I'm here."[14] The North Koreans branded Hollingsworth "a war maniac," and some Americans wondered whether his bluster "was a deterrent or a provocation."[15]

Hollingsworth's aggressive style did not play well in Washington, and his bellicose and somewhat over-the-top rhetoric made him once again seem to some like an "unguided missile." However, not everyone in Washington felt that way; he and his plan received the notice and support of numerous high-ranking military officials and influential congressmen, including Sen. John Tower of Texas and Sen. John Stennis of Mississippi. Additionally, a few in the media were supportive; an article in the *New York Post* described him as "an inspirational leader and innovative strategist in an age of managerial generals."[16]

Hollingsworth's "hell-bent-for-leather" image was more than a little misleading. He was a good soldier and followed orders; he was also very adept at working well with the other senior officers in Korea who were less flamboyant. He read voraciously on politics, international relations, and sociology. However, that was not his public face, which was that of one who was always spoiling for a fight.

This perception seemed to be borne out in a January 1976 interview by Norman Pearlstine of the *Wall Street Journal*. In typical Hollingsworth fashion, he told Pearlstine that he could win any war in Korea in nine days. Holly was quoted as saying, "We'll need five days and five nights of real violence. Our firepower will have a tremendous impact on their ground troops, breaking their will to fight in addition to killing them. After that, we'll need four more days to tidy up the battlefield." The general took the reporter to a forward fortified observation post. He pointed to a broad valley that stretched in front of the position toward the DMZ and North Korea, saying, "This is my killing zone. If the Communists attack, they have to bring their tanks through here. And when they do, I will murder them."

In reporting the general's words, Pearlstine quoted one American military official in Seoul, who said, "Holly is the only general in the world who tells the enemy exactly what his plans are, but that has probably kept the North Koreans from miscalculating when evaluating our defenses."[17]

However, a number of observers were less enamored with Hollingsworth and his statements to the reporter. They believed that his "obsession with violence" was excessive even for a military man. They questioned whether his aggressiveness was appropriate for Korea or anywhere else in the world in the wake of the Vietnam War. Hollingsworth was a creature of World War II, when the enemy was clearly defined and violence was necessary to prevail in a no-holds-barred fight to the finish. In the era of limited war, Hollingsworth made some policy makers uneasy and they feared that his bellicose stance might actually entice the North Koreans to launch a preemptive attack. Even some of Holly's fellow generals were irritated with him about some of the comments he had made to reporters about the original Korean defense plan, which he had scrapped soon after taking command. He was essentially criticizing those generals who had gone before him on the Korean Peninsula.

The *Wall Street Journal* piece came out as Hollingsworth was nearing the end of his assignment at I Corps. He wanted to be reassigned to Europe, where he could advance his "short war" approach. If an assignment in Europe was not possible, then he would not have been disappointed to succeed General Stilwell as commanding general of all troops in South Korea. Either of those commands would have meant a promotion to four-star general.

Gen. Frederick C. Weyand, army chief of staff, was considering what to do with Hollingsworth when Pearlstine's article appeared in the *Wall Street Journal*. Shortly thereafter, he announced that Hollingsworth would be succeeded at I Corps by Lt. Gen. John H. Cushman, then commandant of the Army Command and General Staff College at Fort Leavenworth, Kansas. Cushman later said in an oral history done for the US Army Center of Military History that he "believed that, while Holly's departure for a well-deserved retirement had for some time been visualized, the stir cause by the piece [in the *Wall Street Journal*] had accelerated that departure."[18] After the article came out, Weyand met briefly with General Cushman and told him to get to Korea right away. The short time between the announcement of the change of command and Cushman's hurried departure for Korea seems to bear out Cushman's assessment of the situation. As one reporter noted, "They [the senior army leadership] decided they need a low profile guy instead of a gunslinger."[19]

"Hank" Emerson, by then commander of XVIII Airborne Corps at Fort Bragg, North Carolina, talked up Holly to get his fourth star and recommended that he be given command of Eighth Army in Korea. However, that was not to be.

The End of a Career

Notified of the accelerated date for the change of command, Holly announced that he would retire, saying, "After 35 years' proud service of my country, it's time to make room for someone else." Hollingsworth said his tour in Korea had been "the highlight" of his career. Never one to mince words, he said, "Because of building this new strategy, there's an honest-to-God defense of this country for the first time." In his typically outspoken fashion, he no doubt irritated some of his fellow general officers who had preceded him in Korea when he claimed that the plans he discarded when he arrived might have resulted in the loss of Seoul in any future war.[20]

The announcement of Holly's retirement caused much consternation among his fellow officers, some of whom, like Cushman, speculated that politics had something to do with the removal of the outspoken general. The announcement came at a time when he had come under some criticism for earlier bellicose statements; perhaps the *Wall Street Journal* interview was the straw that broke the camel's back.

Army officials at the Pentagon admitted that the timing of Holly's departure was "an unfortunate coincidence" but denied that Hollingsworth's retirement was anything but routine, noting that the general had stayed in Korea longer than the normal two-year tour of command. Still, it appeared that Hollingsworth was too "warlike" for the Pentagon and the White House. As one reporter put it, "To a nation still spiritually convalescent after Vietnam, his saber-rattling from Korea's DMZ was a jarring sound."[21] It did not help that former defense secretary James Schlesinger, who liked and supported the general, had been fired by the Ford administration just a few months before Hollingsworth announced his retirement.[22] With Schlesinger gone, Holly had no top cover.

Hollingsworth inspired intense loyalty among both Korean and American subordinates. Many among his staff had hoped he would be getting his fourth star and would eventually replace General Stilwell, the supreme commander of UN, US, and South Korean forces. However, that was not to be. Holly's impending departure "cast a pall" over the command. There was a feeling among many of his officers that a fighting general had been benched prematurely; one colonel told a reporter regretfully, "He would have made a fantastic, teaching, inspiring chief of staff."[23] One reporter, writing about Holly's retirement, quoted a Pentagon official, who said, "There aren't many jobs around for combat commanders like Holly. If there was a war, he would definitely get a promotion and a fourth star."[24] However, there was not a war and Hollingsworth had apparently reached the end of his usefulness to the army.

Hollingsworth, for his part, stoically accepted the decision by the army chief of staff. He said he had been prepared to serve on, but retirement came as no surprise. While there is no retirement age for general officers, the most senior posts are presidential appointments contingent on an appropriate vacancy. When he had been promoted to lieutenant general, Abrams had warned him that he might have to retire if there was not a four-start billet for him when he left command in Korea.[25] Apparently that was not in the cards, and Hollingsworth prepared to leave the army. He told a reporter that he would "hunt and fish and try lying in bed till 7 some morning to see what that was like."[26]

After two and a half years in Korea, Holly relinquished command of I ROK/US Corps to Lieutenant General Cushman on 12 February 1976 at Camp Red Cloud. At the change of command, General Stilwell said, "Our service together in Korea magnified my professional admiration for his peerless leadership, incomparable tactical skill and total dedication to mission. . . . We will sorely miss the presence of this complete soldier. But the echo of the footsteps and influence of James F. Hollingsworth will long endure on the Peninsula."[27] The Korean government awarded him the Order of National Security Merit, the first time an American had been so honored.

Hollingsworth could be justifiably proud of what he had accomplished in Korea. He received a congratulatory note from his old friend and commander Gen. William DePuy, who wrote in an August 1975 letter, "I really believe that you have made a bigger impact and done more good for your country and Korea than any other General Officer with the possible exception of General Ridgway when he turned the war around. What also pleases me is that your solution to the problem is a vivid illustration of what I am trying to inject into the doctrine of the US Army. As you know it is nothing new because it involves the concentration of overwhelming force at the point of decision."[28] This was high praise indeed from a man who did not routinely hand out praise of any kind.

Hollingsworth had left his mark on Korea and Korea had left its mark on Hollingsworth. During the course of his time in the country, he had become close friends with South Korean president Park Chung-Hee. As he prepared to leave for the United States, Hollingsworth promised Park that he would return every six months to visit and discuss South Korean defense strategy. That was a promise the American general kept until Park's death in 1979.

Holly's departure from Korea and pending retirement marked the end of a remarkable career. John Saar, in an article in the *Washington Post*, perhaps said it best when he described the general as a "defiant anachronism . . . a swash-buckling, kick-their-asses leader with courage and luck in copious measure; he has been shot at, shot down, wounded, decorated and usually victorious for 35 years . . . his life has been dedicated to warfare and the preparation for it. A professional." Further, "If GIs were fighting somewhere in the world, chances are better than even that Hollingsworth would get a fourth star and a new command. Instead he is headed for the bench to give peace a chance because the United States has run out of wars."[29]

On 18 February, Texas senator Lloyd Bentsen stood before the US Senate and said, "General Hollingsworth is, at 57, a legend within the US Army. He is a soldier's soldier who first demonstrated his capabilities in defending the Siegfried Line in 1944. His leadership then was as it remains today—complete, deeply respected, and capable of instilling confidence in all whom it touches . . . General Hollingsworth has served his nation well. It has made great demands of him, and he has risen to every challenge. I salute this distinguished Aggie, welcome him home to Texas, and wish him well in his future endeavors."[30] Senator Bentsen's speech praising Hollingsworth was printed in full in the Congressional Record, but as it turned out, the general's service to the nation was not over just yet.

9

Retirement

Upon his return to the United States, Lieutenant General Hollingsworth was delayed and assigned as special assistant to the army chief of staff. In March, Sen. Sam Nunn (D, GA) and the Armed Services Committee asked Hollingsworth to go to Europe to evaluate the capability and potential of US and NATO (North Atlantic Treaty Organization) forces to meet the threat of the Warsaw Pact in central Europe. Hollingsworth went to Europe as directed, but he did not like what he found when he got there. For example, in the course of a visit to an 8-inch artillery battalion, he asked the battalion commander how long it would take to get his ammunition and move to his initial defensive position. The battalion commander replied that it would take about four hours, so Holly told him to load out. It took the battalion three days, but it still did not get all of its ammunition out of the storage area, which consisted of old German bunkers without lights. Holly could see that the battalion was nowhere near ready for war. He found similar shortcomings everywhere he went, and he visited a lot of US installations throughout Europe.

When he examined the classified allied defense plans, he found them problematic. For example, the plan called for a German division to cross in front of the V US Corps to join the German corps located north of the American corps. If the plan had been executed, there would have been major problems as one division passed in front of others. In Holly's estimation, the plan was impractical and failed to account sufficiently for the attacking Soviet forces.[1]

Hollingsworth believed that the Soviets and their allies in the Warsaw Pact had achieved an "overwhelming" advance in conventional weapons such as tanks, artillery, and infantry fighting vehicles while the United States had been bogged down in Vietnam. They had positioned their forces to strike with little or no warning. According to Holly's assessment, the US forces in Europe were neither equipped nor adequately prepared for a surprise Soviet attack.

He returned to Washington, anxious to do what he could to remedy the situation. In July, he presented *The Hollingsworth Report: Central Europe Assessment* to the secretary of defense, the National Security Council, and the Senate and House Armed Services Committees. In the report, Hollingsworth said that US forces had to improve their "capability to respond quickly for the simple reason that the Soviets have the capability . . . to strike with little or no warning." He charged that US forces had survived too long "sitting on a credible strategic nuclear deterrent" but had "allowed our conventional capability to just drag along and just barely stay alive." What was needed, according to Hollingsworth, was a wholesale upgrading of US and NATO conventional capability to offset the advantage the Soviet Union and its allies had in tanks, artillery, and infantry. Hollingsworth closed his report with a recommendation for an add-on of $46 billion to the military appropriations bill to correct major deficiencies and enhance the capabilities of US forces in Europe. The report would prove to be very critical in the continuing debate about NATO capabilities in Central Europe.

With his assessment and subsequent report completed, General Hollingsworth retired in August 1976 after thirty-six years of service. He said at the time of his retirement that he planned to take time for hunting and fishing. He purchased a small ranch in Comfort, near San Antonio, and prepared for a life of leisure. However, he soon found, as he said, that "after being on call for 24 hours a day for 36 years, it's not easy to do nothing."[2] Having had a number of offers from government agencies and private research firms, he decided to go back to work, forming Hollingsworth Consultants, Inc., an aerospace consulting firm concerned with projects related to national security. He was also elected to the board of directors of one major corporation and served as a consultant to seven others. However, it was his role as a part-time consultant to Senator Nunn and the Senate Armed Services Committee that kept him busiest, shuttling back and forth between his office in Hurst and Washington, DC. Arnold Punaro, staff director for Senator Nunn's committee, remembered that Hollingsworth was immensely helpful to the senator on defense matters. Nunn put a great premium on Hollingsworth's objectivity and in-depth knowledge of military affairs, and he appreciated the general's unflinching willingness to critique the status quo, even when he had to do so against very senior generals and civilians in the Department of Defense.[3]

On 24 January 1977, the Senate Armed Services Committee published a report by Senator Nunn and Sen. Dewey Bartlett (R, OK) entitled *NATO and the New Soviet Threat*. As a consultant, Hollingsworth played a major role in the preparation of this document, which was based in large part on his earlier report on the capabilities of US forces in central Europe.

The Nunn-Bartlett study concluded that the "Soviet forces deployed in Eastern Europe now possess the ability to launch a potentially devastating conventional attack in Central Europe without warning." The report noted that the Soviets had expanded and modernized their ground forces and substantially increased their frontal aviation to enhance "the capability to wage successfully the kind of blitzkrieg called for in Soviet doctrine."[4] It was estimated that NATO forces in the Central Region would be confronted by five Soviet armies that could move directly to attack without reinforcement and sustain multiple axes of attack at rates of twenty to forty kilometers a day.

This new capability struck at the heart of the NATO alliance and its military and political weaknesses. Senators Nunn and Bartlett advocated for the development of NATO capability at the strategic nuclear, theater nuclear, and conventional levels sufficient to deter and, if necessary, defeat Soviet aggression with their newly revamped forces.

The Nunn-Bartlett report suggested a series of steps designed to produce that capability. Many of these mirrored the recommendations that Hollingsworth had made in his earlier assessment. First, on the political front, the report advocated a meeting of key NATO military and political leaders to find "ways to speed up the political decisions required to meet unexpected Warsaw Pact mobilization." On the military side, the report recommended specific measures meant to increase the capabilities of NATO military forces. First of all, the planning assumptions about prior warning time had to be drastically revised in light of the new Soviet capability. Second, NATO covering forces should be shifted to the east to "compel the Pact forces to deploy for major battle before they enter NATO territory."[5] Third, NATO forces should be provided with more artillery, antitank, and air defense systems. Fourth, ammunition stocks had to be drastically increased. Additionally, the combat readiness of deployed forces and command and control architectures had to be improved.

Effectively, the Senate Armed Services Committee had accepted Hollingsworth's recommendations for a buildup of the US Army in Europe and the concurrent revamping of the entire NATO defense arrangement. Although it did not happen overnight, the subsequent buildup of US forces and its NATO partners no doubt contributed greatly to the fall of the Berlin Wall, the demise of the Warsaw Pact, and the shortening of the Cold War.

Just before Senators Nunn and Bartlett finalized their report, Jimmy Carter was inaugurated as the thirty-ninth president of the United States on 20 January 1977. Early in his tenure in office, Carter told the press that he was thinking about bringing some American troops home from Korea. His plan was to pull out all US forces—ground and air—and to negotiate assurances from China and the Soviet Union that North Korea would not invade south. Hollingsworth, already retired by this time, thought this was incredibly shortsighted and naive. He believed that the defense of Korea was critical to the defense of Japan and the maintenance of stability in Northeast Asia. He did not trust the Soviets or the North Koreans and believed that removing US troops would possibly invite North Korea to invade South Korea. Hollingsworth testified to that fact before the Senate Armed Services Committee. He worked with Sens. Sam Nunn, John Glenn, and Gary Hart to keep the 2nd Division in Korea. In the end, although Carter did reduce the number of US troops in Korea, the president did not order the withdrawal of the 2nd Division.

In retirement, Holly continued to be an advocate for Korea. In May 1979, he was quoted in the *Korea Herald* saying, "It [Korea] is vital to the defense of the United States and members of the Free World. . . . The national interests of the United States in the Pacific and Northeast Asia are tied to the short warning, and little time will be available to react to possible assaults from North Korea against the Republic of Korea."[6] Holly returned to Korea in September 1979 for a visit with his old friend, President Park Chung-Hee, who received him like a returning national hero.

On 26 October 1979, Hollingsworth was stunned and saddened by the news that President Park had been assassinated. Park had been shot by the leader of the Korean Central Intelligence Agency, Kim Jae-Kyu. Hollingsworth also knew Kim and could only speculate on the motives behind the killing. Four days after Park's death, in an interview published by the *Fort*

Worth Star-Telegram, Hollingsworth opined that the threat of a Communist invasion of South Korea in the wake of Park's death was a distinct possibility. He said, "The assassination of Park was a great shock and personal loss to me. It will mean instability to all of Northeast Asia . . . I would not throw out the possibility of an attack from the North Koreans."[7] The North Koreans did not attack, but Hollingsworth continued to watch the situation closely.

Korea was not Hollingsworth's only area of interest during the later years of his retirement; he remained very active in military affairs and was routinely sought out for his opinions on national defense. On 14 April 1983, he received a letter from Melvin Price (D, IL), House Armed Services Committee, inviting him to testify before the joint subcommittee hearings of the Research and Development and the Procurement Subcommittees of the House Armed Services Committee. Specifically, the purpose of these hearings was to continue the examination of the Soviet–Warsaw Pact threat to NATO's Allied Command Europe (ACE), Central Region, and the options available to the United States and NATO to redress the growing asymmetries in NATO–Warsaw Pact conventional military capabilities. Again, Hollingsworth's opinions and counsel were sought.

At the hearings, Hollingsworth provided his assessment of the situation in NATO, elaborating on his earlier European assessment and his observation of more current events. He discussed how he thought that an enemy attack would develop should the Soviets decide to launch an offensive in Europe. He argued for a strong forward defense and a vigorous targeting of the second echelon of the attacking forces. He said that he was encouraged by the many improvements to NATO defensive capabilities that he had observed, but he warned that such improvements might not be enough if the Soviets attacked. He finished his testimony by making a strong case for continuing to increase the credibility of NATO forward defense.[8]

In February of the following year, Hollingsworth published an article in *Armed Forces Journal* titled "Understanding the Conventional Umbrella." In that article, which echoed his testimony before the House Armed Services Committee, he wrote, "What we need now is a 'conventional umbrella' which negates Communist superiority in numbers and allows us to wage a successful conventional battle in selected locations throughout the world . . . it will do little good, however, for US forces to fight a successful conventional battle in Europe if Allied forces on the flanks are overwhelmed. The formation of a conventional umbrella leading to a strong conventional deterrence must be the goal of all of us in support of the SACEUR (Supreme Allied Commander Europe) and the Alliance. Full acceptance of that goal and participation by all member nations in support of SACEUR is needed now. A strong conventional defense is essential to deterrence."[9]

Hollingsworth continued to have a lot of influence on national defense issues. In January 1985, he was invited to attend a three-day conference in Washington with 140 top civilian and military leaders to prepare recommendations for the secretary of defense on force structure in Europe. Hollingsworth remained active in the defense policy arena, writing a number of articles about the defense of Europe, all the time keeping his eye on Korea.

In addition to his activities in the national defense arena, including service on several corporate boards in the defense industry, Hollingsworth was active in other areas. He was a member of the board of trustees at the Marine Military Academy in Harlingen, Texas, and was in great demand as a speaker at universities, high schools, civic clubs, commencements, and Masonic events.

In retirement, Hollingsworth was very involved in activities at his alma mater, Texas A&M. He was very active in Texas A&M development programs and personally endowed several scholarships. He was a member of the A&M Chancellor's 21st Century Council of Advisors and was an adviser to the president of Texas A&M University. More importantly, he routinely acted as an inspirational speaker and mentor with the Corps of Cadets. In an atmosphere that emphasized honor, courage, integrity, and selfless service, he was a perfect role model. His wartime record and garrulous manner won him both the cadets' admiration and affection. In talking with the cadets, he was in his element. He could no longer be with soldiers in uniform, but he could and did influence many of the cadets who would go on to lead soldiers, sailors, airmen, and marines in combat.

In one example of his relationship with the cadets, Hollingsworth was approached at a party near the A&M campus by a young man who was slated to be one of the senior leaders in the Corps of Cadets the following year. The young man requested to meet privately with the general to speak about a personal matter. Behind closed doors, the young man told Holly that he was from a very religious family and did not know how he could reconcile having to kill someone in war with his religious beliefs. Holly said that in 1942, he had asked God the same question, and "God told me to kill all the damned Germans I could and I did."[10] This was typical, over-the-top vintage Hollingsworth. He then explained to the young man about just wars and that sometimes you had to do things in war that were difficult. The young man said he understood, but he was also concerned that he would not be brave enough in battle, that he might be frightened. Hollingsworth told him that most sane humans felt that way, and if anyone told you different, "they were either crazy or lying." The general and the cadet continued to talk and the general was able to help the young man come to terms with his personal concerns. The cadet went on to take a Marine Corps commission, won all the awards at marine officer training, and served four years in the corps before leaving the service. Having served his country, the young man went on to be extremely successful in business and now gives back to the university in the same way that Holly sought to do. There are too many stories like this to recount; he was always approachable and would stop to talk with anyone he encountered on campus. He loved the students and provided an inspirational example of caring leadership and attention to duty. In his later years, the old warrior general in his inimitable fashion touched the lives of countless young men and women at Texas A&M.

In late 1988, Holly's wife, Nickie, became ill with cancer, and she died on 4 March 1989. Throughout Holly's military career, Nickie had been known as "Mrs. H," and she was loved and admired by all she came to know during the general's distinguished career. She had been a gracious hostess among their friends and the dignitaries of foreign countries. She was known for treating everyone, regardless of rank, with sincerity and respect. She had stood by the general from the very beginning and he felt her loss greatly.

Nickie was buried in the Fort Sam Houston National Cemetery. The remains of their son, Jamie, were removed from the Sanger Cemetery and reinterred alongside his mother at Fort Sam Houston.

Hollingsworth married his second wife, Janie Harris, on 24 March 1990 at the First United Methodist Church in Palm Harbor, Florida. He had known Janie for many years since she had been his secretary at the Pentagon. Later, Janie worked as personal secretary for Texas governor William Clements for eighteen years when he was an official in the Defense Department in the Pentagon, as well as at both his SEDCO Corporation office in Dallas and during two terms in the Texas state house. Holly and Janie were inseparable for the rest of their lives.

In 1994, Hollingsworth was inducted into the Corps of Cadets Hall of Honor at Texas A&M. This was a high honor from an institution that had meant so much to Hollingsworth. However, an even higher honor awaited him. On 10 September 1999, the Corps of Cadets and Texas A&M University honored one of its most famous alumni with the dedication of the statue mentioned in the introduction. It was a fitting honor for an old warrior who had come home to the place that played such an important role in molding him as a young man.

Epilogue

Lt. Gen. James F. Hollingsworth passed away quietly on 2 March 2010, Texas Independence Day, at the age of ninety-one. Janie had held a private vigil by his side for several days. He was buried with full military honors in Arlington National Cemetery on 20 May 2010. The funeral was attended by soldiers from all across the United States who had served with the general and wanted to pay their last respects to the old soldier. Additionally, there was a contingent of former South Vietnamese officers in full ARVN dress uniform. The flag covering the general's casket was presented to Janie by Secretary of Defense Robert Gates, who had previously served as president of Texas A&M University. At the reception following the interment, "Plug" Kendregan, Danger 79er's old friend from the Big Red One, regaled those in attendance with humorous tales of his time with the general in Vietnam. This was a fitting tribute from one of Holly's "little fellers"; it said volumes about how the old general was viewed by those with whom he had fought and served.

In death, he received tributes from many other quarters as well. Upon hearing of the general's death, Texas A&M president R. Bowen Loftin said, "Gen. Hollingsworth was unquestionably one of the most distinguished military officers ever produced by Texas A&M—as attested by the fact that a statue honoring him has been prominently placed in the Corps of Cadets quad, where thousands of current and former students have seen it and been inspired by the all-too-brief account of his long and valiant service to his country. Gen. Hollingsworth will be sorely missed."

One eulogy from the Army War College alumni magazine said, "LTG

'Holly' was a Soldier's Soldier. . . . He was no perfumed prince, nor a degreed dandy. . . . He was an old-fashioned General who could talk to Soldiers about something other than ice cream and mail. He spoke their language, often melting the tin ear of eager staff officers. On the other hand, as Chief of Army Legislative Liaison, he could sit at a Senate tea party, pushing the Army program with vigor and success. . . . Those of us privileged to serve with him salute him proudly and smartly. The saber has been sheathed."[1]

Perhaps the plaque on Hollingsworth's statue in the Corps of Cadets area at Texas A&M provides the best epitaph for the old soldier:

> He was revered by his troops and feared by the enemy as a warrior who was always on the scene in times of need or at times of immense peril. A man of character, honor and dignity, he gave a full measure of discipline to every aspect of his life, a role model and a motivator to all who knew and loved him. A great Texas Aggie!

In a last act of loyalty to the institution he so loved, the general left virtually his entire estate to the Texas A&M Foundation. His beloved Janie followed him in death on 9 May 2013, at the age of ninety-two. She was buried beside General Hollingsworth in Arlington Cemetery.

Even after his passing, Hollingsworth continued to be recognized for his service to the nation. In December 2014, a new exhibit opened at the Bastogne War Museum in Belgium. Hollingsworth was one of five Texas A&M graduates whose World War II service was highlighted in the exhibit, which was titled "From Texas to Bastogne, Texas Aggies Go to War."[2] He and the other honorees represented the twenty thousand Aggies that served in World War II. It was a fitting tribute to one of America's greatest soldiers.

In *The Generals*, journalist Tom Ricks wrote about Gen. George S. Patton, saying that "the modern American military probably is worse for not having a few senior commanders with a dose of Patton's dynamism and color in them."[3] His assessment of Patton holds true just as much for James Francis Hollingsworth. Holly was a dynamic and colorful individual made for war, and his like will probably never be seen again.

Appendix 1

James F. Hollingsworth, Lieutenant General, US Army, Awards and Decorations

United States

Distinguished Service Cross (awarded for action in World War II)
Distinguished Service Cross (awarded for action in Vietnam War)
Distinguished Service Cross (awarded for action in Vietnam War)
Army Distinguished Service Medal (awarded for action in Vietnam War)
Army Distinguished Service Medal (awarded for action in Vietnam War)
Army Distinguished Service Medal (awarded for action in Vietnam War)
Army Distinguished Service Medal (awarded for action in Vietnam War)
Silver Star (awarded for action in World War II)
Silver Star (awarded for action in World War II)
Silver Star (awarded for action in World War II)
Silver Star (awarded for action in World War II)
Legion of Merit with 2 OLC*
Soldier's Medal (awarded for action in World War II)
Distinguished Flying Cross (awarded for action in Vietnam War)
Distinguished Flying Cross (awarded for action in Vietnam War)
Distinguished Flying Cross (awarded for action in Vietnam War)
Bronze Star with Valor device and 3 OLC

Air Medal with Valor device and 37 OLC
Army Commendation Medal
Purple Heart with 5 OLC
American Defense Medal
Alaska Distinguished Service Medal
American Campaign Medal
European–African–Middle Eastern Campaign Medal
World War II Victory Medal
Army Occupation Medal (Germany)
National Defense Service Medal with OLC
Armed Forces Expeditionary Medal (Korea)
Republic of Vietnam Campaign Medal with "60" device
Vietnam Service Medal
Glider Badge
General Staff Identification Badge
Office of Secretary of Defense Identification Badge

Belgium

Fourragère and Croix de Guerre

Republic of Vietnam

National Order of Vietnam (Third, Fourth, and Fifth Class)
Distinguished Service Order First Class
Cross of Gallantry with Five Palms
Republic of Vietnam Civil Action Honor Medal with Palm

Republic of Korea

Order of National Security Tong-II
Order of Merit Chung Mu First Class

*Oak Leaf Cluster (OLC) authorized for subsequent awards of the same medal (e.g., Legion of Merit with 2 OLC = 3 awards of the Legion of Merit).

Appendix 2

Award Citations—Distinguished Service Cross

Distinguished Service Cross

James F. Hollingsworth
Lieutenant Colonel, U.S. Army

The President of the United States of America, authorized by Act of Congress, July 9, 1918, takes pleasure in presenting the Distinguished Service Cross to Lieutenant Colonel (Infantry) James Francis Hollingsworth (ASN: 0-34155), United States Army, for extraordinary heroism in connection with military operations against an armed enemy while serving with Headquarters, 2d Battalion, 67th Armored Regiment, in action against enemy forces on 11 April 1945, in Germany. Colonel Hollingsworth personally led, in a 1/4 ton truck, a Task Force of tanks and infantry for fourteen hours in a dash of seventy-one miles from Gr. Douren, Germany, to the Elbe River at Schonebeck, Germany. On three occasions during the day he went into towns with small forces mounted in 1/4 ton trucks and, by surprise, effected a complete surrender without bloodshed of the German garrisons. When stopped by a road block in Schonebeck, near a bridge, he continued to direct the fight, although he was wounded twice and barely able to walk. Only after the bridge had been blown and all hope for its capture had vanished did he consent to evacuation for his wounds. Colonel Hollingsworth's heroic actions and aggressive leadership were directly responsible for the accomplishments of the Task Force under his command and are in keeping with the highest traditions of the armed forces.

General Orders: Headquarters, Seventh U.S. Army, General Orders No. 646 (1945)
Action Date: 11 Apr 45
Service: Army
Rank: Lieutenant Colonel
Company: Headquarters
Battalion: 2d Battalion
Regiment: 67th Armored Regiment

Distinguished Service Cross

Second Award
James F. Hollingsworth
Brigadier General, U.S. Army

The President of the United States of America, authorized by Act of Congress, July 9, 1918 (amended by act of July 25, 1963), takes pleasure in presenting a Bronze Oak Leaf Cluster in lieu of a Second Award of the Distinguished Service Cross to Brigadier General James F. Hollingsworth (ASN: 0-34155), United States Army, for extraordinary heroism in connection with military operations involving conflict with an armed hostile force in the Republic of Vietnam, while serving with Headquarters, 1st Infantry Division. Brigadier General Hollingsworth distinguished himself by exceptionally valorous action during the period 5 November 1966 to 8 November 1966 while serving as Assistant Division Commander of the 1st Infantry Division. On 5 November 1966, three Special Forces units attacked what unexpectedly turned out to be a numerically superior Viet Cong force. Within minutes, General Hollingsworth was airborne over the battle area in his command and control helicopter. To gain an accurate knowledge of the fluid ground situation, he had his pilot fly repeated low level passes over the insurgent positions. During these reconnaissance passes, while receiving intense hostile fire, General Hollingsworth formulated stratagems for the maneuver of the ground units, ordered devastating air strikes and artillery barrages on the Viet Cong emplacements, and enabled them to repel the numerically superior Viet Cong force. On 8 November, one of his battalions engaged several Viet Cong Units. Immediately upon arriving at the scene, General Hollingsworth fearlessly moved about the area of conflict issuing directives, maintaining fire discipline, and encouraging the men to fight with renewed efforts. With complete disregard for his personal safety, he continuously exposed himself to the concentrated Viet Cong fire to coordinate all facets of the battle. His masterful and unerring battle strategy accounted for one of the most significant victories in the current conflict. Brigadier General Hollingsworth's extraordinary heroism and inspiring leadership were in keeping with the finest traditions of the military service and reflect great credit upon himself, the 1st Infantry Division, and the United States Army.

General Orders: Headquarters, U.S. Army, Vietnam, General Orders No. 590 (February 7, 1967)
Action Date: November 5–8, 1966
Service: Army
Rank: Brigadier General
Company: Headquarters
Division: 1st Infantry Division

Distinguished Service Cross

Third Award
James F. Hollingsworth
Brigadier General, U.S. Army

The President of the United States of America, authorized by Act of Congress, July 9, 1918 (amended by act of July 25, 1963), takes pleasure in presenting a Second Bronze Oak Leaf Cluster in lieu of a Third Award of the Distinguished Service Cross to Brigadier General James F. Hollingsworth (ASN: 0-34155), United States Army, for extraordinary heroism in connection with military operations involving conflict with an armed hostile force in the Republic of Vietnam, while serving with Headquarters, 1st Infantry Division. Brigadier General Hollingsworth distinguished himself by exceptionally valorous actions on 20 March 1967 while serving as Acting Commander, 1st Infantry Division when the artillery support base at Bau Bang came under intense enemy mortar attack a few hours after midnight. Taking off in his command helicopter, following a briefing on the situation, General Hollingsworth immediately flew to the besieged unit. Despite the devastating ground fire directed at his aircraft, he ordered his pilot to make repeated low level passes over the ravaged area while he dauntlessly reconnoitered it. Realizing that an insurgent ground assault was imminent, General Hollingsworth called for air strikes as he continued to expose himself to the hail of bullets streaking through the darkness. When flareships illuminated the battlefield, he located the Viet Cong assembly area and, ignoring his vulnerable position, guided the support aircraft in their bombing and strafing runs. At 0500 hours, the insurgents began their mass attack. Contemptuous of the grave dangers, General Hollingsworth flew directly over the assaulting force and adjusted artillery fire into the charging Viet Cong.

During the entire engagement, he continuously risked his own safety to best coordinate and direct the aggressive defense, which finally repulsed the fanatical enemy. Through his boundless courage and tactical ingenuity, he was instrumental in the defeat of the Viet Cong regiment, in which over 250 insurgents were killed. Brigadier General Hollingsworth's extraordinary heroism and devotion to duty were in keeping with the highest traditions of the military service and reflect great credit upon himself, his unit, and the United States Army.

General Orders: Headquarters, U.S. Army, Vietnam, General Orders No. 2075 (May 6, 1967)
Action Date: 20 Mar 67
Service: Army
Rank: Brigadier General
Company: Headquarters
Division: 1st Infantry Division

Notes

Introduction

1. Robert Widener, "Who Is the Most Highly Decorated GI of All Time?" *VFW*, April 2014, 43. To answer the question posed in the title of the article, the author assigned points for each medal awarded for valor. The result was two lists: the first included those who had received the Medal of Honor and the second was based on the total number of points awarded for valorous decorations. Based on these criteria, Hollingsworth was number three on the second list.

Chapter 1

1. The descendants of Valentine Hollingsworth trace their lineage back to Charlemagne.

2. The recollections of Hollingsworth's early life come from Lt. Gen. James F. Hollingsworth, oral history interview by Terry Anderson, Texas A&M University, College Station, TX, 18 August 1982; Gerald Hollingsworth, interview by author, Sanger, TX, 17 January 2014; Jack Hollingsworth, interview by author, Sanger, TX, 17 January 2014; and Ross and Betsy Hollingsworth, interview by author, Phoenix, AZ, 21 February 2015.

3. Sandi Major, "Farmboy to Legendary General," *Fort Worth Press*, 27 November 1966.

4. Public Law 37-108, which established land-grant colleges, Record Group 11, General Records of the US Government, 1778–2006, National Archives and Records Administration, Washington, DC.

5. Henry C. Dethloff, *A Pictorial History of Texas A&M University 1876–1976* (College Station: Texas A&M University Press, 1975), 52.

6. Quote in Henry C. Dethloff, *Texas Aggies Go to War* (College Station: Texas A&M University Press, 2006), 73.

7. *1937 Longhorn* (College Station: Texas A&M University, 1937); *1938 Longhorn* (College Station: Texas A&M University, 1938); *1939 Longhorn* (College Station: Texas A&M University, 1939).

8. Major, "Farmboy to Legendary General."

9. Dethloff, *Texas Aggies Go to War*, 205; John A. Adams Jr., *Keepers of the Spirit: The Corps of Cadets at Texas A&M University, 1876–2001* (College Station: Texas A&M University Press, 2001), 159–60. During the war, twenty-nine A&M graduates reached the rank of general officer; seven Aggies were awarded the congressional Medal of Honor.

Chapter 2

1. Carlo D'Este, *Patton: A Genius for War* (New York: Harper Collins, 1995), 382.

2. Hollingsworth, oral history interview by Anderson, 16–17.

3. D'Este, *Patton*, 384.

4. Quote in D'Este, *Patton*, 385.

5. Ibid., 429.

6. Philip St. John, *Second Armored Division: A History* (Paducah, KY: Turner, 1998), 11.

7. Stanley P. Hirshson, *General Patton: A Soldier's Life* (New York: Harper Collins, 2002), 237.

8. Hollingsworth, oral history interview by Anderson, 15. No official record of this assignment could be located, and he declined to elaborate during his interview.

9. St. John, *Second Armored Division*, 11.

10. Christopher Gabel, *The US Army GHQ Maneuvers of 1941* (Washington, DC: US Army Center of Military History, 1991), 105, 111.

11. Quote in Hirshson, *General Patton*, 249.

12. Quote in Donald E. Houston, *Hell on Wheels: The 2d Armored Division* (Novato, CA: Presidio Press, 1977), 101.

13. In April 1943, Harmon relinquished command of the 2nd Armored Division and assumed command of the 1st Armored Division, relieving Maj. Gen. Orlando Ward.

14. Dethloff, *Texas Aggies Go to War*, 141; James R. Woodall, *Twelve Texas Aggie War Heroes: From World War I to Vietnam* (College Station: Texas A&M University Press, 2016), 181.

15. St. John, *Second Armored Division*, 22.

Chapter 3

1. The Normandy amphibious landings were conducted under Operation NEPTUNE.

2. Houston, *Hell on Wheels*, 157, 189, 191, 195, 199.

3. Steven J. Zaloga, *Operation Cobra 1944: Breakout from Normandy* (Oxford, UK: Osprey, 2001), 26; Woodall, *Twelve Texas Aggie War Heroes*, 181–82.

4. Houston, *Hell on Wheels*, 204.

5. Ibid.

6. Omar Bradley, *A Soldier's Story* (New York: Henry Holt, 1951), 318.

7. The accidental bombing of the 30th Infantry Division caused a major controversy between Bradley and the air corps. His understanding was that the bombers would bomb on a line parallel to the Périers–Saint-Lô highway, not perpendicular to the line of US troops, but the air corps disagreed because it felt that doing so would expose its bombers to German flak since they would be bombing from low altitude.

8. Woodall, *Twelve Texas Aggie War Heroes*, 182.

9. Russell F. Weigley, *Eisenhower's Lieutenants: The Campaign of France and Germany, 1944–1945* (Bloomington: Indiana University Press, 1981), 160.

10. Quote in Christopher Pugsley, *Operation Cobra* (Phoenix Mill, UK: Sutton, 2004), 74.

11. Bradley assumed command of 12th Army Group, and Bradley's deputy, Lt. Gen. Courtney L. Hodges, assumed command of First Army. With the activation of Third Army, there was a major shifting of divisions between corps and of corps between armies during the fluid days following the breakout from Normandy. On 2 August 1944, the 2nd Armored Division was temporarily transferred to the control of XIX Corps under Maj. Gen. Charles Corlett, which was part of Patton's Third Army. The division reverted to VII Corps control on 7 August.

12. When the first US troops entered Germany on 11 September 1944, the Allies had reached a phase line that the OVERLORD planners did not expect to reach until D+330 (2 May 1945).

13. *History 67th Armored Regiment* (Brunswick, Germany: Georg Westermann, 1945), 32.

14. Steven J. Zaloga, *The Siegfried Line 1944–45: Battles on the German Frontier* (Oxford, UK: Osprey, 2007), 27.

15. Operation MARKET-GARDEN was a plan by British general Bernard Montgomery for a combined airborne-mechanized operation to seize a key bridge across the Rhine at Arnhem, thus facilitating a 21st Army Group attack into the vital German Ruhr region. The operation was launched on 17 September and

proved to be a disappointing failure when the British armored column was unable to link up with the airborne troops.

16. Houston, *Hell on Wheels*, 301.

17. "Time on target" is a fire coordination technique whereby artillery fire from many weapons arrives at the target at precisely the same time.

18. Lt. Gen. James F. Hollingsworth, oral history interview by John Votaw, 1st Infantry Division Museum, Naperville, IL, 14 July 1999, Tape 1, 77.

19. LTG James Hollingsworth, "Commander's Hatch: Remembering Some Hard-Fought Lessons of World War II, Part 2," *Armor*, March–April 1989, 5.

20. St. John, *Second Armored Division*, 35–36.

21. Zaloga, *Siegfried Line*, 80.

22. Hollingsworth, "Commander's Hatch," 6.

23. There is no intention here to go into detail about the Battle of the Bulge; for a recent and detailed discussion of the battle from beginning to end, see Antony Beevor, *Ardennes 1944: The Battle of the Bulge* (New York: Viking, 2014).

24. Houston, *Hell on Wheels*, 335–42; Beevor, *Ardennes 1944*, 273; Charles B. MacDonald, *A Time for Trumpets: The Untold Story of the Battle of the Bulge* (New York: William Morrow, 1985), 579–81; William K. Goolrick and Ogden Tanner, *The Battle of the Bulge* (New York: Time-Life Books, 1979), 180. After this action, Harmon was given command of a corps, but he never received his third star. After the war, Holly, in his usual candid fashion, said he did not think much of Collins: "I thought he was a weak sister."

25. Quoted in Beevor, *Ardennes 1944*, 295.

26. Max Hastings, *Armageddon: The Battle for Germany, 1944–1945* (New York: Alfred A. Knopf, 2004), 228.

27. Houston, *Hell on Wheels*, 351.

28. Goolrick and Tanner, *Battle of the Bulge*, 181.

29. Houston, *Hell on Wheels*, 374; St. John, *Second Armored Division*, 43.

30. Hollingsworth, oral history interview by Anderson, 34; Cornelius Ryan, *The Last Battle: The Classic History of the Battle for Berlin* (New York: Simon and Schuster, 1994), 289.

31. Ryan, *Last Battle*, 289–90.

32. Robert LaGuardia, "Lt. Gen. James F. Hollingsworth—Meanest General in the US Army," *Stag*, October 1975, 64.

33. Ryan, *Last Battle*, 305.

34. Ibid., 307.

35. Houston, *Hell on Wheels*, 417. The 67th Armored Regiment was the first US unit to reach the Elbe.

36. Ryan, *Last Battle*, 309.

37. Houston, *Hell on Wheels*, 417. Colonel Disney himself would be severely wounded by German artillery less than thirty-six hours later.

38. During World War II, the men of the 2nd Armored Division were recognized for distinguished service and bravery under fire with 9,369 awards, including 2 Medals of Honor, 23 Distinguished Service Crosses (one to Hollingsworth), and 2,302 Silver Stars, as well as nearly 6,000 Purple Hearts. In 238 days of battle, the division suffered 7,348 casualties, including 1,160 killed in action.

39. The 2nd Armored Division served as an occupation force in Berlin until 9 August, when it was replaced by the 82nd Airborne Division. The division then moved to the Bad Orb–Hanau area near Frankfurt, about 120 miles east of the Luxembourg border. Although it was unknown to most of the division, it was scheduled for transfer to southern France to assimilate replacements and new arrivals in preparation for a new amphibious operation—the invasion of the Japanese home islands. However, on 2 September 1945, after atomic bombs were dropped on Hiroshima and Nagasaki, the Japanese formally surrendered in Tokyo Bay and World War II was over. The division remained in the Frankfurt area on occupation duty until the end of December 1945.

40. Hollingsworth, oral history interview by Anderson, 42–43.

Chapter 4

1. Many officers reverted to lesser rank after the war was over, but Hollingsworth was promoted, no doubt largely because of his combat record.

2. Officer Efficiency Report, 31 January 1946, Box 14, Hollingsworth Papers, Cushing Library, Texas A&M University, College Station, TX.

3. He was also a 32nd Degree Mason in the Army Consistory of the Ancient and Accepted Scottish Rite, Fort Leavenworth, Kansas. He was a Shriner and member of Karem Temple, Waco, Texas.

4. Maj. Gen. I. D. White to Maj. Gen. F. A. Irving, letter, 10 November 1948, Box 14, Hollingsworth Papers.

5. Col. Walter Burnside to Maj. Gen. I. D. White, letter, 23 November 1948, Box 14, Hollingsworth Papers.

6. Maj. Gen. I. D. White to Hollingsworth, letter, 23 November 1948, Box 14, Hollingsworth Papers.

7. Maj. Gen. E. N. Harmon, *Combat Commander: Autobiography of a Soldier* (Englewood Cliffs, NJ: Prentice-Hall, 1970), 281.

8. Maj. Gen. I. D. White to Hollingsworth, letter, 1 March 1951, Box 8, Hollingsworth Papers.

9. He received his 33rd Degree in Washington, DC, in 1999. After retiring from the service, he became a member of the Alzafar Shrine in San Antonio, Texas. His parents were buried in a Masonic cemetery in Valley View, Texas.

10. Briefing announcement, Subject: Precautions for Atomic War, 4 October 1952, Fort Leavenworth, Kansas, Box 14, Hollingsworth Papers.

11. Dick Sugg, e-mail message to author, Subject: GEN Hollingsworth, 30 November 2013.

12. Text of message, Box 19, Hollingsworth Papers.

13. Alexander M. Haig Jr., *Inner Circles: How America Changed the World; A Memoir* (New York: Warner Books, 1992), 157.

14. Ibid.

15. Gen. H. Norman Schwarzkopf, *It Doesn't Take a Hero* (New York: Linda Grey Bantam Books, 1992), 62.

16. Ibid., 63.

17. Brig. Gen. Hamilton Howze to Hollingsworth, letter, 22 December 1952, Box 19, Hollingsworth Papers.

18. Hollingsworth to Brig. Gen. Einar B. Gjelsteen, letter, 10 February 1953, Box 19, Hollingsworth Papers.

19. Allan R. Millett and Peter Maslowski, *For the Common Defense*, rev. ed. (New York: Free Press, 1994), 535.

20. Lyman L. Lemnitzer, "This Is a Significant Beginning," *Army Combat Forces Journal*, November 1955, 62.

21. A. J. Bacevich, *The Pentomic Era: The US Army between Korea and Vietnam* (Washington, DC: National Defense University Press, 1986), 38.

22. Matthew B. Ridgway, *Soldier: The Memoirs of Matthew B. Ridgway* (New York: Harper Brothers, 1956), 320, 323–41; Stephen E. Ambrose, *Eisenhower*, vol. 2, *The President* (New York: Simon and Schuster, 1984), 223–24.

23. Bacevich, *Pentomic Era*, 41.

24. James E. Hewes Jr., *From Root to McNamara: Army Organization and Administration, 1900–1963* (Washington, DC: US Army Center of Military History, 1975), 239–41.

25. Woodall, *Twelve Texas Aggie War Heroes*, 188.

26. "Wilson Marshals Services' Chiefs to Decry Rivalry," *New York Times*, 22 May 1956.

27. "Military Forces Split by Conflict on Arms Policies," *New York Times*, 19 May 1956.

28. "Transcript of News Conference Held by Wilson and His Military and Civilian Aides," *New York Times*, 22 May 1956.

29. Lt. Col. Lewis F. Shull, letter, 27 March 1956, reprinted in *The Pointer*, 20 April 1956, Box 19, Hollingsworth Papers.

30. Hollingsworth, oral history interview by Anderson, 60.

31. Newspaper reports differ as to who was driving the car. In "J. F. Hollingsworth," *Denton (TX) Record-Chronicle*, 11 October 1960, the obituary reads that the younger Hollingsworth was teaching the other boy to drive. The other article about the accident, "Killeen Youth Killed in Sunday Sportscar Mishap," *Gatesville (TX) Messenger*, 14 October 1960, does not mention who was driving the car.

32. "Killeen Youth Killed." After his mother's death in 1989, James's remains were removed from the Sanger Cemetery and reinterred beside those of his mother at Fort Sam Houston National Cemetery.

33. Hollingsworth, oral history interview by Anderson, 64.

34. Assistant Secretary of Defense Norman Paul to Gen. Earle Wheeler, letter, 8 August 1963, Box 7, Hollingsworth Papers.

35. Zia took office in 1977 as a result of a coup against the government of Prime Minister Zulfikar Ali Bhutto in July 1977. Zia died in a plane crash in August 1988.

36. Both letter and memo response can be found in Box 7, Hollingsworth Papers.

37. Hollingsworth to Assistant Secretary of Defense Norman Paul, letter, 19 July 1965, Box 7, Hollingsworth Papers.

38. Norman Paul to Cyrus Vance, memorandum, 24 August 1965, Box 7, Hollingsworth Papers.

39. Distinguished Service Medal Citation, Department of Defense, September 1965, Box 7, Hollingsworth Papers.

40. Hollingsworth to Lt. Col. Earl W. Bell, letter, 12 September 1965, Box 7, Hollingsworth Papers.

41. Cyrus R. Vance to Hollingsworth, letter, 15 October 1965, Box 15, Hollingsworth Papers.

42. Hollingsworth, oral history interview by Anderson, 65.

43. Hollingsworth to Assistant Secretary of Defense Norman Paul, letter, 8 December 1965, Box 8, Hollingsworth Papers.

44. Maj. Gen. G. V. Underwood to Hollingsworth, letter, 1 December 1965, Box 13, Hollingsworth Papers.

Chapter 5

1. For a detailed discussion of the early US combat deployments, see John Carland, *Stemming the Tide: May 1965 to October 1966* (Washington, DC: US Army Center of Military History, 2000).

2. James Scott Wheeler, *The Big Red One* (Lawrence: University Press of Kansas, 2007), 431.

3. II Field Force, numbering more than 100,000 troops, was the senior US command in the III Corps Tactical Zone and included the 25th and 1st Infantry Divisions, as well as a number of combat support and combat service support units. As the II Field Force commander, Seaman would be DePuy's boss.

4. Maj. Paul H. Herbert, *Deciding What Has to Be Done: General William E. DePuy and the 1976 Edition of FM 100-5, Operations* (Fort Leavenworth, KS: Combat Studies Institute, 1988), 11.

5. Lt. Col. Romie Brownlee and Lt. Col. William Mullen, *Changing an Army: An Oral History of General William E. DePuy, USA Retired* (Carlisle Barracks, PA: US Army Military History Institute, 1985), 90.

6. Quotations of Hollingsworth, unless otherwise noted, are from Lt. Gen. James F. Hollingsworth, senior officer oral history interview by Henry Gole, 18 January 2005.

7. Henry G. Gole, *General William E. DePuy: Preparing the Army for Modern War* (Lexington: University Press of Kentucky, 2008), 190.

8. Phillip B. Davidson, *Vietnam at War: The History 1946–1975* (Novato, CA: Presidio Press, 1988), 699–700.

9. Quoted in James E. Parker, *Last Man Out* (Camden, SC: John Culler and Sons, 1996), 244–45.

10. Glenn Infield, "'Danger 79er' Toughest General the Cong Ever Faced," *Stag*, April 1968, 64.

11. Peter Arnett, "Exacting Commander Wants 1st Division Best in Army," *Lubbock (TX) Avalanche-Journal*, 30 August 1966.

12. Brig. Gen. James E. Shelton, *The Beast Was Out There* (Naperville, IL: Cantigny First Division Foundation, 2002), 16.

13. Unless otherwise stated, the Hollingsworth quotes in this chapter come from the general's letters to his wife, which can be found in Box 11, Hollingsworth Papers.

14. Quoted in Carland, *Stemming the Tide*, 305.

15. Haig, *Inner Circles*, 156.

16. Quoted in Steven Weingartner, ed., *Blue Spaders: The 26th Infantry Regiment,*

1917–1967 (Wheaton, IL: Cantigny First Division Foundation, 1996), 133–34.

17. Quoted in George C. Wilson, *Mud Soldiers* (New York: Charles Scribner's Sons, 1989), 12.

18. Quoted in Gole, *General William E. DePuy*, 163.

19. Henry Gole, "General William DePuy: His Relief of Subordinates in Combat," unpublished paper (Lexington, VA: Virginia Military Institute Archives, 2007), 4–6.

20. When Holly's brother asked him why he kept the same call sign rather than change it frequently, as was the normal practice in Vietnam, Holly replied, "Because I want the enemy to know I am there."

21. Hollingsworth, oral history interview by Votaw, 77, 95.

22. Carland, *Stemming the Tide*, 306.

23. Ibid. Also see Gen. (Ret.) Paul F. Gorman, interview by James Scott Wheeler, First Division Museum, Wheaton, IL, 6–8 April 2004, 17–18.

24. Gole, *General William E. DePuy*, 170.

25. Gorman, interview, 34–35.

26. Wilson, *Mud Soldiers*, 40.

27. Keith Shelton, "Sanger General Goes Where Action Is," *Denton (TX) Record-Chronicle*, 19 June 1966.

28. Wheeler, *Big Red One*, 435.

29. Ibid., 436.

30. Hollingsworth, oral history interview by Votaw, Tape 2, 30.

31. Wheeler, *Big Red One*, 431–50; Carland, *Stemming the Tide*, 305–36.

32. Gole, *General William E. DePuy*, 173.

33. Nicholas Tomalin, "The General Goes Zapping Charlie Cong," *Sunday Times* (London, UK), 5 June 1966. This story was reprinted in Thomas Wolfe, *The New Journalism* (New York: Harper and Row, 1973).

34. Norman Pearlstine, "'Tiger in the Forest': U.S. General Envisions 'A Short, Violent War' If Korean Reds Attack," *Wall Street Journal*, 13 January 1976.

35. Hollingsworth, senior officer oral history interview by Gole, 28.

36. Lewis Sorley, *Honorable Warrior: General Harold K. Johnson and the Ethics of Command* (Lawrence: University Press of Kansas, 1998), 256.

37. Hollingsworth, oral history interview by Votaw, Tape 2, 3.

38. Quoted in Gole, "General William DePuy."

39. Quoted in Gole, *General William E. DePuy*, 175.

40. Gole, "General William DePuy," 26.

41. Lt. Gen. (Ret.) Richard Keller, interview by author, Fort Leavenworth, KS, 1 September 2015.

42. Quoted in Gole, "General William DePuy," 25.

43. Ibid., 22; General Donn A. Starry, senior officer oral history interview by LTC Matthias A. Spruill and LTC Edwin T. Vernon, in Lewis Sorley, ed., *Press On! Selected Works of General Donn A. Starry* (Fort Leavenworth, KS: Combat Studies Institute Press, 2009), 1055.

44. Quote in Gole, "General William DePuy," 29.

45. Quotes in William A. Cohen, *Heroic Leadership: Leading with Integrity and Honor* (San Francisco: Jossey-Bass, 2010), 74–75.

46. Norman Ross, e-mail message to author, 24 August 2015.

47. "General Hollingsworth Stars in 'Soldier,'" *Pacific Stars and Stripes*, 28 July 1975.

48. Hollingsworth, oral history interview by Votaw, Tape 1, 94.

49. Hollingsworth, oral history interview by Anderson, 108.

50. Hollingsworth, oral history interview by Votaw, Tape 1, 72.

51. "Communists Down General's Copter," *San Francisco Examiner*, 10 November 1966.

52. John Baum, telephone conversation with author, 18 August 2015. Baum was an artillery battery commander under DePuy and Hollingsworth.

53. John Lesko, telephone conversation with author, 27 August 2015.

54. Randy House, e-mail message to author, 12 September 2015.

55. George Fielding Eliot to Nickie Hollingsworth, letter, 11 November 1966, Box 15, Hollingsworth Papers.

56. Gole, *General William E. DePuy*, 189.

57. Thomas E. Ricks, *The Generals* (New York: Penguin Press, 2012), 242.

58. Other accounts of the confrontation between Johnson, DePuy, and Hollingsworth describe the incident as a "shouting match" (Gole, *General William E. DePuy*, 91). One observer to the confrontation was cited as being "fascinated and astounded by the acrimony of the dialogue" (Sorley, *Honorable Warrior*, 256–57). While no one will ever know for sure exactly what went on behind closed doors,

it is clear that this was a serious clash between the chief of staff of the army and two of his subordinate generals.

59. Gole, *General William E. DePuy*, 190; Ricks, *Generals*, 245.

60. Quote in Gole, "General William DePuy," 12.

61. Gole, *General William E. DePuy*, 171, 185.

62. Gole, "General William DePuy," 10.

63. Hollingsworth described Seaman as a "very lightweight fellow. Probably a fine staff officer. Fine man, but not a fighter." Hollingsworth, oral history interview by Votaw, Tape 1, 90.

64. Gole, *General William E. DePuy*, 197. DePuy went on to receive four stars and was the very influential first commander of the US Army Training and Doctrine Command, where he played a key role in the revitalization of the army after Vietnam.

65. Lt. Col. (Ret.) Warren R. Silva to author, letter, 26 August 2015.

66. William Schreiber, e-mail message to author, 2 September 2015.

67. Silva to author.

68. Chaplain (Col.) (Ret.) Wesley Geary, telephone interview by author, 13 August 2015.

69. Holly apparently held no rancor for General Johnson; after the war, he described Johnson as "a hell of a fine man. Just a fine man." Hollingsworth, oral history interview by Votaw, Tape 2, 5.

70. More than thirty officers who served in the 1st Division under DePuy and Hollingsworth went on to achieve general officer rank.

Chapter 6

1. Quoted in Paul J. Scheips, *The Role of Federal Military Forces in Domestic Disorders, 1945–1992* (Fort McNair, Washington, DC: US Army Center of Military History, 2005), 216.

2. Hollingsworth to Lt. Gen. Bruce Palmer, letter, 6 May 1968, Box 17, Hollingsworth Papers.

3. Hollingsworth to Col. William B. Caldwell, letter, 14 August 1968, Box 17, Hollingsworth Papers.

4. Lt. Gen. Bruce Palmer to Hollingsworth, letter, 7 June 1968, Box 17, Hollingsworth Papers.

5. Douglas E. Kneeland, "War Stirs More Dissent among G.I.'s," *New York Times*, 6 June 1970.

6. Andrew H. Meyers, *Black, White, and Olive Drab: Racial Integration at Fort Jackson, South Carolina, and the Civil Rights Movement* (Charlottesville: University of Virginia Press, 2006), 190–97. Levy was released from prison in 1969. In 1974, the US Supreme Court upheld Levy's conviction.

7. Ibid., 204.

8. Kneeland, "War Stirs More Dissent."

9. Copy of remarks by Maj. Gen. James F. Hollingsworth to South Carolina Law Enforcement Officers' Association, 11 June 1970, Box 17, Hollingsworth Papers.

10. Meyers, *Black, White, and Olive Drab*, 208.

11. Notes, command and staff meeting, Fort Jackson, SC, 15 June 1970, Box 13, Hollingsworth Papers.

12. H. A. Boucher to Gen. William C. Westmoreland, letter, 2 April 1971, Box 18, Hollingsworth Papers.

13. Hollingsworth to Congressman Herman Badillo, letter, 27 June 1971, Box 2, Hollingsworth Papers.

14. Hollingsworth to Mrs. R. Barry, letter, 13 February 1971, Box 18, Hollingsworth Papers.

15. Brig. Gen. Willard Latham, *The Modern Volunteer Army Program: The Benning Experiment, 1970–1972* (Washington, DC: Department of the Army, 1974), iii.

16. Hollingsworth to J. R. Blandford, letter, 25 January 1971, Box 18, Hollingsworth Papers.

17. Hollingsworth to Gen. William C. Westmoreland, letter, 27 January 1973, Box 19, Hollingsworth Papers.

Chapter 7

1. Maj. John D. Howard, "The War We Came to Fight: A Study of the Battle of An Loc, April–June 1972," unpublished student paper (Fort Leavenworth, KS: US Army Command and General Staff College, June 1974), 1. Howard was speaking about American forces in general, but the description is certainly true regarding Hollingsworth; for his whole life he had been preparing for this type of large-scale fight to the finish.

2. William M. Hammond, *Public Affairs: The Military and the Media, 1968–1973* (Washington, DC: US Army Center of Military History, 1996), 371–72.

3. Hollingsworth to Col. Eugene M. Perry, letter, 25 November 1971, Box 2, Hollingsworth Papers.

4. Hollingsworth to Maj. Michael J. Rosenberg, letter, 29 November 1971, Box 2, Hollingsworth Papers.

5. Hollingsworth to Brig. Gen. Sam S. Walker, letter, 25 November 1971, Box 2, Hollingsworth Papers.

6. US advisers had actually been in Vietnam since 1950, when the Military Assistance Advisory Group Indochina was established in Saigon in September to supervise the use of $10 million worth of US military equipment provided to the French in their fight against the Communist Viet Minh forces. After France was defeated at the Battle of Dien Bien Phu in 1954, US personnel were involved in a cooperative effort with the French to bolster the forces of the newly declared Republic of Vietnam. When the French departed Vietnam in 1956, the burden of providing assistance to Saigon fell on the United States, which provided advisers down to the battalion level.

7. At this point, there were only four US infantry battalions left in Vietnam: two from the 1st Cavalry Division and two from the Americal Division.

8. The CORDS program, established in May 1967, was originally called the Civil Operations and Revolutionary Development Support, but "Revolutionary" was later changed to "Rural." The objective of the CORDS program was to assist the Saigon government in spreading its influence in the provinces at the grassroots level.

9. For a full discussion of the operation, see James H. Willbanks, *A Raid Too Far: Operation Lam Son 719 and Vietnamization in Laos* (College Station: Texas A&M University Press, 2014).

10. Donald P. Gregg, *Pot Shards: Fragments of a Life Lived in CIA, the White House, and the Two Koreas* (Washington, DC: New Academia Publishing/Vellum Books, 2014), 114.

11. Lewis Sorley, *A Better War: The Unexamined Victories and Final Tragedy of America's Last Years in Vietnam* (New York: Harcourt Brace, 1999), 307–9.

12. Headquarters, Pacific Command, Directorate of Operations Analysis, *Contemporary Historical Examination of Current Operations Report (CHECO): The Battle for An Loc, 5 April–26 June 1972* (Honolulu, 1973), xiii. Hereafter referred to as *CHECO Report.*

13. Military History Institute of Vietnam, *Victory in Vietnam: The Official History of the People's Army of Vietnam, 1954–1975,* translated by Merle L. Pribbenow (Lawrence: University Press of Kansas, 2002), 283–84.

14. The regular ground forces of North Vietnam were officially named the People's Army of Vietnam (PAVN), but US troops generally called them the North Vietnamese Army, or "NVA." Thus, the more commonly accepted terminology from that time will be used here.

15. US Military Assistance Command, Vietnam, special intelligence report: "The Nguyen Hue Offensive—Historical Study of Lessons Learned" (Saigon, January 1973), C-1.

16. "The War That Won't Go Away," *Newsweek*, 17 April 1972.

17. Military History Institute of Vietnam, *Victory in Vietnam*, 295; Military History Institute of Vietnam, *Chien Dich Tien Cong Nguyen Hue Mien Dong Bo—Nam 1972—Luu Hanh Noi Bo* [The Nguyen Hue Offensive Campaign in Eastern Cochin China, 18–19 April 1972—For Internal Distribution Only], translated by Merle L. Pribbenow (Hanoi: Military History Institute of the Ministry of Defense, 1988), 15.

18. US Military Assistance Command, Vietnam, Military History Branch, *Command History, 1972–1973* (Saigon: US Military Assistance Command, Vietnam, 1973), J-1.

19. RF/PF were a form of South Vietnamese militia. Recruited locally, they fell into two broad groups—Regional Forces and Popular Forces (RFPFs, called Ruff-Puffs by American forces).

20. Except where noted, this account of Hollingsworth's actions during the battle for Loc Ninh and An Loc are drawn from Maj. Gen. James F. Hollingsworth, "Communist Invasion in Military Region III," unpublished narrative, Microfiche Reel 44 (University Publications of America: Records of the Military Assistance Command, Vietnam, 1972).

21. The attack helicopters were from Task Force Garry Owen, which was the only US ground unit left in Military Region III; it was built around the nucleus of the 3rd Brigade, 1st Cavalry Division, and included the 229th Aviation Battalion, from which the attack helicopters came.

22. Maj. Gen. James F. Hollingsworth, backchannel message to Gen. Creighton C. Abrams, "Daily Commander's Evaluation," Microfiche Reel 44 (University Publications of America: Records of the Military Assistance Command, Vietnam, 6 April 1972).

23. US Military Assistance Command, Vietnam, *Command History, 1972–1973*, J-5.

24. The rest of the American advisers were either killed or captured; those who were captured, including Captain Smith, were not released until after the Paris Peace Accords were signed in January 1973.

25. Hollingsworth, backchannel message, 7 April 1972.

26. Hollingsworth, "Communist Invasion," 21.

27. The task force was composed of the 2nd Battalion, 52nd Regiment, and the 1st Battalion, 48th Regiment, with attachments from the 52nd Intelligence and Reconnaissance Company, C Battery, 182nd Artillery (105-mm howitzer), a platoon of 155-mm howitzers, and B Company, 18th Engineer Battalion. Their parent organization, 18th ARVN Division, was headquartered in Xuan Loc in Long Khanh Province.

28. Whitehead's award was later upgraded to the Distinguished Service Cross.

29. Lam Quang Thi, *Hell in An Loc: The 1972 Easter Invasion and the Battle That Saved South Viet Nam* (Denton: University of North Texas Press, 2009), 78.

30. Quoted in US Military Assistance Command, Vietnam, *Command History, 1972–1973*, J-7.

31. Mike McDermott, *True Faith and Allegiance: An American Paratrooper and the 1972 Battle of An Loc* (Tuscaloosa: University of Alabama Press, 2012), 32–35.

32. Quoted in US Military Assistance Command, Vietnam, *Command History, 1972–1973*, J-7.

33. The only part of the 1st Cavalry Division that remained in Vietnam by this time was Task Force Garry Owen, which was built around the 3rd Brigade. The helicopters that flew in support of the coming battle in An Loc were flown by those under Garry Owen control.

34. The survivors of Task Force 52 withdrew to An Loc, arriving on 12 April. In the process of withdrawing, the three advisers with the task force were wounded and were evacuated by helicopter. The author and Maj. Raymond Haney, adviser with the 18th ARVN Division's cavalry squadron, flew from Lai Khe to An Loc on the afternoon of 12 April to join the task force for the coming battle. Before the battle was over, both the author and Major Haney would be wounded and evacuated to 3rd Field Hospital in Saigon.

35. Howard, "War We Came To Fight," 29.

36. Quoted in *CHECO Report*, 16.

37. Brig. Gen. John R. McGiffert, deputy commanding general, Third Regional Assistance Command, interview by Major Walter S. Dillard, US Military Assistance Command, Vietnam, SJSHistory (Saigon, 10 October 1972), 17. The author was present in An Loc when Hollingsworth radioed the advisers that they were there for the duration.

38. *CHECO Report*, 16.

39. US Military Assistance Command, Vietnam, *Command History, 1972–1973*, J-12.

40. Ibid.

41. Philip. C. Clarke, "The Battle That Saved Saigon," *Reader's Digest*, March 1973, 153.

42. Truong Nhu Tang, *Vietcong Memoir: An Inside Account of the Vietnam War and Its Aftermath* (New York: Harcourt Brace Jovanovich, 1983), 167–68.

43. Hollingsworth, backchannel message, 15 April 1972.

44. Hollingsworth, backchannel message, 16 April 1972.

45. Quoted in Headquarters, 5th Division Combat Assistance Team, Advisory Team 70, "After-Action Report, Binh Long Campaign, 1972," TRAC, 20 July 1972, D-12.

46. Hollingsworth, "Communist Invasion," 10.

47. US Military Assistance Command, Vietnam, *Command History, 1972–1973*, J-15.

48. "An Adviser's Three-Month Nightmare Ends," *Pacific Stars and Stripes*, 4 June 1972, 1.

49. Ian Ward, "North Vietnam's Blitzkrieg—Why Giap Did It: Report from Saigon," *Conflict Studies*, October 1972, 5.

50. Pham Nhat Nam, "An Loc: The Unquiet East," translated by John C. Shafer (DeKalb: Northern Illinois University, n.d.), 10–11.

51. Hollingsworth, "Communist Invasion," 13.

52. "The Battle for An Loc Goes On." *Pacific Stars and Stripes*, 19 April 1972.

53. "In Furious Battle," *Newsweek*, 24 April 1972, 32; David Fulghum, Terrence Maitland, and the editors of Boston Publishing, *The Vietnam Experience: South Vietnam on Trial* (Boston: Boston Publishing, 1984), 152.

54. William M. Hammond, *Reporting Viet Nam: Media and Military at War* (Lawrence: University Press of Kansas, 1998), 269, 270.

55. Daniel Southerland, "US General Talked Too Rough—Rebuked," *Christian Science Monitor*, 15 April 1972; "Reprimand Gen. for Remarks," *Pacific Stars and Stripes*, 17 April 1972.

56. Msgr. Marvin Bordelon to Hollingsworth, letter, 19 April 1972, Box 2, Hollingsworth Papers.

57. Hal Drake, "Viets on Way to Victory at An Loc—Top Adviser." *Pacific Stars and Stripes*, 23 April 1972.

58. Hollingsworth, "Communist Invasion," 15–16.

59. Ibid., 16–17.

60. Hollingsworth, backchannel message, 23 April 1972; Hollingsworth, "Communist Invasion," 17.

61. Hollingsworth, "Communist Invasion," 17–18.

62. US Military Assistance Command, Vietnam, *Command History, 1972–1973*, J-22.

63. "Biggest B-52 Raids of War Pound Reds Besieging An Loc," *Los Angeles Times*,

12 May 1972; Headquarters, 5th Division Combat Assistance Team, "After-Action Report," 25.

64. Quoted in Fulghum, Maitland, and editors of Boston Publishing, *Vietnam Experience*, 154.

65. Lewis Sorley, ed., *Vietnam Chronicles: The Abrams Tapes, 1968–1972* (Lubbock: Texas Tech University Press, 2004), 847.

66. Hollingsworth, backchannel message, 16 May 1972.

67. Lt. Gen. Ngo Quang Truong, *Indochina Monographs: The Easter Offensive of 1972* (Washington, DC: US Army Center of Military History, 1980), 134.

68. Lam Quang Thi, *Hell in An Loc*, 176. Dien Bien Phu was the battle that was won by the Viet Minh in 1954 and resulted in the withdrawal of France from Southeast Asia.

69. "Media Fail to Convey Good News from An Loc," *Baltimore Sun*, 16 June 1972.

70. Headquarters, 21st Infantry Division (ARVN), "After-Action Report—Binh Long Campaign, 1972" (Saigon, July 1972), C-1.

71. Howard, "War We Came to Fight," 1.

72. Lt. Col. Arthur E. Taylor Jr. to Hollingsworth, letter, 17 July 1972, Box 2, Hollingsworth Papers.

73. McDermott, *True Faith and Allegiance*, 34–35.

74. Davidson, *Vietnam at War*, 629.

75. In addition to Brigadier General Tallman, Lt. Col. Stanley Kuick, Maj. Peter Bentson, 1st Lt. John Todd, and ARVN Master Sergeant Son were killed by the enemy artillery round. In addition to the author, Maj. Joe Hallum was also wounded in the incident. The only other American to die in An Loc in 1972–1973 was Lt. Col. William Nolde, who was also killed in the city by enemy artillery, just hours before the cease-fire on 27 January 1973.

76. John Saar, "Gen. Hollingsworth Retiring—Blunt, Decorated Vietnam Veteran Revised Korea Strategy," *Washington Post*, 24 January 1975; "Controversial General Announces End of Career," *San Antonio Express-News*, 24 January 1976.

Chapter 8

1. Don Oberdorfer, *The Two Koreas: A Contemporary History* (New York: Basic Books, 1997), 9.

2. Ibid., 61.

3. LaGuardia, "Lt. Gen. James F. Hollingsworth," 65.

4. Message to President Park Chung-Hee and Korean people, n.d., Box 5, Hollingsworth Papers.

5. Pearlstine, "'Tiger in the Forest.'"

6. LaGuardia, "Lt. Gen. James F. Hollingsworth," 65.

7. Lewis Sorley, *Thunderbolt, General Creighton Abrams and the Army of His Times* (New York: Simon and Schuster, 1992). Among the other honorary pallbearers were Harold K. Johnson, Bruce Clark, Don Cowles, Jimmie Leach, Bill Potts, "Dutch" Kerwin, George Patton, Bruce Palmer, and Bob Bernstein.

8. John Saar, "The Army's Defiant Anachronism," *Washington Post*, 15 February 1976, K-2. After he retired, Hollingsworth elaborated on the reasons for the fall of South Vietnam, saying, "Our Congress, our President, our government, our administration, and our people collapsed at the time of victory [1972]" (Hollingsworth, oral history interview by Anderson).

9. Quote in Woodall, *Twelve Texas Aggie War Heroes*, 197.

10. John Saar, "A Texas Gunslinger Retires . . . Reluctantly," *Dallas Times Herald*, 15 February 1976.

11. Hollingsworth to Starry, letter, 29 March 1975, Donn A. Starry Papers, Box 3, Folder 5, US Army Heritage and Education Center, Carlisle Barracks, PA.

12. Keyes Beech, "Steel Trap Awaits Korean 'Moles,'" *Omaha (NE) World-Herald*, 27 November 1975.

13. Quoted in Woodall, *Twelve Texas Aggie War Heroes*, 197.

14. Beech, "Steel Trap Awaits Korean 'Moles.'"

15. Saar, "Army's Defiant Anachronism," K-1.

16. Rowland Evans and Robert Novak, "Evans and Nowak: Korean Strategy," *New York Post*, 16 June 1975.

17. Pearlstine, "'Tiger in the Forest.'"

18. Lt. Gen. John H. Cushman, oral history interview by Robert Mages, US Army Center of Military History, Fort McNair, Washington, DC, 2009, 2011, 22-1.

19. Saar, "Army's Defiant Anachronism," K-1.

20. "Controversial General Announces End of Army Career," *San Antonio Express-News*, 24 January 1975.

21. Saar, "Texas Gunslinger Retires."

22. Ibid.

23. Saar, "Gen. Hollingsworth Retiring."

24. LaGuardia, "Lt. Gen. James F. Hollingsworth," 62; Saar, "Texas Gunslinger Retires."

25. Abrams to Hollingsworth, letter, 6 June 1973, Box 5, Hollingsworth Papers.

26. Saar, "Texas Gunslinger Retires."

27. *Korea Report* (Seoul: 8th Army Public Affairs, March 1976), 17.

28. Gen. William DePuy to Hollingsworth, letter, 27 August 1975, Box 6, Hollingsworth Papers. DePuy was at the time of his writing commander of US Army Training and Doctrine Command. 29. Saar, "Gen. Hollingsworth Retiring."

30. "Hollingsworth Retirement Postponed," *Texas Aggie*, May 1976, 15.

Chapter 9

1. Hollingsworth, oral history interview by Votaw, Tape 2, 54–55.

2. Tom Moran, "Hollingsworth Now with Research Firm after Army Career," *Houston Chronicle*, 1 May 1978.

3. Arnold Punaro, telephone interview by author, 1 March 2017.

4. Sen. Sam Nunn and Sen. Dewey F. Bartlett, *NATO and the New Soviet Threat* (Washington, DC: US Government Printing Office, 1977), 4, 16.

5. Ibid., 19.

6. "Korea Integrity Essential to Security of the Free World," *Korea Herald*, 11 May 1979.

7. Bill Deener, "Former US Commander in Korea Says Invasion by North Possible," *Fort Worth Star-Telegram*, 30 October 1979.

8. Remarks before the US House of Representatives Armed Services Committee, 24 April 1983, Box 4, Hollingsworth Papers.

9. Lt. Gen. James F. Hollingsworth, "Understanding the Conventional Umbrella," *Armed Forces Journal*, February 1984.

10. Story related by Frank Muller, telephone conversation with author, 9 September 2015.

Epilogue

1. "A Tribute to LTG (Ret) James F. Hollingsworth," *U.S. Army War College Foundation and Alumni Magazine*, Spring 2010, 6.

2. *From Texas to Bastogne, Texas Aggies Go to War*. Bastogne, Belgium: Bastogne War Museum, n.d.

3. Ricks, *Generals*, 64.

Bibliography

Author Interviews

Bahm, John, 18 August 2015 (telephone).
Geary, Chaplain (Col.) (Ret.) Wesley, 13 August 2015 (telephone).
Hollingsworth, Gerald, Keller, TX, 17 January 2014.
Hollingsworth, Jack, Sanger, TX, 17 January 2014.
Hollingsworth, Ross and Betsy, Phoenix, AZ, 21 February 2015.
Keller, Lt. Gen. (Ret.) Richard, Fort Leavenworth, KS, 1 September 2016.
Lesko, John, 25 August 2015 (telephone).
Punaro, Arnold, 1 March 2017 (telephone).
Rhodes, Col. (Ret.) Dusty, 20 August 2015 (telephone).
Rogan, Thomas C., 28 August 2015 (telephone).
Smith, Raymond, 19 August 2015 (telephone).
Sprause, Command Sgt. Maj. (Ret.) Clarence, San Antonio, TX, 15 January 2014.

Email Messages and Telephone Conversations

Dale Andrade, John Bahm, Bob Baker, Phil Bakke, Clif Berry, Victor Binkoski, Timothy Carey, Joe Carroll, Dan Feather, Eric Gillespie, Henry Gole, William Hardy, Paul Herbert, Mike Hoffman, Jim Holland, Randy Hollingsworth, Randy House, John Howard, Bernard Kenan, John Lesko, Mike McDermott, Pep McPhillips, Frank Muller, Lew Murray, Jack Nicholson, Rusty Pickens, Merle Pribbenow, Lowell Reese, Dusty Rhodes, Steve Robinette, Thomas Rogan, Norman Ross, Stephen Ruth, William Schreiber, Harv Shein, Jim Shelton, Warren Silva, Mike Sloniker, Raymond Smith, Dick Sugg, Jim Tucker, Walter Ulmer, Beau Voelkel, Trevor Voelkel, Fred Wagner, Dave Weber, Jerry Whiteker, Jim Woodall

Oral Histories and Archived Interviews

Cushman, Lt. Gen. John H., oral history interview by Robert Mages, US Army Center of Military History, Fort McNair, Washington, DC, 2009, 2011.

Emerson, LTG Henry E., senior officer oral history interview by LTC Jonathan Jackson, US Army Military History Institute, Carlisle Barracks, PA, 2004.

Gorman, Gen. (Ret.) Paul F., interview by James Scott Wheeler, First Division Museum, Wheaton, IL, 6–8 April 2004.

Hollingsworth, Lt. Gen. James F., oral history interview by Terry Anderson, Texas A&M University, College Station, TX, 18 August 1982.

Hollingsworth, Lt. Gen. James F., oral history interview by John Votaw, 1st Infantry Division Museum, Naperville, IL, 14 July 1999.

Hollingsworth, Lt. Gen. James F., senior officer oral history interview by Henry Gole, Carlisle Barracks, PA, 18 January 2005.

Hollingsworth Papers, Cushing Library, Texas A&M University, College Station, TX.

McGiffert, Brig. Gen. John R., deputy commanding general, Third Regional Assistance Command, interview by Maj. Walter S. Dillard, US Military Assistance Command, Vietnam, SJSHistory, Saigon, 10 October 1972.

Unpublished Material

DiMarco, Louis. "Restoring Order: The U.S. Army Experience with Occupation Operations, 1865–1952." PhD diss., Kansas State University, 2010.

Gole, Henry. "General William DePuy: His Relief of Subordinates in Combat." Unpublished paper. Lexington, VA: Virginia Military Institute Archives, 2007.

Gorman, Gen. Paul F. "Strategy & Tactics for Learning: The Papers of General Paul F. Gorman, USA Ret." Fort Leavenworth, KS: US Army Command and General Staff College, n.d.

Headquarters, 3rd Regional Assistance Command. "Debriefing Reports of Advisers Returning from An Loc." Long Binh, 1972.

Headquarters, 3rd Squadron, 5th Cavalry. "After-Action Report, Battle of Ap Bau Bang, 1 May 1967."

Headquarters, 5th Division Combat Assistance Team, Advisory Team 70. "After-Action Report, Binh Long Campaign, 1972." TRAC, 20 July 1972.

Headquarters, 21st Infantry Division (ARVN). "After-Action Report—Binh Long Campaign, 1972." Saigon, July 1972.

Headquarters, Pacific Command, Directorate of Operations Analysis. *Contemporary Historical Examination of Current Operations Report (CHECO): The Battle for An Loc, 5 April–26 June 1972.* Honolulu, 1973.

Headquarters, US Military Assistance Command, Vietnam. *Command History, 1966.* Saigon: Military History Branch, Office of the Secretary, Joint Staff, MACV, June 1967.

———. *Command History, 1967.* 3 vols. Saigon: Military History Branch, Office of the Secretary, Joint Staff, MACV, 16 September 1968.

———. *Command History, 1972–1973.* 2 vols. Saigon: Military History Branch, Office of the Secretary, Joint Staff, MACV, July 1973.

Hollingsworth, Maj. Gen. James F. Backchannel messages to Gen. Creighton C. Abrams. "Daily Commander's Evaluation." Microfiche Reel 44. University Publications of America: Records of the Military Assistance Command, Vietnam, April–July 1972.

———. "Communist Invasion in Military Region III." Unpublished narrative. Microfiche Reel 44. University Publications of America: Records of the Military Assistance Command, Vietnam, 1972.

———. Statement before the Joint Hearings of the Subcommittee on Research and Development and the Subcommittee on Procurement and Military Nuclear Systems of the House Armed Services Committee, 26 April 1983.

Hollingsworth Report: Review of ARNG Federal Recognition Standards and Procedures and Promotion Procedures for Reserve Component Officers. Washington, DC: Department of the Army, 1967.

Howard, Maj. John D. "The War We Came to Fight: A Study of the Battle of An Loc, April–June 1972." Unpublished student paper. Fort Leavenworth, KS: US Army Command and General Staff College, June 1974.

Military History Institute of Vietnam. *Chien Dich Tien Cong Nguyen Hue Mien Dong Bo—Nam 1972—Luu Hanh Noi Bo* [The Nguyen Hue Offensive Campaign in Eastern Cochin China 18–19 April 1972]. Translated by Merle L. Pribbenow. Hanoi: Military History Institute of the Ministry of Defense, 1988.

Parker, Jay M. "The Colonels' Revolt: Eisenhower, the Army, and the Politics of National Security." Unpublished student paper. Newport, RI: Naval War College, 1994.

Pham Nhat Nam. "An Loc: The Unquiet East." Translated by John C. Shafer. DeKalb: Northern Illinois University, n.d.

———. "Remembering Viet Nam." Lecture delivered at the National Archives, Washington, DC, 30 April 2002.

Smith, Capt. Mark A. "Battle of Loc Ninh, RVN, 5–7 April 1972." Unpublished narrative. Fort Bragg, NC, 21 October 1976.

Sorley, Lewis. "Reassessing Viet Nam." Lecture delivered at the Vietnam Center, Texas Tech University, 17 March 2006.

Timberlake, Capt. Ron, F Troop, 9th Cavalry, and Capt. Michael Sloniker, A Company, 229th Aviation, 3rd Brigade, 1st Cavalry Division. Unpublished narrative, 1999.

Ulmer, Col. W. F. Senior officer debriefing report. Third Regional Assistance Command, Long Binh, 10 January 1973.

US Military Assistance Command, Vietnam. Military History Branch. *Command History, 1972–1973.* Saigon: US Military Assistance Command, Vietnam, 1973.

———. Special intelligence report (declassified): "The Nguyen Hue Offensive—Historical Study of Lessons Learned." Saigon, January 1973.

Books

Adams, John A., Jr. *Keepers of the Spirit: The Corps of Cadets at Texas A&M University, 1876–2001.* College Station: Texas A&M University Press, 2001.

Ambrose, Stephen E. *Citizen Soldiers: The U.S. Army from the Normandy Beaches to the Bulge to the Surrender of Germany. New York:* Simon and Schuster, 1998.

_____. *Eisenhower.* Vol. 1, *Soldier, General of the Army, President-Elect, 1890–1952.* New York: Simon and Schuster, 1983.

_____. *Eisenhower.* Vol. 2, *The President.* New York: Simon and Schuster, 1984.

_____. *Eisenhower: Soldier and President.* Rev. ed. New York: Simon and Schuster, 1991.

Andradé, Dale. *America's Last Vietnam Battle: Halting Hanoi's 1972 Easter Offensive.* Lawrence: University Press of Kansas, 2001.

Bacevich, A. J. *The Pentomic Era: The U.S. Army between Korea and Vietnam.* Washington, DC: National Defense University Press, 1986.

Bando, Mark A. *Breakout at Normandy: The 2nd Armored Division in the Land of the Dead.* Oswego, WI: MBI Publishing, 1999.

Baumer, Robert W. *Aachen: The U.S. Army's Battle for Charlemagne's City in World War II.* Mechanicsburg, PA: Stackpole Books, 2015.

Beevor, Antony. *Ardennes 1944: The Battle of the Bulge.* New York: Viking, 2014.

Bounds, Helen, Tona Payne, Nancy Smith, and Sanger Area Historical Society. *Images around America: Around Sanger.* Charleston, SC: Arcadia Publishing, 2011.

Bradley, Omar. *A Soldier's Story.* New York: Henry Holt, 1951.

Brownlee, Lt. Col. Romie, and Lt. Col. William Mullen. *Changing an Army: An Oral History of General William E. DePuy, USA Retired.* Carlisle Barracks, PA: US Army Military History Institute, 1985.

Caddick-Adams, Peter. *Snow & Steel: The Battle of the Bulge, 1944–45.* New York: Oxford University Press, 2015.

Carafano, James J. *After D-Day: Operation Cobra and the Normandy Breakout.* Mechanicsburg, PA: Stackpole Books, 2008.

Carland, John. *Stemming the Tide: May 1965 to October 1966.* Washington, DC: US Army Center of Military History, 2000.

Clark, Allen. *Wounded Soldier, Healing Warrior.* St. Paul, MN: Zenith Press, 2007.

Clarke, Jeffrey J. *Advice and Support: The Final Years, 1965–1973.* Washington, DC: US Army Center of Military History, 1988.

Cohen, William A. *Heroic Leadership: Leading with Integrity and Honor.* San Francisco: Jossey-Bass, 2010.

Cole, Hugh M. *The Ardennes: Battle of the Bulge.* Washington, DC: US Army Center of Military History, 1965.

Collier, Richard. *The War in the Desert.* New York: Time-Life Books, 1977.

Collins, J. Lawton. *Lightning Joe.* Novato, CA: Presidio Press, 1994.

Davidson, Phillip B. *Vietnam at War: The History 1946–1975.* Novato, CA: Presidio Press, 1988.

Davis, Franklin M., Jr. *Across the Rhine.* New York: Time-Life Books, 1980.

DePuy, Gen. William E. *Selected Papers.* Compiled by Col. Richard Swain. Fort Leavenworth, KS: Combat Studies Institute, US Army Command and General Staff College, 1993.

D'Este, Carlo. *Patton: A Genius for War.* New York: Harper Collins, 1995.

Dethloff, Henry C. *A Centennial History of Texas A&M University 1876–1976.* 2 vols. College Station: Texas A&M University Press, 1975.

______. *A Pictorial History of Texas A&M University 1876–1976.* College Station: Texas A&M University Press, 1975.

______. *Texas Aggies Go to War.* College Station: Texas A&M University Press, 2006.

First Infantry Division in Vietnam: "Big Red One." Paducah, KY: Turner, 1993.

First Infantry Division in Vietnam. Vol. 1, *July 1965–April 1967.* n.p., n.d.

First Infantry Division in Vietnam. Vol. 2, *1 May 1967–31 Dec 1968.* n.p., n.d.

Ford, Ken. *Falaise 1944: Death of an Army*. Oxford, UK: Osprey, 2005.
From Texas to Bastogne, Texas Aggies Go to War. Bastogne, Belgium: Bastogne War Museum, n.d.
Fulghum, David, Terrence Maitland, and the editors of Boston Publishing. *The Vietnam Experience: South Vietnam on Trial.* Boston: Boston Publishing, 1984.
Gabel, Christopher. *The U.S. Army GHQ Maneuvers of 1941*. Washington, DC: US Army Center of Military History, 1991.
Galvin, John R. *Fighting the Cold War: A Soldier's Memoir*. Lexington: University Press of Kentucky, 2015.
Gavin, James M. *War and Peace in the Space Age.* New York: Harper and Brothers, 1958.
Geelhoed, E. Bruce. *Charles F. Wilson and Controversy in the Pentagon, 1953–1957.* Detroit: Wayne State University Press, 1979.
Gilmore, Donald L., with D. M. Giangreco. *Eyewitness Vietnam.* New York: Sterling, 2006.
Gimbel, John. *The American Occupation of Germany: Politics and the Military, 1945–1949.* Stanford, CA: Stanford University Press, 1961.
Gole, Henry G. *General William E. DePuy: Preparing the Army for Modern War.* Lexington: University Press of Kentucky, 2008.
Goolrick, William K., and Ogden Tanner. *The Battle of the Bulge.* New York: Time-Life Books, 1979.
Grandolini, Albert. *The Easter Offensive Vietnam 1972.* Vol. 1, *Tanks in the Streets.* West Midlands, UK: Helion, 2015.
Gregg, Donald P. *Pot Shards: Fragments of a Life Lived in CIA, the White House, and the Two Koreas.* Washington, DC: New Academia/Vellum Books, 2014.
Haig, Alexander M., Jr. *Inner Circles: How America Changed the World; A Memoir.* New York: Warner Books, 1992.
Hammond, William M. *Public Affairs: The Military and the Media, 1968–1973.* Washington, DC: US Army Center of Military History, 1996.
______. *Reporting Viet Nam: Media and Military at War.* Lawrence: University Press of Kansas, 1998.
Harmon, Maj. Gen. E. N. *Combat Commander: Autobiography of a Soldier.* Englewood Cliffs, NJ: Prentice-Hall, 1970.
Hastings, Max. *Armageddon: The Battle for Germany, 1944–1945.* New York: Alfred A. Knopf, 2004.
Hatfield, Thomas M. *Rudder: From Leader to Legend.* College Station: Texas A&M University Press, 2011.
Herbert, Gen. Paul, ed. *Dogface Charlie: Soldiers' Recollections of Vietnam and the Big Red One.* Wheaton, IL: First Division Museum, 2012.
Herbert, Maj. Paul H. *Deciding What Has to Be Done: General William E. DePuy and the 1976 Edition of FM 100-5, Operations.* Fort Leavenworth, KS: Combat Studies Institute, US Army Command and General Staff College, 1988.
The Heroic Battle of An Loc. Saigon: Ministry of Foreign Affairs, 1972.
Hewes, James E., Jr. *From Root to McNamara: Army Organization and Administra-*

tion, 1900–1963. Washington, DC: US Army Center of Military History, 1975.

Hirshson, Stanley P. *General Patton: A Soldier's Life.* New York: Harper Collins, 2002.

History 67th Armored Regiment. Brunswick, Germany: Georg Westermann, 1945.

Houston, Donald E. *Hell on Wheels: The 2d Armored Division.* Novato, CA: Presidio Press, 1977.

Lam Quang Thi. *Hell in An Loc: The 1972 Easter Invasion and the Battle That Saved South Viet Nam.* Denton: University of North Texas Press, 2009.

Latham, Brig. Gen. Willard. *The Modern Volunteer Army Program: The Benning Experiment, 1970–1972.* Washington, DC: Department of the Army, 1974.

Leftwich, Bill J. *The Corps at Aggieland.* Lubbock, TX: Smoke Signal Publishing, 1976.

Linn, Brian McAllister. *Elvis's Army: Cold War GIs and the Atomic Battlefield.* Cambridge, MA: Harvard University Press, 2016.

MacDonald, Charles B. *A Time for Trumpets: The Untold Story of the Battle of the Bulge.* New York: William Morrow, 1985.

_____. *U.S. Army in WWII: The European Theater of Operations; The Last Offensive.* Washington, DC: US Army Center of Military History, 1973.

_____. *U.S. Army in WWII: The European Theater of Operations; The Siegfried Line Campaign.* Washington, DC: US Army Center of Military History, 1993.

MacGarrigle, George L. *Taking the Offensive: October 1966 to October 1967.* Washington, DC: US Army Center of Military History, 1998.

Mauer, Harry. *Strange Ground: Americans in Vietnam, 1945–1975; An Oral History.* New York: Henry Holt, 1989.

McDermott, Mike. *True Faith and Allegiance: An American Paratrooper and the 1972 Battle of An Loc.* Tuscaloosa: University of Alabama Press, 2012.

Meyers, Andrew H. *Black, White, and Olive Drab: Racial Integration at Fort Jackson, South Carolina, and the Civil Rights Movement.* Charlottesville: University of Virginia Press, 2006.

Military History Institute of Vietnam. *Victory in Vietnam: The Official History of the People's Army of Vietnam, 1954–1975.* Translated by Merle L. Pribbenow. Lawrence: University Press of Kansas, 2002.

Millett, Allan R., and Peter Maslowski. *For the Common Defense.* Rev. ed. New York: Free Press, 1994.

Ngo Quang Truong, Lt. Gen. *Indochina Monographs: The Easter Offensive of 1972.* Washington, DC: US Army Center of Military History, 1980.

Nguyen Van Quy. *Hoi ky An Loc: 86 ngay cua mot bac si giai phau tai mat tran* [Memoir of An Loc: 86 days of a surgeon in battle]. Westminster, CA: Van Nghe Publishing, 2002.

Nunn, Sen. Sam, and Sen. Dewey F. Bartlett. *NATO and the New Soviet Threat.* Washington, DC: US Government Printing Office, 1977.

Oberdorfer, Don. *The Two Koreas: A Contemporary History.* New York: Basic Books, 1997.

Parker, James E. *Last Man Out.* Camden, SC: John Culler and Sons, 1996.

Patch, Chester, and Elmo Richardson. *The Presidency of Dwight D. Eisenhower.*

Lawrence: University Press of Kansas, 1991.
Peterson, Edward. *The American Occupation of Germany: Retreat to Victory*. Detroit: Wayne State University Press, 1978.
Pugsley, Christopher. *Operation Cobra*. Phoenix Mill, UK: Sutton, 2004.
Ricks, Thomas E. *The Generals*. New York: Penguin Press, 2012.
Ridgway, Matthew B. *Soldier: The Memoirs of Matthew B. Ridgway*. New York: Harper and Brothers, 1956.
Rogers, Lt. Gen. Bernard William. *Cedar Falls-Junction City: A Turning Point*. Washington, DC: US Army Center of Military History, 1989.
Ryan, Cornelius. *The Last Battle: The Classic History of the Battle for Berlin*. Reprint ed. New York: Simon and Schuster, 1994.
Scheips, Paul J. *The Role of Federal Military Forces in Domestic Disorders, 1945–1992*. Fort McNair, Washington, DC: US Army Center of Military History, 2005.
Schwarzkopf, Gen. H. Norman. *It Doesn't Take a Hero*. New York: Linda Grey Bantam Books, 1992.
Sevy, Grace. *The American Experience in Vietnam*. Norman: University of Oklahoma Press, 1989.
Shelton, Brig. Gen. James E. *The Beast Was Out There*. Naperville, IL: Cantigny First Division Foundation, 2002.
Sorley, Lewis. *A Better War: The Unexamined Victories and Final Tragedy of America's Last Years in Vietnam*. New York: Harcourt Brace, 1999.
_____. *Honorable Warrior: General Harold K. Johnson and the Ethics of Command*. Lawrence: University Press of Kansas, 1998.
_____, ed. *Press On! Selected Works of General Donn A. Starry*. Fort Leavenworth, KS: Combat Studies Institute Press, 2009.
_____. *Thunderbolt: General Creighton Abrams and the Army of His Times*. New York: Simon and Schuster, 1992.
_____, ed. *Vietnam Chronicles: The Abrams Tapes, 1968–1972*. Lubbock: Texas Tech University Press, 2004.
St. John, Philip. *Second Armored Division: A History. 1991*. Paducah, KY: Turner, 1998.
Taylor, John M. *General Maxwell Taylor: The Sword and the Pen*. New York: Doubleday, 1989.
Taylor, Maxwell D. *The Uncertain Trumpet*. New York: Harper and Brothers, 1959.
Tevington, William M., comp. *The United States Constabulary: A History*. Paducah, KY: Turner, 1998.
Tran Van Nhut, Gen., with Christian L. Arevian. *An Loc: The Unfinished War*. Lubbock: Texas Tech University Press, 2009.
Truong Nhu Tang, *Vietcong Memoir: An Inside Account of the Vietnam War and Its Aftermath*. New York: Harcourt Brace Jovanovich, 1983.
Wallace, Robert. *The Italian Campaign*. New York: Time-Life Books, 1978.
Weigley, Russell F. *The American Way of War: A History of United States Military Strategy and Policy*. Bloomington: Indiana University Press, 1973.
———. *Eisenhower's Lieutenants: The Campaign of France and Germany, 1944–*

1945. Bloomington: Indiana University Press, 1981.

———. *History of the United States Army.* New York: Macmillan, 1967.

Weingartner, Steven, ed. *Blue Spaders: The 26th Infantry Regiment, 1917–1967.* Wheaton, IL: Cantigny First Division Foundation, 1996.

Wheeler, James Scott. *The Big Red One.* Lawrence: University Press of Kansas, 2007.

Whiting, Charles. *The End of the War, Europe: April 15–May 23, 1945.* New York: Stein and Day, 1973.

Willbanks, James H. *Abandoning Vietnam: How America Left and South Vietnam Lost Its War.* Lawrence: University Press of Kansas, 2008.

———. *The Battle of An Loc.* Bloomington: Indiana University Press, 2005.

———. *A Raid Too Far: Operation Lam Son 719 and Vietnamization in Laos.* College Station: Texas A&M University Press, 2014.

Wilson, George C. *Mud Soldiers.* New York: Charles Scribner's Sons, 1989.

Wolfe, Thomas. *The New Journalism.* New York: Harper and Row, 1973.

Woodall, James R. *Twelve Texas Aggie War Heroes: From World War I to Vietnam.* College Station: Texas A&M University Press, 2016.

Zaloga, Steven J. *Battle of the Bulge 1944.* Oxford, UK: Osprey, 2004.

———. *Operation Cobra 1944: Breakout from Normandy.* Oxford, UK: Osprey, 2001.

———. *The Siegfried Line 1944–45: Battles on the German Frontier.* Oxford, UK: Osprey, 2007.

Periodicals and Newspapers

"An Adviser's Three-Month Nightmare Ends." *Pacific Stars and Stripes*, 4 June 1972.

Alsop, Joseph. "Fighting of the ARVN at An Loc." *Los Angeles Times*, 9 May 1972.

———. "Lack of Reserves in South Vietnam." *Pacific Stars and Stripes*, 10 May 1972.

———. "The South's Heroic Defense of An Loc." *Pacific Stars and Stripes*, 30 May 1972.

"An Loc: A Battlefield in Hell." *Pacific Stars and Stripes*, 1 May 1972.

Arnett, Peter. "Exacting Commander Wants 1st Division Best in Army." *Lubbock (TX) Avalanche-Journal*, 30 August 1966.

Atkins, Ken. "Retired General Still Watching Soviets." *Dallas Morning News*, 11 November 1979.

Ayala, Elaine. "Famous A&M Grad 'Danger 79er' Dies." *San Antonio Express-News*, 7 March 2010.

"The Battle for An Loc Goes On." *Pacific Stars and Stripes*, 19 April 1972.

"Battle of An Loc Ends." *Pacific Stars and Stripes*, 18 June 1972.

Beech, Keyes. "Steel Trap Awaits Korean 'Moles.'" *Omaha (NE) World-Herald*, 27 November 1975.

"Biggest B-52 Raids of War Pound Reds Besieging An Loc." *Los Angeles Times*, 12 May 1972.

Black, Charles. "An Loc Is Key to Saigon," *Columbus Enquirer*, 17 May 1972.

"Both Sides Claim An Loc," *Pacific Stars and Stripes*, 18 April 1972.
"Brig. Gen. James F. Hollingsworth Assumes New Duties." *Denton (TX) Record-Chronicle*, 22 June 1967.
Clarke, Philip C. "The Battle That Saved Saigon." *Reader's Digest*, March 1973, 151–56.
———. "Defying the Odds at An Loc." *American Legion Magazine*, April 2000, 39.
"Communists Down General's Copter," *San Francisco Examiner*, 10 November 1966.
"Controversial General Announces End of Career." *San Antonio Express-News*, 24 January 1976.
Cooley, John K. "How American, Russian Armored Capabilities Match Up." *Christian Science Monitor*, 5 March 1980.
Deener, Bill. "Former US Commander in Korea Says Invasion by North Possible." *Fort Worth (TX) Star-Telegram*, 30 October 1979.
Drake, Hal. "The Road to An Loc—Alive and Flashing with Death." *Pacific Stars and Stripes*, 21 April 1972.
———. "Viets on Way to Victory at An Loc—Top Adviser." *Pacific Stars and Stripes*, 23 April 1972.
Ellithorpe, Harold. "'Can You Hold Out for Just Eight More Minutes?'" *Life*, 21 April 1972, 51.
Evans, Rowland, and Robert Novak. "Evans and Novak: Korean Strategy." *New York Post*, 16 June 1975.
Faas, Horst. "Communists Down General's Copter." *Abilene (TX) Reporter*, 10 November 1966.
"Ford Reaffirms U.S. Ties with South Korea." *Pacific Stars and Stripes*, 12 August 1974.
"Former US Commander in Korea Says Invasion by North Possible." *Fort Worth (TX) Star-Telegram*, 30 October 1979.
Fournier, Richard. "Donnybrook in the Bong Trang Woods." *VFW*, August 2016, 36–38, 40–41.
"General aboard Downed 'Copter." *Odessa American*, 16 November 1966.
"General Hollingsworth Stars in 'Soldier,'" *Pacific Stars and Stripes*, 28 July 1975.
"General Led Tank Attack." *Denton (TX) Record-Chronicle*, 20 June 1966.
"General's Chopper Speeds MEDEVAC," *American Traveler*, 17 September 1966.
"Gen. Hollingsworth Retiring." *Dallas Morning News*, 24 January 1976.
"Gen. James Hollingsworth Nominated for Third Star." *Denton (TX) Record-Chronicle*, 3 July 1973.
"The G.I.s: 60,000 Miles to Breakfast." *Time*, 30 June 1975, 41.
Halstead, Fred. "Antiwar GIs Speak: Interviews with Fort Jackson GIs United against the War." *International Socialist Review*, July–August 1969, 1–47.
Heinl, Robert D., Jr. "The Collapse of the Armed Forces." *Armed Forces Journal*, June 1971, 30–38.
Hollingsworth, Lt. Gen. James F. "Understanding the Conventional Umbrella." *Armed Forces Journal*, February 1984.

Hollingsworth, LTG James. "Commander's Hatch: Guest Column," *Armor*, January–February 1989, 6.

———. "Commander's Hatch: Remembering Some Hard-Fought Lessons of World War II, Part 2." *Armor*, March–April 1989, 5–6, 45–46.

"Hollingsworth Heads TRAC." *Pacific Stars and Stripes*, 17 December 1971.

"The Hollingsworth Report." *National Guardsman*, March 1969, 22–23.

"Hollingsworth Retirement Postponed." *Texas Aggie*, May 1976, 15.

Howard, Maj. John D. "An Loc: A Study in U.S. Power." *Army*, September 1975, 18–24.

———. "They Were Good Ol' Boys!" *Air University Review*, January–February 1975, 26–39.

Infield, Glenn. "'Danger 79er' Toughest General the Cong Ever Faced." *Stag*, April 1968, 17–19, 64–66.

"In Furious Battle." *Newsweek*, 24 April 1972, 31–33.

"J. F. Hollingsworth." *Denton (TX) Record-Chronicle*, 11 October 1960.

"Killeen Youth Killed in Sunday Sportscar Mishap." *Gatesville (TX) Messenger*, 14 October 1960.

Kneeland, Douglas E. "War Stirs More Dissent among G.I.'s." *New York Times*, 6 June 1970.

"Korea Integrity Essential to Security of the Free World," *Korea Herald*, 11 May 1979.

Korea Report. Seoul: 8th Army Public Affairs, March 1976.

"Korea/Special Report: The Long Siege." *Time*, 30 June 1975, 34–40, 42–43.

Kutsky, Diana. "Sanger Native Advances toward 4-Star Status." *Denton (TX) Record-Chronicle*, 22 March 1976.

LaGuardia, Robert. "Lt. Gen. James F. Hollingsworth—Meanest General in the U.S. Army." *Stag*, October 1975, 32–33, 62–65.

Lemnitzer, Lyman L. "This Is a Significant Beginning." *Army Combat Forces Journal*, November 1955, 62.

Major, Sandi. "Farmboy to Legendary General." *Fort Worth (TX) Press*, 27 November 1966.

"Media Fail to Convey Good News from An Loc." *Baltimore Sun*, 16 June 1972.

Melcher, David F., and John C. Siemer. "How to Build the Wrong Army." *Military Review*, September 1992, 66–76.

"Military Forces Split by Conflict on Arms Policies." *New York Times*, 19 May 1956.

Moran, Tom. "Hollingsworth Now with Research Firm after Army Career." *Houston Chronicle*, 1 May 1978.

"New General Is Assigned to 1st Division," *American Traveler*, 11 March 1966.

"Not Much Left to Defend in War-Shattered An Loc," *Pacific Stars and Stripes*, 24 April 1972.

"On Highway 13: The Long Road to An Loc." *Time*, 24 April 1972, 27.

Pearlstine, Norman. "'Tiger in the Forest': U.S. General Envisions 'A Short, Violent War' If Korean Reds Attack." *Wall Street Journal*, 13 January 1976.

"Pentagon Weighs a Guard Shake-Up." *New York Times*, 16 May 1964.

"The Race against Disaster." *Life*, 21 April 1972, 42–46, 51–53.
Rauch, Rudolph. "A Record of Sheer Endurance." *Time*, 26 June 1972, 25–26.
"Reds Launch New Tank Attack on An Loc." *Pacific Stars and Stripes*, 13 May 1972.
"Report on NATO and New Soviet Threat." Congressional Record, Proceedings of 95th Congress, First Session, Senate, 25 January 1977, vol. 123, no. 13.
"Reprimand Gen. for Remarks." *Pacific Stars and Stripes*, 17 April 1972.
"Retirement Life Proving Calmer for Fiery General." *Fort Worth (TX) Star-Telegram*, 4 July 1979.
Saar, John. "The Army's Defiant Anachronism." *Washington Post*, 15 February 1976.
———. "Gen. Hollingsworth Retiring—Blunt, Decorated Vietnam Veteran Revised Korea Strategy." *Washington Post*, 24 January 1975.
———. "A Nervous Air Mission to Anloc and Back." *Life*, 12 May 1972, 36–37.
———. "A Texas Gunslinger Retires . . . Reluctantly." *Dallas Times Herald*, 15 February 1976.
Schaefer, Allen. "Death in the Afternoon—The Route 13 Battle." *Pacific Stars and Stripes*, 13 May 1972.
Schemmer, Benjamin F. "Bien Hoa Air Base: Short of Toilet Paper but Long on Teamwork." *Armed Forces Journal*, June 1972, 15–18.
Shelton, Keith. "Sanger General Goes Where Action Is." *Denton (TX) Record-Chronicle*, 19 June 1966.
"Shock of War." *Life*, 12 May 1972, 34–38.
"A Soldier's Farewell." *Washington Post*, 15 February 15 1976.
Southerland, Daniel. "U.S. General Talked Too Rough—Rebuked." *Christian Science Monitor*, 15 April 1972, 1–2.
Stachurski, Lt. Col. Richard J. "The Nunn-Bartlett Report: A Realistic Prescription for NATO?" *Air University Review*, July–August 1978, 21–25.
"A Tale of Two Broken Cities." *Time*, 15 January 1972, 25–26.
Tomalin, Nicholas. "The General Goes Zapping Charlie Cong." *Sunday Times* (London, UK), 5 June 1966.
"Transcript of News Conference Held by Wilson and His Military and Civilian Aides," *New York Times*, 22 May 1956.
Trauschweizer, Ingo. "Back to the Cold War: The U.S. Army after Vietnam." *U.S. Military History Review*, December 2015, 18–37.
"A Tribute to LTG (Ret) James F. Hollingsworth." *U.S. Army War College Foundation and Alumni Magazine*, Spring 2010, 6.
"U.S. General Dies in An Loc Shelling." *New York Times*, 10 July 1972.
"Viet General Vows to Defend An Loc." *Pacific Stars and Stripes*, 5 May 1972.
"Vietnam: The Specter of Defeat." *Newsweek*, 15 May 1972, 20–22.
Ward, Ian. "North Vietnam's Blitzkrieg—Why Giap Did It: Report from Saigon." *Conflict Studies*, October 1972, 1–11.
"The War That Won't Go Away." *Newsweek*, 17 April 1972, 16–21.
Widener, Robert. "Who Is the Most Highly Decorated GI of All Time?" *VFW*, April 2014, 42–43.

Willbanks, James H. "The Battle of An Loc 1972." *Armchair General*, September 2009, 40–49.

———. "Tribute: General James F. Hollingsworth." *Vietnam*, October 2010, 51.

"Young Hollingsworth Takes Up Army Duty." *Denton (TX) Record-Chronicle*, 5 October 1939.

Index

Page numbers in *italics* refer to illustrations.